# DON'T LOOK BACK IN ANGER

## CARL H SPIERS

EMPIRE
PUBLICATIONS

First published in 2012

EMPIRE PUBLICATIONS
1 Newton Street, Manchester M1 1HW
© Carl H Spiers 2012

ISBN: 1901746 836 - 9781901746839

Printed in Great Britain by 4edge Ltd, Hockley, Essex.

# CONTENTS

# INTRODUCTION

WHAT YOU ARE ABOUT TO READ may shock you, it may make you smile, it may take you back to those mad crazy days of the 70's & 80's when hundreds of thousands of football hooligans rampaged up and down the country week in week out. There were various kinds of hooligans; you had the majority of whom were just chanters, pushers n shovers making the numbers up but adding to the wonderful atmospheres on various kops. Then there were the stylists: lads and girls who dressed the part looked the part or even sported tattoos of their chosen club and had to be seen to be part of the mob. Then you had the front liners, the lads who shed blood, who showed incredibly feats of bravery and loyalty and many whom got badly damaged both physically and mentally, without blowing my trumpet.

For most of my teenage years and early twenties I was a front line football hooligan for my home town team Oldham Athletic and have the scars both physical and mentally to show for it. Along the way I have lost many friends who once stood side by side with me fighting for our team, town and in many cases our lives. Many of these were lost to drugs or drink and even depression, as they tried in vain to find the buzz/adrenaline that football violence gave us for so long. I was one of the lucky ones. I survived to tell the tale.

This book is a bit different from most other football hooligan related books as most of it is based on the lower leagues and most of it on the back foot, as it took us many years of toil, blood, sweat and tears to establish our team and reputation. We did well considering our numbers and lack of success and being on the doorstep of Man United, Man City, Leeds and Liverpool, all of whom attracted fans from Oldham - traitors one and all...

But the real lionhearts and loyalists stayed by their home town team and perhaps that gave us an edge because a lad who fights through sheer loyalty and love of his home town will give far more than someone who jumps on another team's bandwagon! Never the less any lad/girl who stood and fought will always get my respect for many chose the easier option to run and fade away...

I would like to thank Colin Blaney for his support and

encouragement, Rick Milnes photographer, my beloved son Jack now aged 25 who steered clear of the footy violence but loves my old tales, my lovely Lana and my many friends from the terraces. RIP to all those no longer with us, OAFC for being such a big part of my life and my late great father Hughie who never once questioned me for being a wild one, and to all the terrace legends who inspired me.

*We don't carry hammers*
*We don't carry lead*
*We only carry hatchets*
*To bury in your head*
*We are all supporters*
*Fanatics everyone*
*We all hate Man City*
*Leeds and Everton*

This book is dedicated to the memory of all football hooligans who stood and fought for their team and town and mates.

# LOVE AT FIRST FIGHT

I WAS 8 AND A HALF YEARS OLD and due to go to my first ever away game watching my beloved Oldham Athletic. I'd already been to a few home matches with my mam dad or older brother Peter, we were a big Latics supporting family and lived within earshot of Boundary Park and could often hear the "Boundary Park roar". I begged me mam to let me go to an away game and she relented and instructed my older brother Peter to take me on Barlow's coaches which was based ten minutes walk from our house in Northmoor. Peter was then 13 and an avid Latics fan, this very game was nearby at Stockport County, a town only 12 miles away and half a hour on the coach. Nevertheless I was very excited and proudly wore my tangerine blue and white scarf as we walked to Barlow's coach station.

The coach was due to leave at 6pm for this Friday evening match, it was a nice night late summer evening and still light. Pete wore his scarf n bobble hat, as we got nearer I noticed more and more Latics fans mainly youths or young men. We got on one of the half a dozen or so coaches and there seemed great excitement as youths chanted and chatted away, many of the youths I noticed had long hair and wore denim jackets and leather jackets, and big working boots. I asked Peter why are they dressed like that, he informed they were greasers, I also noticed a few smart dressed youths with short smart cut styled hair windjammer jackets  white jeans and desert boots, Peter told me these were Mods. This all went over my head...

I was fascinated though with the lads chanting rude songs with swear words and as we get near Stockport's ground more and more coaches from Oldham were arriving - Yelloway's and Stott's coaches, there must have been 25 or so coaches all lined up outside Edgeley Park. As we got off a big mob got together and marched defiantly across the car park taunting Stockport fans who taunted them back, this was really exciting and scary at the same time. Peter looked worried as both mobs approached each other, there were no cops about and all of a sudden a roar went up and they charged into each other. My brother dragged me to one side and we watched as the mass brawl ensued, Oldham with their bigger numbers soon overwhelmed Stockport who ran off but a few got caught and beaten up which I did not enjoy seeing. Eventually a couple of police came with big sticks and started whacking some Oldham fans.

We soon got into the ground and we were in an end behind the goal. It was just a big shed with a big hill full of dust to stand on, Oldham soon filled this ramshackle end up and seemed to have many more fans than Stockport who were congregated in the opposite end across the pitch. Both sets of fans chanted and taunted each other, the chanting fascinated me also, 'Zigger Zagger Zigger Zagger ATH LET TIC!', '1 - 2 - 3 - 4 Listen to the Chaddy roar' – both me and Peter joined in – I was buzzing and watching the fans more than the game, I was in awe, the game was pretty boring but just before half time Latics scored and the crowd surged forward with many going onto the pitch before a handful of cops got em off and back into this stand.

The goal produced wild scenes of celebration and even more taunting of the Stockport fans in the opposite end, who by now were making their way up the side of the pitch towards the Oldham end in a mob of 200 or so Oldham fans were goading them and surged towards the paddock wall to meet them head on. It was so exciting but my brother Peter dragged me back to a good but safer vantage point, for although he wasn't gonna get involved, he wanted to see this clash, Oldham had the bigger mob but Stockport came running up the last few yards and Oldham ran into them surging over this little wall which collapsed under the strain.

The Oldham lads picked up broken masonry and lobbed it at the now fleeing Stockport mob who fled en masse with Oldham in pursuit, meanwhile I was on my hands and knees scooping up loads of loose change off the floor... there was over a fiver's worth of thruppeny bits, tanners, shillings and pennies, a tidy sum which kept me in sweets for weeks... the average working wage of a man back then would have been a fiver.

The Oldham fans made their way back all jubilant at running Stockport off and smashing that wall down and a new chant was begun to the tune of the popular Soul hit in the charts back then, *Breaking Down the Walls of Heartache* by Johnny Johnson and the Bandwagon. Oldham fans chanted 'Breaking down the walls of Stockport County' – this chant lasted many years at Oldham.

When the half-time whistle blew the light had faded and now the floodlights were turned on adding to the atmosphere. All the Oldham fans are talking about how they ran Stockport and how they would 'do them' after the game. I went to the cafe bar and bought pop, chocolate and crisps, with my new found wealth – this money was to last me a few more weeks.

The second half flew by and Stockport equalised and Oldham fans were mobbing up near the end of the game to take them on once more many suggesting they run across the pitch but the sight of half a dozen burly coppers put paid to this. At the final whistle, the mob surged toward the exit chanting their new song with great gusto. I could also see Stockport's mob making for the same way. Peter held my hand tight and I was a bit scared but clung onto him and my pocket full of change as the half a dozen cops escorted the Oldham fans to their coaches but with an almighty roar a big crew of about 100 Oldham fans broke away and charged across the car park into the fleeing Stockport mob.

Only a few stayed and slugged it out which impressed me, I saw two men fighting one to one, the Stockport fan was very tall and thin with bushy ginger hair, he was wearing a full length afghan coat, the Oldham lad fighting him was very small but looked hard and was swinging his fists and in a whirlwind motion and he soon had his taller opponent on the deck. I heard Oldham fans saying "That's Slouk". He came back into the escort with many backslaps and congratulations, I admired him for his bravery and toughness despite his size. He got on a coach with a big gang of very hard looking lads, this was the Glodwick (Gloddick) mob - Oldham's toughest gang in the 1970's. They made their mark and would continue to so for many more years.

All the talk on the coach home was about the trouble rather than the game. The wall breaking the chasing off of Stockport fans during and after the game and little Slouk battering the big ginger lad, I loved all the football banter the chanting and the hero worshipping, it gripped me as much as everyone else, it was exciting and I couldn't wait to get to Richmond juniors school on Monday morning to tell my pals. When we got back to Barlow's coach station we walked the short 10 minute journey back home to Northmoor along Rochdale Road past Oldham College. In front of us were a small group of long haired youths who lived on the nearby Clarkwell estate, Bryn Rose whose brother Nigel was in my class, Charlie, - Ste Charlesworth, Ste Hurst, Mad John and Barry Ten Bellies, a big fat lad whose mam had a sweet shop and ran trips to Blackpool. Me and Pete were only a few yards behind them and they were going on about the trouble with Slouk and the Glodwick mob.

That night in bed I could not stop thinking about the game - well the fighting to tell you the truth and the chanting, it gripped me and I yearned to be a football fan and maybe one day have a fight with away fans. It was all a bit disturbing for a 8 year old lad but it was very exciting, next day I rolled my jeans up like the bovver boys did, ha ha that's what the older people called them, bovver boys with their big boots and rolled up jeans.

On Monday morning at 8.30m my best pal Paul Sykes who was a year less a day older than me, calls me en route to Richmond junior school a quarter of a mile away. I excitedly told him all about going to Stockport on the Friday night and all the trouble I witnessed, he listened intently and was laughing as I regaled in some of the song/ chants etc as we nicked our usual bottle of milk off a random doorstep as we did every school morning. We both decided we were going to be bovver boys one day following our beloved Oldham Athletic. That was the very beginning of a very long and colourful career as a football hooligan for both of us. Once at school the talk in the yard was all about what I saw at Stockport as more and more young 8/9 and 10 yr old lads listened to me rabbitting on, I must have made an impact because out of those primary school kids at Richmond quite a lot became football hooligans during the 1970's and 80's.

For the next couple of years at Richmond Juniors every time it rained, the kids all piled into a big covered area under the Art block which we called the Chaddy End Oldham's Kop and we'd all sing and chant football songs we had heard at Latics, or on Match of the Day, we would split into 2 gangs Oldham and Man United, we made sure all the tougher kids were on the Oldham side and we would try and out chant each other and have toy barneys. Mock fights - a bit like British bulldog. We played at the Cubs and Scouts and Boys Brigade, we would make a hell of a racket and it was all great fun and now and then a fight would break out as someone got hurt or went too far.

It was during these brawls that sorted out who was cock of the class or even the whole school, I was rated 4th cock of the school after Robert McConkie, a wild Scottish lad from a huge rough Scottish family, he arrived down from Scotland when he was 8 (his family were rumoured to have 13 kids!) and lived in a derelict house nearby. They were really scruffy and rough, Rob soon made his mark battering big John Wild on his first day - a heavily built lad with jam jar glasses who we all assumed was cock of our class because he was bigger than anyone else. Well Rob, who was only small, soon put that to bed. He also beat quite a few more up to confirm he was the cock and even though me and Rob were best of mates we fought 3 times, each time it got broke up but Rob would have won me because he would go a lot further.

The 2nd cock was Terry Forsyth - a very strong lad who I fought but proved too strong for me. He soon had me pinned down and was pummelling me, until Rob dragged him off then beat him, but Terry was tough and he was another future football hooligan. The 3rd cock was a lad called Dean Lord who was our best footballer and good at all sports I don't know why he was rated 3rd cock but he was and I was rated the 4th cock, which I was proud of as it was a large school, I loved my junior school days, in the 3rd and 4th years our teacher was Terry Taylor, a trendy young man in his twenties who wore fashionable clothes large kipper tie flared pants and had long blown dry hair, "Trendy Terry" we called him, he was very modern and funny although if you crossed him you would get his "little friend "an old plimsoll he kept in his drawer but would whack you over the arse with, which stung terribly. Also another weapon of Terry Taylor's was a West Indian girl called Lorita who was heavily built and Mr. Taylor would order her to crack anyone being cheeky across the head, which would send you flying cross the room, Lorita's younger brother Stephen Morgan ended up playing professional football for Blackpool, Plymouth and Coventry City. Terry Taylor was a great teacher and he was our football team manager and Richmond Street won many trophies under him including our team who won the double, the league and cup in 1971/2.

Other great memories from Richmond were the school discos held every dinner time in the yard during that wonderful summer of 1970, when England were playing in the World Cup in Mexico, and the England football Squad had the brilliant song Back Home in the charts, we'd all sing-along to it and chant "England" Mr. Taylor would be laughing his head off. Other popular tunes that summer were The Archies' "Sugar Sugar" - Dave Edmunds "I hear you knocking" - Marvin Gaye and Tammi Terrelles "Onion Song "and The Supremes "Stoned Love".

We all thought we were Pan's People off Top of the Pops as we danced along in formation, and then chasing the girls in a game of 'Kiss Catch' I once had the most embarrassing experience when during one game of 'Kiss Catch' I set my sights on the best looking girl in school Lyn Mcdermott who was a couple of years older than me and beautiful, and I caught her wrestled her to the ground and began to stick my lips on her but she spun me round kicked me in the balls and as I got up slapped me across the face, I could have died I was that embarrassed, everyone was falling about laughing. Bitch!

It was whilst at junior school I formed my first ever gang, WEBB....

West end Boot Boys, 1971, we painted this on a few walls in the district. I was 10 years old, and West End street was where I lived, I recruited a few lads who lived in and around there, we had about 15 lads and a couple of girls and we would brick rival gangs and raid bonfires, and do daring things like knock a door runaway, members of my first ever gang included Gary Lazenbury, Paul Lazenbury and their little brother John – John (RIP) Keith Pemberton, Gary and Mark Rothera, Ste Howe (RIP), my sister Karen a very tough tomboy (RIP) Andy Kershaw, Willy Sullivan, John Moo Sullivan (nicknamed moo because everytime he lost his temper he would making a mooing sound like a cow!) Dave Turver, Ste Bailey, John Bardsley, the three Alt brothers, Tony Michael and Pip... (Pip – Philip as a dwarf, he was about 3 ft tall but a cheeky bleeder and a great stone thrower). We were not to last long but it gave me a taste for gangs and organisation as we defended our area..

# THE ROOTS OF FOOTBALL VIOLENCE

FOOTBALL AGGRO HAS BEEN AROUND for many more years than people imagine. Going back to the 1920's, reports of Millwall fans attacking rival fans were common place but it really took off properly in the 1960's, as Mods and Rockers clashed up and down the country especially on Bank Holidays in resorts like Clacton, Brighton, Margate, Rhyl and Blackpool the massive media coverage of these mass brawls influenced football teams to mob up and attack rival fans as they defended or tried to take over kops up and down the country, typically the Scousers were at the fore-front of football aggro in the early 1960's wrecking trains and taking over ends, including the Stretford End when Everton took over the Stretford End in 1966 the last team to do so although Oldham can also lay claim to that as Geoff Smith confirms.

"It was 1969 and a Lancashire senior cup tie, where teams from the North West played each other during the season for a chance to lift a trophy, the big teams like United, City, Liverpool and Everton would play their reserves but the smaller teams like Latics would play their first teams for a chance of a trophy and prestige. This night Latics were drawn away at United current European champions and best supported team in the land, that night there was a crowd over 25,000 in Old Trafford as many supporters wanted to see the next generation of United players which included many who were to star for United for years to come, it was a prestigious match for the Latics and a couple of thousand made the short half a hour journey and settled into the away end facing the famous Stretford End, after about twenty minutes there was a big roar from the Stretford End and a huge gap appeared in the middle and United fans clambered onto the pitch as a mob of around fifty Oldham hooligans began chanting 'Oldham! Oldham! Oldham!' led by their leader the massive Gil Doc, king of the Chaddy End, this mob held their own for the next 15 minutes until the cops arrived and escorted them around the pitch to put them in with the rest of the Oldham fans, they got a standing ovation and even United fans clapped them because this was one of the most feared ends in the country, now let's not kid ourselves there is no way this mob would have even got in on a normal match day and I'm sure very few of United's hooligans were even at this match but the fact is for a short time Oldham Athletic took the Stretford End and it has gone down in Oldham folklore."

Oldham's hooligans had already been making a good name for themselves for a few years up and down the country and by the end of the 1960's had taken several ends including QPR, Doncaster, Mansfield Rochdale, Chesterfield, Southport, Man United (ha ha) and few more, back then most hooligan firms had leaders and Oldham were lucky to have Gil Doc has their leader, a huge powerful youth who by the time he was 13 was sporting a beard and was a big very strong and hard youth and was already cock of North Chadderton school and boozing up town and brawling with men much older than him.

Gill was a Rocker as were most youths in Oldham during the early 1960's, his gang was the notorious Sewer Mob who mostly came from Chadderton and could when needed pull a mob of 100 together, this Mob supported Oldham Athletic and would congregate the top of the Chaddy End on the wooden boards, they defended this end against all comers and many tried in vain to take over the Chaddy End in the 1960's only one team managed it, little Stockport who took over on Tuesday night when no-one expected any of them to come as earlier that season Oldham had taken over Stockport's end, this was 1968 when Oldham were rock bottom of the league and crowds down to 3000, the season after Oldham fans got their act together.

They avenged that the season after, but many other teams did try and take the Chaddy End and perhaps the greatest success of Oldham's hooligans was when they somehow retrieved the Chaddy End in 1966 when the mighty Wolves of Division One took over the Chaddy End in a 3rd round FA Cup tie. Wolves were a massive club back then with a massive following and by 1.30pm they had taken over the Chaddy End with hundreds of youths, many blacks amongst them and most of them Mods as opposed to Oldham's Rockers, word soon spread to Chadderton and Gil Doc who gathered his troops together and marched up to Boundary Park, they could hear the Wolves fans chanting and goading them as they approached the ground, Gil gave the big speech that no one takes a backward step as we get our Chaddy End back off these Wolves bastards! Gill and his Sewer Mob aided by other gangs from around Oldham entered the Chaddy End and slowly but surely made their way up to the top of the end which was full of Wolves hooligans, Gil smashed his way through dozens of Wolves fans with his mob and followers behind him, it took twenty minutes of non stop brawling before the final charge scattered Wolves fans, many jumping out of the open back windows at the back of the Chaddy End leaping 30 feet to escape the wrath of the Oldham thugs, quite a few got thrown out and were hurt badly, the rest of the Wolves ran away across the pitch... Oldham led by Big Gil Doc retrieved the Chaddy End in an amazing show of courage and pride... it has gone down as one of the greatest days in Oldham's hooligan history....

Such was the level of violence that a lot of Wolves fans wrote to the Oldham Chronicle complaining: here are a couple of examples....

*"I feel I must stress my disgust and shock at the way Oldham Athletic supporters acted on our recent visit to Boundary Park, they acted like animals and attacked innocent supporters of Wolves with sticks fists and boots, so many of us got bloody noses and having travelled all over the country have to say these are the worst fans we have come across, thank god we will not have to go back to that godforsaken hole ever again!"*

Alan Butterworth, Stafford.

*"I can assure you that I nor any of my family and friends will ever venture to Boundary Park again, the way your supporters behaved was shameful and totally uncalled for, my uncle got his nose broken and thrown out of the back the stand and was lucky not to have broken his legs only he landed on other Wolves fans who had been thrown out, there are many other cases of Wolves fans being hurt half of the people on our coach were sporting cuts and bruises, where were the police? Why are your supporters so violent? I have reported your club to the football league and informed the police, it was only a football match for Christ's sake!"*

Kenneth Mooney, Bilston, Wolverhampton.

There were many more letter of disgust, funny how none of them mention Wolves taking over the Chaddy End though eh? However this elevated Oldham into the big hooligan league as word spread around the country of Oldham doing the mighty Wolves, their name and reputation was growing fast.

Someone who was there right at the beginning of football violence was the charismatic Jimmy Kirton, one of the Sewer Mob, great pal of Gil Doc and without doubt THE most influential Oldham supporter of all time. Jimmy Kirton was born in 1948 the eldest of four boys and one girl, brought up in Chadderton he first ventured to Boundary Park in the late 1950's, he met Gil Doc at North Chadd senior school in 1959 and soon became pals with him and together with Gil, John Farrell and others formed the Sewer Mob in the early 1960's and also they were all Latics fans, this mob grew and grew as did it's reputation, with Big Gil and Big Faz being the main men, two very hard youths respected all over Oldham, Jimmy Kirt who was only slightly built and was the mouthpiece, very cocky very confident and a great one to whip up the lads and girls, Jimmy loved being centre of attention with his rants and wit and knew he had the best back up in town with Gil and Faz, Jimmy took to the football violence like a duck to water, he loved a scrap and was very loyal to his beloved Latics..

Throughout the 1960's Oldham were at the forefront of football violence and by the end of the decade as most of them reached their early twenties and retired due to marriage, responsibilities and the odd one imprisoned although that was a rarity back then, it was time for new blood to defend the Chaddy End and to try and take rivals ends, gangs like the Glodwick Mob, Royton, Chadderton, Derker, Northmoor, Abbeyhills, Limeside, Werneth, Fitton Hill and others who put aside local rivalries and joined as one huge mob to take on all comers. It was not going to be easy as more and more rival supporters built up large mobs some with huge numbers and over the next ten years in the 1970's many teams attempted to take the Chaddy End quite a few did but Oldham fought off many more.

The first violence I saw at Boundary Park was early 1970 on a night match when Latics played Bradford Park Avenue, a mob of about 30 of them all long haired Rockers congregated at the top of the Chaddy an hour before kick off and before any Oldham youths were there. Bradford were attacking anyone who came near them, they were very aggressive and chanting, other mobs from Oldham came in and tried in vain to take them on but Bradford's mob were tough, at kick off they still held the top of the Chaddy End but then the Glodwick Mob arrived about 30 strong and marched up defiantly with all the other mobs now tagging onto them. Glodwick piled right into the Bradford lads who fought gallantly and did not take a backward step but were soon overwhelmed and it seemed everyone of them were battered and the Chaddy End was back in the hands of Oldham, it was scary to see. Me and Paul Sykes saw it all unfold and we had new heroes, the Glodwick Mob, who seemed to be the most feared mob in Oldham although many thought that the infamous Crossley Skins were, that night after the match the Oldham mob marched up Sheepfoot Lane onto Rochdale Road and the mile walk into the town centre, they smashed the window of Chan's chippy, our local Chinese, and they walked up Barker Street were they attacked a group of Pakis who were stood outside a cafe they owned. The Pakis fought back with knives, brushes and machetes, it was brutal stuff and quite a few were cut but Oldham's numbers once more overwhelmed the dozen or so Pakis who fled into the cafe which was then smashed up, then the cops came and everyone fled. Me and Paul were gobsmacked, here we were 9 and 10 years old witnessing all this violence.

The Glodwick mob were mainly made up of Greasers, who were like the 60's Rockers with their long hair, denims or leather jackets and wearing heavy steel toe cap boots, they looked fearsome and were fearsome, most of them were also Ukrainians and Polish as their parents settled in Glodwick after the war as did most of Oldham's West Indian community. The Glodwick mob attracted youths from all over Oldham to tag along with them, a few from my area of Northmoor did, Mad John a heavily built 60's Rocker who in 1970 would be in his twenties, heavily tattooed and justified his nickname, Charlie who by now was a Skinhead, a tall youth who was fond of paint spraying his and his best pals name on walls all over town, his best mate being Bryn Rose, he was a bit older than Charlie and made a good name for himself at Oldham Athletic on the terraces, he was our local hero, he looked the part with his long mane of dark hair and me and Paul got to know him well because Bryn's younger brother Nigel was in my class and a pal of ours and we were often at their flat on Clarkwell estate, their mam was great with us and she ran a chippy on Rochdale Road, which was full of scarves many that Bryn had nicked on his travels and pennants which I assumed he bought, it was a great chippy.

One day walking home from Richmond junior school me and Paul bumped into some lads our age from Werneth and soon we were bragging to each other whom we knew, so me and Paul said our mate Nigel's brother Bryn is the King of the Chaddy End, these lads laughed and said their mates brother Fred Hewitt was, we said Bryn would kill him. Next day Nigel tells me and Paul that Bryn wants to see us. Bryn would be 19 then we were 10/11, we called to Nigel's flat and Bryn calmly but firmly told us never to use his name again and that Fred was his mate etc... it was only years later that I realised that Fred Hewitt was one of the town's toughest lads and Bryn certainly wasn't, although we all looked up to him at Northmoor cos he looked the part... oops. I became friends with two of Fred's younger brothers at Grange seniors,

This season 1970/71 saw plenty of violence at Boundary Park and on the streets surrounding the ground, one set of violent fans I witnessed were Grimsby Town who arrived in the town centre early one Saturday morning. I was with my mam as she always took me up town every Saturday morning and at around 10 am I saw this big gang of skinheads with black and white scarves mostly tied around their wrists or dangling for the jeans belt loops, they looked so smart and were the first skinheads I had seen apart for the odd one at Latics, most of these were wearing Harrington jackets, faded Levi jeans with turn ups at ankle length and cherry red Doc Martins, their heads were not shaved but cropped, a few of them wore bowler hats and carried brollies, there must have been around 40 of them. That morning I was wearing Wellington boots and they spotted me and began singing 'These boots are made for walking' laughing at me, even my mam chuckled....I went to Latics later that day and this mob of skins came into the Chaddy End with more Grimsby fans and attempted to take the Chaddy End but once again were repelled by the combined mobs of Oldham, although they stayed in all the match chanting away in the top corner, but as they were leaving the ground at the end of the game the Oldham mob engulfed them from all sides and kicked fuck out of them, a few of them trying to clamber over the walls of the stadium, all exciting stuff.

Another set of fans to come into the Chaddy End were Chesterfield who were mainly skinheads and were led by a big ginger haired skin with mutton chop sidies (sideburns), he was very gobby, he was wearing a blue and white striped cardigan which looked his grandma had knitted for him, they mobbed up midway up the Chaddy End and lasted about half a hour until the Glodwick Mob arrived late as usual and stinking of beer, they soon set about these Chesterfield skins and one of the Glodwick mob nutted the big ginger skin and dropped him, the mob then booted them all the way down the terraces where they clambered onto the pitch to get away.

Port Vale also appeared in the Chaddy End with about 50 lads and one of them stood out, a tall lad with shoulder length blonde hair with a centre parting, he wore one leather glove and a full length leather trench coat bottle green - he looked very impressive and he was obviously their main man because he was giving the orders out and they seemed to look up to him, they tried and failed to take the top of the Chaddy End once more the bigger numbers of the home fans engulfing them but they went down fighting, a few got arrested from both sides and it made great viewing, the big smoothie was targeted and got hammered but he fought back.

That season Latics played Rochdale away in the 2nd round of the FA Cup, Rochdale being the nearest team to Oldham, only 5 miles away, it was in the papers all week that thousands of Oldham fans would be making the short journey. I was desperate to go but mam and dad, who were going, expected there to be a lot of trouble and did not want me going, same with my brother Peter who went, he also feared there would be large scale violence as it was the talk of the town that Oldham were gonna wreck Rochdale and take over their ground. Rochdale were actually in the 3rd Division back then while we were in the 4th so Dale were favourites; mam, dad and Peter left our house at midday to get the bus to Rochdale which was just around the corner from our house on Rochdale Road. Meanwhile I was crying and so frustrated, but as soon as they went I had my hands down the back of the settee to see if there was any loose change there - me and my younger sister Karen often found coppers there after mam or dad had been drunk and kipped on there, and so it was found about ten bob (50p) - I was on my way! The bus fare was only a tanner and it was only about a shilling in the game, I boarded one of the dozens of buses that was hurtling towards Rochdale all full of Oldham fans chanting and singing. I caught the one o'clock bus and was in Rochdale for 1.30pm - the double decker was full of chanting youths many sticking their heads out of the window and everyone it seemed wearing doc marten boots and half mast jeans... this was the era of the boot boys.

In Rochdale town centre it was mayhem, as hundreds of Oldham youths rampaged, overturning market stalls, robbing shops, attacking men, the police sirens were going non stop and loads got arrested, I joined in a big march of a massive mob up to the ground Spotland which was a mile n half away, it looked great and I didn't see any Dale fans. As we neared the ground all you could hear was the Oldham fans chanting who had already taken the Sandy Lane end Rochdale's kop, the queues outside the ground were huge and the Sandy Lane was full so I with many others queued up at the paddock next to it. The ground was a ramshackle decrepit old stadium and it didn't take long for the Oldham thugs to burst a gate open and in we all piled - freemans. The

scenes were incredible as Oldham filled 3/4 of the stadium, the crowd
was 13,000 and it is said 10,000 were from Oldham, the Sandy Lane
End looked full of Oldham fans with their banners and scarves a sea of
tangerine, blue and white, shortly after kick off there was a big battle in
the middle of the Sandy Lane as a group of 20 or so Dale fans got in
the middle and began chanting 'Rochdale Aggro'. They were swamped
and kicked to fuck, the cops piled and made a few arrests including
Bryn and Peter Rose who lived close to me, they were dragged around
the pitch right past where I was stood, I was so proud of them, the
cops arrested loads that afternoon, the Dale fans were in the opposite
end but even they were being attacked by the much bigger number of
Oldham fans.......we lost the game 2—0 and after the game Oldham
fans rampaged through the town centre and smashed up several trains
taking them back to Oldham.

The 1970/71 season was one of the best ever as we won promotion
and there were so many big games and we were a free scoring team
and even won the Ford Sporting trophy which was given to the highest
scoring team in the country but also the team with the best discipline,
the FA awarded us £70,000 which enable us to build a brand new stand
which was known as the Ford Stand, - we were a team going places
and had great players like the legendary Jimmy Fryatt a big balding
bruiser of a centre forward who had big mutton chop sidies. He looked
fearsome and was the best header of a ball I ever saw, alongside him was
the lightning quick David Shaw who a few years later got a big move to
West Bromwich Albion who were in the First Division. We had Tommy
Bryceland, a Scottish inside right and a very clever footballer, Keith
Bebbington on the wing and Don Heath on the other wing, Harry
Dowd in goals who the season before played in F A Cup final for Man
City, full backs Ian Wood and Maurice Whittle who had the hardest
shot in the league and scored loads of long range free kicks, it was
an exciting team and time, the crowd got bigger and bigger and the
Chaddy End was full most games as the mob grew and grew.

Me and Paul would be outside the ground on match days at 1 pm
waiting for the gates to open at 1.30pm and the surge of youths making
their way up to the top of the Chaddy End, these same lads would
congregate in the same spot for years. Each different mob having their
own little area every home game unless the Chaddy got took which

only happened about 10 times over the next decade, despite so many teams trying many with much greater numbers.

The youths and indeed young men were all ages ranging from lads our age 10-13, then you had the bigger lads 14-17 then what we called The Dockers god knows why but these were the young men aged 18 upwards, grown men who still liked a fight, the Glodwick mob were Dockers and they always arrived late at the game which back then kicked off at 3.15pm as opposed to the rest of the country kicking off at 3pm. The Glodwick mob were renowned drinkers and had been on the piss since lunch time and would come roaring into the Chaddy End at 3.30pm, retrieving the Chaddy the odd time it had been taken, not that Glodwick were the only good mob but when they arrived they did seem to inspire the other mobs.

It was great in the early 1970's early pre match because this is were many of the youths would practise their new chants they had made up and test them out, some were laughed at, some lasted forever, I loved the mobbing up and bouncing up and down on the wooden terracing at the top of the Chaddy and the big surge down the terracing, it was a fantastic era to be a teenager with so much going on, the music and fashions were brill and it was like a University of Life as you learned to look after yourself, make new friends and build up your confidence, we grew up fast but we had to do, it was a dangerous place on them terraces and you would have to be very cute to avoid the aggro back in those heady days.

Fashions came and went but the longest running style and the one linked to the terraces was the Boot Boys, originally called Bovver Boys by the media in the 1960's, it was all about the Boots, which back in the 60's would be crude working boots, often steel toe caps and a lethal weapon, these would be exposed by rolling the jeans up above the ankles and rockers mods skinheads all wore boots at the football although by the end of the 60's skinheads who prided themselves on being a lot smarter than their rival greasers began wearing polished doc marten air ware boots, known as "docs "up north, and "DM's" in the south.....whilst the greasers or "greebo's "as we knew them still wore crude working boots, the skins wore the very smart highly polished  "docs "and polished them in colours like all black, ox blood and cherry red, they were 8 holes and ankle length and denims like Levis or wrangler jeans would be worn with turn ups hanging at the ankle to show off the precious Docs.

There was also a boot called the Monkey boot worn mainly by Boot Girls, and a very poor imitation of the Doc Marten called the Major Domos, which had a square toe, they were awful looking and very few lads wore them but the Doc was so iconic and surely THE most popular footwear of the 1970's. I yearned for a pair and had to wait until I was 12 and even then had to get the smallest size which was 5's my mam bought me a pair from the Army & Navy store in 1973, ox blood and they were 2 sizes too big and I had to wear 2 pairs of football socks to make em half fit. I cherished them and spent hours polishing them in ox blood polish, they took ages to break in and soften up, I loved the smell of the polish and was so proud of them even though it seemed half the country was wearing Docs!

The sight of hundreds of youths parading the Chaddy End in their docs was a sight to behold, it was a fabulous sight and it made you feel you had arrived and were part of something special I was now a fully fledged boot boy with my half mast skinners - baggy parallel denims with turn up worn half mast to show off the docs, wrangler jacket with sleeves rolled up and Latics scarf dangling from wrist although this was tied around the neck once you got older and began fighting because it was too easy for your enemy to grab your scarf dangling from the wrist… it was a striking image most boot boys dressed similar especially for the match it was one of many fashions/images of the early 1970's but the main one on the terraces and every Saturday up and down the country thousands of boot boys and girls were travelling up and down the country on coaches trains and vans ready for battle with rival supporters.

There were boot boy gangs all over Oldham in the early 1970's our local gang was called Northmoor boot boys and lads like Crops, Ste Hurst, Ste "Ned" Kelly, Chris Marsh, John Gallagher, Pete Logan, Mick Chan, Paul David Heap, Vic Scantlebury, Loyd Scantlebury, Jimmy Harper, Mick Dunlea, Sean Gagan, Ray Mayall, Brian Horsfall, Mick Chan, Andy Nuttall, Ste Walsh,, Gary Walsh, Paul Sykes, Hoof Hurst, Dozy Dunc, Dave Heeny, Phil Heeny were amongst them, they hung about on the estate on some steps known as the Power House an Electrical sub station which was their base, most of these became football hooligans at Latics and were my first influences, I was a year of two younger than most of these and I looked up to them as a 12 year old.

The other gang in our area was the Westwood Mob, who hung about around the vibrant Featherstall Road with it's paki cafes and chippies. It was a much livelier place than the Powerhouse steps where the Northmoor lads hung about, there wasn't as many lads but they were easier to get along and more into the fashion and birds than the Northmoor lads. They were  always having parties and attracting birds into the area - it was much more exciting for me and we even formed our own little crew Westwood juniors, when we were 12/13.....the old Westwood lads were 15/16/17 early 70's and included lads like Hunty, Cunny, Ted Legg. Cozzy, Micky Platt, Gaz Rees, Kev Mullins, Fat Eddy, Neil Donaldson, John Caldicott. The juniors were me, Paul Sykes, Geoff Noble, Mark and Nicky Dixon, Terry Forsyth, Dave Hibbert, Rob McConkie, we hung about the paki cafes Yazz's on Middleton road and Meahs on Featherstall Road, also we all went to Cannon Streetreet youth club during the week.

The paki cafes were really dodgy places. Yazz was a stern looking man, who was married to a large built white lady Joan who was good looking with long jet black hair. She had three West Indian kids and three Asian kids, Yazz was grumpy but straight and we tried our best to respect especially Joan who was really good with us, the other main paki cafe nearby was Meah's cafe which was owned by a Bengali gangster called Abu Meah, a very small slightly built but violent young man in his twenties, he had only been in Oldham 3 months in 1969 before opening the East Pakistan social club on the top of Barker street in Oldham town centre. It was long rumoured he had fled East Pakistan because if his criminal activities, the East Pakistan social club was the scene of many violent confrontations with Oldham's hooligans after the games, the pakis always carried weapons and were not soft and only got beaten back by larger numbers,.

One Saturday afternoon in 1970 me and Paul Sykes were walking past when for a dare we ran in chanting 'the Stretford End is always full the Stretford End is always full, full of what? full of coons full of chinks full of pakis, the Stretford End is always full' It was a chant we had heard the older youths chant at Latics, we were 9 & 10 years old, well a couple of paki men grabbed us and dragged us into the back room were Abu Meah was playing cards, we were pleading for mercy especially as one paki brandished a machete, a white prossie with bleached blonde hair black roots and a skirt up her arse told them to let us go if we apologised - which we did several times. Abu Meah swore at us and told us never to come near again! He let us go, we shit ourselves but ran off giggling,

Abu Meah was to see a lot more of us in the next few years when he moved down to Feathertsall Road.

In 1971 East Pakistan had a civil war with Pakistan and won its independence and became Bangladesh and the Pakis that moved in around Featherstall were in the main Bangladeshis or Bengalis as they were known, other areas in Oldham Like Werneth Coppice and Glodwick were predominantly Pakistanis...the Pakistanis saw the Bengalis as the lowest caste. - the dregs of the Asian race. It was way above our tiny heads - Abu Meah soon established himself in Oldham and fought many times and not afraid to use a knife, he wouldn't take any shit despite his size and he ruled his own cafes and communities with an iron fist, often beating his pals with sticks in front of everyone to let us know he was not one to be messed with. The Paki cafes were exciting places for us teenagers, with their pinball machines that paid out a £1 for five in a line, also table football and snacks, they were very scruffy and very dodgy places full of prostitutes and wannabe gangsters but Meah ruled the roost..

The Westwood lads were a lot more fashionable than the Northmoor lads and attracted more birds, especially Hunty, Micky Platt and Cunny, with their blown dry long hair, French flares leather bombers and Jaytex shirts, they were smart lads and were soon to get Lambretta Scooters in the mid 1970's and formed the first scooter club in Oldham, the Globe-trotters, and influenced so many of us, they were not fighters apart from Cunny, but now and then would join forces with Northmoor boot boys to take on Ashe Dene and Chaddy skins...

But the biggest influence and most respected lad from Northmoor/ Westwood was Crops - John Crowther a real one off character. Crops was 5 years older than me and would be 17 in 1972, he was the spit of Marc Bolan with shoulder length long dark natural curls, he was only average build maybe 5ft 7ins, always trendy in latest fashions and the birds loved him and most lads respected and admired him, although not the toughest he was seen as the leader of Northmoors mob. He was well known around Oldham, if you ever mentioned Northmoor people would say "oh that's were Crops come from". He put Northmoor onto the map so to speak. He was great and took me under his wing giving me advice and introducing me to his hero David Bowie on his Dansette record player in his flat. He was game as fuck also and often sported bruises from the many fights/brawls he got involved in, but by the time he was 19/20 he had got involved with a notorious hard drug crowd that had began squatting on Clarkwell estate (Northmoor).

These blokes and women were heroin users in their late 20's, proper fucked up druggies, they looked like Zombies walking about, the main one amongst them was called Joey Magnuss, a half caste Indian bloke, he looked scary. Crops soon spiralled downhill. It was in this era that during a fight with rivals Ashe Dene he ran into a speeding bus and spent months in hospital, he was crippled for years when he came out, and sank into this awful drug scene even further....like all those heroin users/abusers, Crops eventually died in his mid 30's. It was awful seeing this once proud very smart and street wise youth on his arse, begging in the town centre, school kids spitting on him and taking the piss. I last saw him a few months before he passed away, I took him for a breakfast in a cafe in Shaw, slipped him a tenner, he hugged me with tears in his eyes, and said thanks a lot mate, he didn't even recognise me, a few months later he passed away in hospital. His body could take no more, it was very sad and a message to anybody that drugs are evil... RIP Crops.

Oldham in the early 1970's was very much gang related, almost every area/district and council estate had mobs of lads who during the summer months especially would clash with each other often trying to invade each other districts or clashing in the town centre youths clubs or parks around the town. Yet ironically come the beginning of the season at Boundary Park most of these mobs would join forces to repel and take on others teams who came to Oldham. There was always an underlying tension still between a few Oldham mobs, and every now and then this would surface especially if there was a quiet match and boredom set in, some of the Oldham mobs joined up with each other and some would never get along as long standing feuds were set in stone.

Oldham mobs of the early 1970's include. Chaddy Skins...Ash Dene boot boys, Hollinwood, Derker boot boys, Fitton Hill boot boys, Failsworth, Royton skins... (these 4 mobs joined forces briefly and were known as D.F.F.R). Shaw Gawbies, Royton Shed, Shaw Road Boot Boys, Barrowshaw Boot Boys, Sholver Leathers, Lees Boot Boys, Holts Boot Boys, Abbeyhills Greebo's, Limeside Angels, Collier Hill Boot Boys, Crete St Skins, Primmy Nutters, Westwood Mob, Northmoor Boot Boys, Coldhurst Razors, Stottfield, Town Hall Mob and Saddleworth.

The town hall mob were a gang of lads and girls who came from various areas of Oldham but spent a lot of time in the vibrant town centre hanging about in the market hall and cafes and the odd pubs that sold under aged drinkers, this would be around 1972/3 lads like Les

Trelfa, Al Frew, Dave Frew, Dave Pass, Shane Clegg, Tony Stirrup, Eddie Mcguirk, Tommy McConkie, Jimbo Tupman, Lenny Miscievich, there were many more but these names stood out, they wore long leather trench coats platform shoes and had centre parting haircuts with long shoulder length hair...

Oldham's then huge Victorian market hall was a hang out for many gangs on a Saturday when it was at its busiest, there were a few cafes in there where the teenagers would hang about before heading toward Boundary Park during the football season, the best cafe was Brian's Vimto stall in the middle there would be loads hanging about here, and it would kick off now and then with rival mobs. I remember Royton clashing with Fitton Hill one day in there, all wearing the half mast skinners jeans and Doc Martens - there were a few punches and kicks but nothing serious as it spilled outside and the cops were soon onto it. Fitton Hill and Royton clashed many times over the years even though they began being a coalition in the D.F.F.R.

# THE SONGS AND CHANTS OF O.A.F.C.

AS MUCH AS THE VIOLENCE and the gangs impressed me at the football, the chanting of the whole mob at the top of the Chaddy End fascinated me. As a 10/12 year old I wasn't getting involved in all the aggro but I loved and got involved in the chanting and singing, the early 70's was a fantastic time for chanting as the kops up and down the country filled up with hundreds and sometimes thousands of youths, many song were made up and tried and tested at the match most were rejected but some are still going strong today 40 years on... A lot were copied from match of the day from the Stretford End, the Kop of Liverpool FC, The North Bank Highbury, the Kippax of Man City and all the Division One teams. The chanting was so exciting for such a young buck like me, the bouncing up and down the surging down and the incredible noise they made the Chaddy End had ideal acoustics, with its high roof covering most of the stand, you could hear the Chaddy End from afar away as the town centre over a mile away, the Chaddy End roar... I was brought up on that as a boy, I always remember asking my next door neighbour Harry what was all that noise I could hear one summer's evening, he said, "that's the Chaddy End roar lad". Harry was 70 odd, I was about 4 and we lived maybe 4 miles away from Boundary Park.

As exciting as the chanting was it reached fever pitch when rival fans came into the Chaddy End and even more so if they stayed and shared it, all trying to out chant each other it was fantastic and grew and grew through the decade. Certain chants songs were linked to individual teams like Bolton's "whose that marching up the hill boys", Burnley's "No nae never" which Oldham pinched and was one of the most popular chants for decades at Boundary Park. Sheffield United had the strange "ee aye ee aye yo" chant. Man United had the wonderful... "We shall overcome", the Joan Baez classic 60's folk rock song, United fans sang this all way through their 2nd Division campaign in 1974/75, also another United classic was "We are one of those teams that you see now" and then the Geordie's "Blaydon Races "of course which was stolen by every team as was Liverpool's "You'll Never Walk Alone," even Man United fans sang this in the 70's (although technically United fans sang it before scousers but that's a different story!). Then there was West Ham's "I'm forever blowing Bubbles" a very popular ditty with all teams also but it never sounded as good as when the Hammers sang it.

The co-ordination of these massed ranks of youths singing/chanting and clapping in unison was a fantastic sight to behold the rhythmic clapping with arms aloft amazed me hundreds in perfect timing and thousands at the larger clubs, it must have lifted the footballers, it put the hairs on me neck many a time, as much as the buzz of the aggro thrilled so to did the chanting as every game I wondered which new chants would appear, we young teenagers would chant these songs on the streets during the week and at the youth clubs and play grounds. It was a case of monkey see monkey do - all harmless unlike the violence which was spreading throughout the country and would engulf so many of us but as a 11-12, year old that would be in the near future at the moment I was a mere onlooker encouraging the older lads to get into them.

## "YOUR GONNA GET YOUR FUCKIN HEADS KICKED IN!"

1970/71 season was promotion season from the 4th to the 3rd Division. Oldham were up near the top all season and were confident of going up, the crowds increased significantly as did the mob in the Chaddy End, also many other fans were coming into the Chaddy which added to the excitement, any sightings of away fans the roar would go up "AG.. AGR...AGRO!" this alerted everyone and within moments the big charge into the invaders would occur, pies brews and fags would go up in the air as the battling commenced, Oldham were strong that season, no one took the Chaddy End that season despite several attempts, we felt invincible.

Last game of the 70/71 season was Stockport at home we only need a point to confirm promotion, Bournemouth had already won the league, so it was pretty nail biting, it was a great crowd 13,000 and the excitement was at fever pitch with the Chaddy End full to the rafters, it was rocking with all the songs and chants, there were loads of home made banners and just before kick off our local heroes from Northmoor, Bryn Rose, Ste Hurst and Mad John made a presentation on the pitch to Jimmy Frizzell our manager with a huge magnum of champagne. These three were hooligans yet here they were on the pitch, it's not as if they dressed up, Mad John was dressed like a Hell's Angel, Bryn with his match day attire of studded leather jacket and half mast jeans and boots and Hursty who was by now a fully fledged skinhead in Ben Sherman checked shirt braces half mast jeans and docs and a trilby..

Stockport brought a good following but made no attempt on the Chaddy End, they would not have stood a chance this day, too many Oldham lads were packed in and no-one was gonna spoil our day. The match went to plan, we won 2 −1 despite our goalie Harry Dowd throwing the ball into his own net! At the final whistle thousands pour onto the pitch, it was a lovely sunny day and a carnival atmosphere, we all sang "We've won promotion, We've won promotion, We are the greatest team the world has ever seen!" to the tune of recent Eurovision song contest winner by Cliff Richard, Congratulations..

It was wonderful on the pitch as people danced jigged and hugged each other and demanded our tangerine heroes come back out and take their applause, which eventually they did, we then poured out onto the streets en masse and up the long Sheepfoot Lane towards the town centre, the police got a bit heavy handed and the hooligans clashed with them, throwing bricks and bottles a couple of cars got overturned on Sheepfoot Lane and things turned ugly. This baying mob was 500 strong and were attacking police and shops on the way up town, when they reached the town centre the mob went on the rampage, running the through the market hall robbing stalls and then down the two covered Victorian arcades making a hell of a racket, it must have been very scary for the shoppers and traders, the cops despite having dogs out could not control the mob and as wrong as it was it was very exciting for a 10 and half year old wannabe.

Eventually a couple of hours later things subsided as the older lads went into the pubs and the younger boot boys returned to their estates and districts, it was the talk of the summer, bring on Division Three and all it can bring, the fixtures came out in the last week of June every year and was always an exciting time to see who we would be playing first game of the season. We got a local derby at home Bolton Wanderers, who the fuck are they. We smirked, ah well they should bring a few and should be some fun and games, bring em on - "Wanky Wanky Wanky Wanky Wanderers!"

The summer of 1970 really stands out in my mind, apart from the great songs we played at the dinner time school discos, I began to establish myself at Richmond juniors not just in my year but the year above as I was big pals with Martin Golding a chubby Scouse kid who was cock of the school and walked to school with me and our best mate Paul Sykes and home again after school, we also went to Boy's Brigade twice a week the glorious 19th ran by the loveliest man I ever knew Jimmy Mottley. Mr Mottley aas we called him was like Mr. Chips around the Northmoor area, he taught our parents, uncles, cousins and neighbours families for many years, he was the perfect gentleman, he called all the ladies ma'am, and the men sir. The Boy's Brigade was brilliant, we were always playing five a side, British Bulldog and other sports, it was very competitive, Martin and Paul were always setting me up for fights with other lads, it amused them and toughened me up and it wasn't long before I was tougher than them, Martin was a heavily built lad and had that in built Scouse confidence but he wasn't naturally hard and really a bit of a bully, he had an older brother Ringo who made a good name for himself in our district Northmoor.

But in 1970 me, Martin and Paul knocked about together and it built my confidence and reputation up, but Paul and Martin were thieves and even at the tender age of 9 /10 I wasn't comfortable thieving. I didn't mind the bottle of milk off the doorsteps or the minesweeping of the sweets at Woolworths, but they went much further. Thankfully their influence didn't work on me when it came to that, but they were good company, funny lads and adventurous, we were always nicking into the pictures for free, ABC and Odeon on Union Street. Martin would intimidate some kid to pay in and open the exit doors and we would charge in and lay low for a few moments then watch the film for free.

1970 was a big year for football in that the world cup was held that year in Mexico and in many and especially mine *the* biggest and best World Cup of all time, with the fantastic Brazil and their coffee coloured genius footballers Jarzinho, Tostao, Rivelino, Albertos and the best player of all time Pele in those majestic yellow and pale blue shirts. The sun shone all summer but them wonderful multi-skilled footballers shone more... I was only 5 in 1966 when England won the World Cup on home soil but have no recollections yet I recall almost every game from 1970.

# WHO'S THAT MARCHING UP THE HILL BOYS?

OLDHAM'S FIRST GAME of season 1971/72 was against Bolton Wanderers a town only 15 miles away a team with a proud history in FA Cups and Division One but now in freefall. We expected a decent crowd especially as it was the first game in Division 3 and the town was buzzing. We thought we could take on all comers and were looking forward to the season's challenges. I wondered if Bolton would bring a lot as I left my house that sunny morning at 10.30 am as I did every Saturday morning to go up town shopping with me mam. It was only a few hundred yards away up brew (hill), I was buzzing for the game later.. As we got into the town centre I noticed a gang of Bolton fans with their navy blue and white bar scarves dangling from their wrists and their half mast jeans and docs, there was about twenty of them maybe 15/16 years old, they were cocky - laughing and joking and chanting "Wanderers, Wanderers", every few seconds. No one said owt, I thought it won't be long before someone fills them in - an hour later me and mam are walking back home and now there are loads of different gangs of Bolton fans swanning about, but no Oldham fans, I couldn't understand this.

At 1.30pm I left my house to set off for Latics and I could hear this almighty noise, chanting "We are the Wanderers, We are the Wanderers", even half a mile away the noise was deafening, my heart raced and so did I down to Boundary Park, as I got nearer the noise increased, it was deafening, the loudest I had ever heard from a football game. The sound of police and ambulance sirens added to all this, 'what the fuck was going on?' I wondered, as I approached the ground I saw hundreds of Bolton youths running rampage, fighting police and smashing windows etc, the queues outside the Chaddy End snaked halfway up the road and they were all Bolton fans, I got into the Chaddy at about 2.15pm and Bolton had taken it big style - there were hundreds of them all at the top chanting "We are the Wanderers, We are the Wanderers!" Their arms aloft punching the air, it was very impressive if not sickening, where are the Oldham fans I wondered? That massive mob who rampaged after the final game of the season only 3 months ago? The ground filled up and you could see mobs of Oldham boot boys dotted about Boundary Park but very few in the Chaddy End, as the Bolton mob grew and grew, I was praying the Glodwick mob would retrieve the Chaddy End like they had done so many times before and fair play to them bang on kick off in they came backed by a hundred so other Oldham thugs but Bolton heavily outnumbered them and Bolton had so many bigger lads and blokes with them - Skinheads, Greasers, Hells Angels, Teddy boys. They all came charging down to take on the Oldham lads who fought in vain and got over ran and battered to fuck, many clambering onto the pitch to get away. I witnessed all this from a safe distance, it was very scary and I 'd never seen violence of this magnitude up until then. Bolton fans returned to the top of the Chaddy End once more and mocked and taunted the Oldham fans all the game. A few Bolton got ambushed going to the bogs which were behind the stand but they had taken the Chaddy End and battered loads of Oldham fans many innocents and made such an impact they were for many years the most hated fans ever to come to Oldham. It was the start of many violent confrontations between these two Lancashire towns over the next two decades. That August day though Oldham were well out of Bolton's league.

That game versus Bolton Wanderers had a massive impact on so many Oldham fans, a few never ventured to Boundary Park again such was the level of violence unleashed by Bolton fans. Some chose the easier option of supporting Manchester United, with their massive Red Army of thousands of Boot Boys, you could easily melt into such a massive mob, a few chose to follow Man City, a few chose to play amateur football on Saturday afternoons and quite a lot gritted their teeth got a grip toughened up and vowed to seek revenge against these evil Bolton bullying bastards! We would have to take a lot of pain blood tears and guts along the way but we did avenge but it was a rough ride because there is no doubting that during the 1970's Bolton Wanderers were very rough and the "cocks" of the Lancashire clubs.

The lads of Northmoor the area where I came from particularly wanted revenge especially as one of the most sickening attacks took place on one of our pals, Barry Wood who aged 14 took a severe beating off Bolton fans and Barry wasn't even a football fan. What happened was because Northmoor was near Boundary Park there were loads of Bolton thugs in the area that morning and Barry was just completing his paper round, his leg was in plaster due to a recent accident where he broke his ankle, he saw this gang of Bolton fans and tried to make his way away from them but they clocked Barry and moved in on him. They could see he was in plaster and he pleaded with them not to hurt his recovering ankle, it fell on deaf ears, these bastards were not for showing any compassion, any Oldhamer's was fair game and they set about him, beating him to a pulp, so bad that Barry spent weeks in hospital with broken bones, which gave him a permanent limp all his life, prevented him playing football and rugby with his mates and limited his job opportunities. In saying that Barry was made of stern stuff and went onto be a proud family man and worked all his life despite the hindrance. His Northmoor pals and many more were livid and the hatred they had for Bolton Wanderers never waned and much revenge was exacted.

Bolton didn't have it their own way that day though as the main Bolton face and Lever End legend Fred Dickie Dickinson recalls, "we arrived about mid day at Boundary Park and were waiting for the gates to open at 1pm so we could set about taking the Chaddy End. There were half a dozen of us, me and my mates and we were sat on the garden walls in those houses facing the main entrance of the ground. We were being loud and boisterous when a middle aged bloke told us to piss off and move away from his garden, obviously we gave him a load of abuse, yet a few moments later he returned with a baseball bat and set about Mick Godding, hitting him over the head. The lads set about this bloke and filled him in, I watched this and actually felt sorry for him, the cops were soon on the scene and we had to get away rapid, that wound us up no end and set me up for a lot of aggro in the Chaddy End, but there was very little opposition as we took over in no time, but fair play to the old bloke with the baseball bat, he was protecting his home!

"I only wished the Oldham fans had shown the same bottle and aggression as the old neighbour ha ha, could have done with him swinging his bat in the Chaddy that day."

Oldham fans were shocked and embarrassed by the taking of the Chaddy End so easily by Bolton and without any defence, lots of questions were asked - such as why wasn't Oldham fans in there before Bolton? Why didn't all the combined mobs come in together as one to challenge Bolton? Why did the Glodwick mob come in as usual after kick off full as mops and way too late to do anything about it, surely they must have heard Bolton were all over town from mid-morning? The cold hard facts are Bolton were a big club with a big rough tough following only 2 seasons previously they were a Division One club and still had a huge following, Latics were way out of their depth and they had to get their act sorted and sorted soon!! Fortunately 3 days later they played Bury away in the League Cup 1st round and took a couple of thousand fans and took over Bury's end who to be fair offered very little resistance apart from a mob of 50 Bury Reds chanting United, United – they soon got routed and beaten up. Bury's few lads were in the paddocks hiding behind the police chanting "Wanderers "trying to wind us up, it was an easy take over as Bolton's was of our Chaddy End a few days prior, but Bury were soft and Oldham always took over their end as we did with nearby Rochdale..

A few weeks later though the Chaddy End once more got taken over as we played Blackburn Rovers on a Tuesday night, they had the top of the Chaddy End all the game and could not be shifted, even though they didn't have anywhere near the numbers of Bolton but they were solid and stuck together, maybe 300 of them, mostly greasers I recall, they had this mad chant of singing "gree bo, gree bo, gree bo!" with one arm aloft, it looked good and sounded good, Oldham surrounded them on both sides and in front but could not move them and Blackburn came piling in to Oldham throughout the game, after the match Oldham's much bigger numbers got the better of them on the car park and ran them and beat the one's they caught, they were the last team to take the Chaddy End that season, but both our Lancastrian rivals had taken our beloved Chaddy End and it hurt.

I went to both Bolton and Blackburn away that season both very rough grounds, when we played at Bolton I went with my Uncle Jack a big burly barrelled chested man, very strong, he took me in the Lever End, don't know why, ha, but it was packed full of Skins Boot boys and Greasers, they had probably fives times as many thugs as Oldham it was very impressive and they made an incredible noise, I felt safe with Uncle Jack, no one would be taking him on. Oldham's paltry away following was in the opposite end the Railway Embankment also known as the Warbies end, I could see them getting attacked by Bolton fans throughout the game, many running away, a few fought back, it looked pitiful, after the match me and Uncle Jack were heading back to our coach and Bolton fans were picking Oldham fans off at will, many getting bloody noses.

Blackburn away was equally rough we took a lot more there but got kicked to fuck we had about 15 coaches parked a mile from the ground next to a bleeding fun fair, so not only did Rovers fans chase and batter us all when we got to the coaches the fairground emptied and all the gypos and young lads attacked us as well, we couldn't get out of Blackburn fast enough, the coppers there did fuck all to help us, they just laughed, loads of Oldham got twatted there - we were to avenge this many times also.

That season of 71/72 Oldham fans grew in confidence and after Bolton and Blackburn had taken over nobody else did and Oldham even took away ends at Bury, Barrow, Southport, Halifax, Rochdale, York, Mansfield and Chesterfield to name a few, the mob grew and the atmosphere was superb at most home games. We finished that season halfway up the league and safe, I was now 11 and went to every home game and a lot of away games and witnessed the violence and it was gripping me, I saw the respect certain lads got for leading the battles and showing great courage, their reputations were made on the terraces and kept them in good stead for many years, lads like Herby – Steven Jones who in 1972 would have been 17 he had been a skinhead but by now his hair and grown, he wore the latest fashions and although not big he was a strong looking youth who looked hard with his flat nose, he was very vocal and often started the chanting off but he had loads of bottle and never took a backward step, often getting a bloody nose at least and arrested many times during the 70's. He had a younger brother Ray a lot bigger not as vocal as Herby but a big tough lad who followed his brother into battle, both smart dressers the came off Crete St estate and both had good reputations, one of their mates was Shane Clegg same age as Herby average size but very game also although not one to got screaming into battle like Herby, he was more measured with his assaults of away fans, he was very trendy and had the best afro in town but Shane's was natural shoulder length dark blonde curls, gave him a striking image, Shane was big into the Northern Soul scene.

One lad who did stand out from the crowd was Kenny Jones who'd be 18/19 then and was a right nut case, he came from Failsworth and had a strong Manc accent, he had knocked about with the famous Crossley skinheads for a while also, the first time I saw him was at York City. Oldham had taken over the end and after the match the big mob made their way through the town centre toward the train station, Kenny was at the front of the Oldham mob with his long jet black hair flowing behind him his long leather trench coat and blue and white Oldham scarf tied around his neck, at the station on the opposite side were a big gang of Leeds fans who had been to back up York to no avail,

Kenny and his crew of about twenty ran over the bridge and piled in to the Leeds fans who all scattered Kenny was launching milk bottles at them, he got wrestled to the ground by cops and arrested, but this did not deter him for the next game at home he came bouncing into the Chaddy End with his crew laughing and joking and demanding where the away fans were. He was without doubt one of Oldham's top lads in the 70's and 80's and holds the record for most charge sheets, 24 at last count - he was a great and inspirational character.

Ever since I first went to Latics I always noticed this skinhead stood on his own or more often than not mooching about looking for away fans, he looked the part he'd be 19/20 in 1970, he had the skinhead look off to a tee, crew cut perfect sideburns, Barathea blazer with a Lancashire rose, immaculate faded Levi's and cherry red docs, and he always wore one leather glove, something to do with going to Soul Nights. He looked a tough nut and many a time he'd go into the away fans, he came from Royton and everyone seem to know him even though he seemed a loner, his name was Dave Rabbich.

One away game where I was very impressed with Oldham's away following was Halifax Town in April 1972, there was loads of trouble, me and Paul went on one of the many coaches leaving Barlow's coach station, maybe 15 or more, most of them Boot Boys, Halifax is only 17 miles away and we were there within 30 minutes, the coaches for some reason dropped us in the nearby town centre and it was only 1.30pm, it was pissing down and here were maybe 300 Oldham Boot Boys swanning about Halifax, it didn't take long for some locals to challenge us and a mob of Yorkies bricked the Oldham mob, who then gave chase through the busy market, overturning a few stalls for good measure, chanting and putting the fear of god up the shoppers.

We marched triumphantly towards the Shay, arguably the worst ever football ground in the Football League, it was so basic and scruffy with just three stands and one big steep hill were the local bus drivers could watch the match for free. Oldham filled their allocated end and also had about 100 lads in Halifax's end which was the paddock opposite, Halifax had double them numbers and as soon as the match kicked off the mass brawling began, the bigger numbers of Halifax were getting the upper hand forcing Oldham's mob further towards the halfway line, come half - time Halifax were really piling the pressure on the Oldham mob and they were taking some serious hammer, a few Oldham in our end ran across the wet muddy pitch to join in the fray, and Halifax met them on the pitch so the rest of us in our end went across the pitch including me and Paul and it was our first taste of football violence as we targeted young Boot Boys our age, we found some and set about them, booting them up their arses as they fled. Oldham soon had Halifax on the run and by the time the 2nd half kicked off we had cleared their end, Halifax had fled albeit for a brave few who got kicked to fuck, it was then I hear a wonderful chant to the tune of American Pie.... "Bye Bye Mr. Halifax Town, took my hatchet to the Shay and chopped it right down, the Oldham boys had you down on the ground, singing this will be the day that you die, this will be the day that you die" - that song was made up within moments of Oldham taking Halifax's end by the legendary original 60's thug Jimmy Kirt, Jimmy made many wonderful chants and songs up he truly was one of the best Oldham characters of all time.

After the game Oldham rampaged out of the ground and into the town centre to were the coaches were parked, chasing any Halifax fans they spotted which were not many, we boarded our coaches and as Paul went to claim the back seat a big stocky Glodwick lad called Adam grabbed Paul and squeezed his face telling him to fuck off he was sitting there! Paul shit himself and moved away, Paul was only 12 Adam was 19, we were both a long way from gaining respect from the older lads especially the Glodwick Mob, Paul never forgot that but did not avenge it, we both had a lot of respect for Adam and the Glodwick Mob, and put it down to experience. Funnily enough another Glodwick lad cracked me a couple of years later when we played Villa at home, I was only 13 he'd be 22, Keith Partridge a top lad whom I had tons of respect for, a good man, apparently I was being a cheeky little fucker, ah well no surprise there - we fought side by side many times years later.

# I GOT A ROLLS ROYCE COS IT'S GOOD FOR MY VOICE..

**A**S FAST AS I WAS LEARNING on the terraces it was at the Youth Club which I began attending in 1972 that I learned about the finer things in life away from football violence – although I certainly got onto a few scraps there. My youth club was Cannon Streetreet a ten minute walk from my house, it had opened in the early 1960's and was one of the towns biggest and most popular youth centres, it attracted youths from all over Oldham but mainly from Northmoor, Westwood and the tough Primrose bank council estate, an estate that housed many large mainly Irish families such as the Diveneys, Mcghees, Kenways, Bakers, Jones, Swords, Standrings, Brennans, Mcgarrigles, Shearings, Cleary's, Cunliffes, Morrows, these Primmy lot were a lot rougher than us from Northmoor/Westwood, but most of us knew them from School the Proddies went to Grange the Catholics went to St Anselms, a lot of the Primmy lot ended up marrying each other.

I remember my first night there vividly – it was a Friday night late September 1972, I went along with Neil Wood who was a year above me and so called cock of the year, and Paul Sykes also a year older than me, they'd be 12, I was 11, you were supposed to be aged 12 to 17. I was very nervous one for being under aged and looking it, both Paul and Neil were big lads and looked older but secondly Cannon Streetreet had a bad reputation for violence, now I know I'd already seen a lot at the football but this was lads 16 and older beating kids up. Paul and Neil said they'd back me if there was any trouble, the doors opened at 7pm but even at 6.30pm there was a massive queue of teenagers all piled up on the steps outside, I recognised a few from school and even more from Latics, there were also loads of girls there in the feather cuts and monkey boots, all effin and jeffin. There were some really rough birds, scary fuckers, when the doors finally opened a big roar went up and they all charged for the entrance, we waited until the rush had calmed down, when we got there we had to sign a membership form where I lied and told them I was born in 1960 to make me 12 but I got in no problems and I was gobsmacked at the size of the place and how many teenagers were in there.

Cannon Streetreet had a great atmosphere, loads of giggling girls loads of running about and so much activity, table tennis, pool, 5 a side. a huge trampoline, a TV room (were all the snogging went on with the lights out) a big disco room, I was very impressed, most of the lads were Oldham fans with a few United and City, the first night flew but at the end of the night I saw a sickening sight that I never forgot, the word was that there was gonna be a fight at the end of the night between a black lad called Crook and a white Rocker called Stan, who looked fearsome and scary but Crooky only had a couple of mates backing him, loads were rooting for Stan, it seemed the whole club some 200 plus wanted to see this fight apparently to see who was the cock of Cannon Street. The fight was right outside the club and the big crowd made a circle, I got a good view, well this black lad was knocking Stan all over, he kept being knocked down but Crooky would let him back up, Stan was bleeding heavily from his nose and around his eyes, all of a sudden someone hands Stan a bottle which he smashes on Crook's head and down he goes then Stan plunges the bottle into the back of his neck pulled it out and a torrent of dark red blood spurted everywhere, it was sickening. Girls began screaming, most of us walked away many in disgust, then we saw Stan's mates all pile into Crooky and his 2 mates and batter fuck out of them, the screams the black lads let out haunted me, I know I'd already seen a lot of violence at the football but this sickened me, I never saw Crooky again, but that Stan thought he was King Kong for a few weeks bullying and intimidating lads at the youth club, until another lad came from another youth club offered him out and battered fuck out of him and most of the Cannon Street regulars were cheering and that was the end of Stan, we never saw him again.

Me, Neil and Paul all lived a ten minute walk away from Cannon Street and at the end of Mondays. Weds, and Friday nights we'd walk the same route home across Rochdale Road and cut through the College grounds, we used to always sing the same song playing our air guitars, "Children of the Revolution" by T. Rex, one of our favourite lines was, "I've got a Rolls Royce, der der der der, because it's good for my voice, der der der der, but you can't beat the Children of the Revolution oh no!" another thing we always did was piss on the very powerful spot lights that lit up the Oldham College signs, this would give off a horrendous hissing noise and smell like a mini explosion. Daft stuff.

All in all the Primmy and Northmoor lads got on and would even mob up to go to Latics games, Northmoor lads back then included Pete

Logan a big tall lad with fantastic dark ginger hair cut perfectly into a Feather cut just like David Bowies, it looked very impressive, Log as he was known also wore all the latest fashions, Ste 'Ned' Kelly, a typically Boot Boy with the wranglers and perfectly highly polished Docs, he was very loud and funny and wasn't shy at getting stuck in at the football, Andy Nuttall, another Doc Marten wearing boot boy, John Gall, Ray Mayall, Chris Marsh, Mick Dunlea, Ste Newton, Mick Chan, Jimmy Harper. Of the Primmy lads I remember Nicky Baker, a wild youth who would fight anyone and not back down despite his slight build, Tony Diveny, a small lad 2 years older than me but very cocky,confident and street wise, Johnny 'Loopy' Morrow, Donty Shearing, Danny "Eggy" Standring, The Cleary brothers, Big Tony Diggle, Dessie Curley, Paddy Brennan, Johnny Cunliffe who even though only 15 had the best sideburns in town, a few Curleys and a lot more besides...

I spent 5 happy years going to Cannon Street youth clubs and indeed a few more dotted around Oldham they were very busy places back in the 70's, but there were always fights many times over girls or football, I had quite a few one to ones and one night in 1974 got jumped by 4 lads who waited for me outside, they were from St.Mary's estate and pounced onto me and booted me in the hea. I was hammered but got up all groggy and smashed a bottle on the lamp post and shouted at them to come back which they did and I stuck it into one lads fore-ars. Blood spurted everywhere and he screamed and his mates ran off. I'm so glad he put his arm out and I didn't stick in his chest, God forbid! I got a caution from the Juvenile courts for that, I was treated leniently because the cops knew I had been jumped, and it was self-defence. I also got a life ban from Cannon Street which was bang out of order given I was jumped and from lads from another area who never came again, I was reinstated a couple of months later when a new man took over the reigns, a giant 6 foot 6 inches Barbadian former police man who gave everyone who had been barred a fresh start, which was a lot, thanks Charles a great man indeed. I never saw them lads again who jumped me.

The 1971/72 season was certainly a eye opener for the Chaddy Enders having seen our end taken over by both Bolton and Blackburn, and shared with a few teams but we took some serious kickings away from home, in saying that the mobs grew and by the end of the season the Chaddy End had its biggest combined mob up to date....We all looked forward to the new football season of 1972/73 and were confident nobody would take the Chaddy End again, as most lads would be in from 1.30pm ready to take on any invaders, once again in the summer we eagerly awaited this forthcoming seasons fixtures, one big game we looked forward to was the mighty Aston Villa who had been relegated to the 3rd Division but were still getting crowds of 30,000 plus! That game was in October, no big home games before then but a couple of potentially big friendlies pre season at home Burnley and Man City both in Division One.

Burnley was our first pre season friendly and as I left my house at 1pm that sunny Sat afternoon I could hear the Burnley fans loud as fuck and already in the Chaddy End in their hundreds, the cops let them in rather than have them wandering the streets, the noise they made was incredible on par with Bolton the season before. I was so excited and called for Paul and we bombed it down to Boundary Park, when we got there, there were hundreds of Oldham Boot Boys queuing up to get into the Chaddy End and take Burnley on, we all get in and there was a good hour mass brawling as both set's of fans charged into each other, eventually Oldham's bigger mobs finally ran Burnley out of the Chaddy End and into the paddocks, although a few stayed, these were long haired bikers with leather jackets with all the studs etc, they were game as fuck but the Glodwick mob nailed them and booted them down the terracing, the Chaddy End was bouncing and full of confidence at re - taking our end back off such a big club as Burnley, we sang our songs of war and defiance all the match and at 3/4 time went round to the away end to confront Burnley en masse a huge mob of 500, but Burnley would not come out to play and hid behind the cops, Oldham taunted them and thought this season we were unbeatable bring on the Villa Bolton and Blackburn...we are Oldham super Oldham.

# AG - AGR - AGRO - AGRO!

**A**LL WEEK THE TALK was how Oldham fucked Burnley off and bring on Man fucking City who didn't have a big reputation back then unlike Man United's Red Army who were rampaging up and down the country - well how fucking wrong were we! That Saturday afternoon by 2pm the Chaddy End was full to bursting point. Within an hour City had filled the whole stand which held over 6000 and most of these were hooligans or so it seemed. "We took the Chaddy End!" they taunted us, "Manchester la la la, Manchester la la la" no Oldham fans got in the Chaddy End that day, they couldn't if they wanted to, it was full up and full of gloating Mancs,.." Oh Rodney Rodney Rodney Rodney Rodney Marsh!" it looked and sounded and was an amazing sight, a fantastic sea of sky blue... the Oldham fans were in the opposite end the Rochdale Road End accompanied by a mob of a couple of hundred Man United fans, it was a kind of coalition, the Reds were from Oldham, Rochdale, Middleton and Moston. There was a big gap between the Oldham and the United fans the coalition was uneasy the United fans were just chanting "United, United" all the time looking down on little Oldham. At half-time thousands of City came across the pitch United fans fled en masse most climbing out of the ground.

City to be fair did not attack us the Oldham fans but just returned triumphantly back to the Chaddy End, after the game thousands of City marched up Sheepfoot Lane back to the train stations at Werneth and Oldham Mumps in the town centre, I saw no resistance from Oldham that day - it was a very impressive take over and it was only a friendly!

Talk about being brought back down to earth, ah well we were lucky that no other big teams came to Oldham the first few games of the season and the Chaddy End was soon bouncing with confidence and taking big mobs away to Chesterfield Southport, Bury, York, Halifax, Rochdale, Tranmere, Wrexham and Crewe.

We took loads to Wrexham and took their end but after the game we came unstuck as half the town turned on us, our ten coaches got smashed to fuck, most of the Welsh mob after the game were Hell's Angels, and wielding chains and iron bars, it was fucking scary! On our coach that day was Meat Pie Fred, a 30 stone fat fucker, MPF was a bit slow and the Glodwick mob took him under their wing. We called him Meat Pie Fred cos he was always scoffin pies and drank beer like a fish drinks water, he was a great character always singing songs and always wore his 1950's blue and white barred scarf with the 1950's players name sewn in, well that day when the Hell's Angels began attacking our coach and trying to get on we shoved Meat Pie Fred to the entrance, his back was jammed in the door hole and he took some terrible blows but bought us enough time until the cops came. When we finally left Wrexham under police escort loads of lads gave Meat Pie Fred cans of beer and he got pissed on the back seat and pissed his pants and a torrent of piss ran down the aisles on the coach we all lifted our legs up, it was hilarious, the driver was not happy though as half the windows were put through and the coach stank of piss !!!

So late 1972 the town is up for the big one the mighty Aston Villa were due in town, the biggest club in the Third Division with the biggest crowds and following. It was a very wet miserable day that Saturday and as usual I was with me mam uptown from 10 am having a mooch, saw loads of Villa youths milling about, a few wearing Crombies and carrying brollies, I just knew there would be loads of trouble at the game later that day, me and Paul were down there for 12.30pm, and already hundreds of Villa fans were arriving on coaches, also the cameras were there from Granada. It was shown on the Big Match on that Sunday, the turnstiles opened at 1pm and the hundreds of Villa fans piled into the Chaddy and the cops didn't do a thing about it, they soon began their chanting and roaring letting everyone know they had taken the Chaddy End.

Very few Oldham youths/thugs went into the Chaddy End, they could hear on the way down just how many Villa fans were in the Chaddy and it must have seemed a lost cause, the few who did bravely go in got attacked by Villa and forced into the paddocks, it was an awesome mob, me and Paul were in but kept a safe distance, and were no threat anyhow, the Oldham fans congregated in the away end the huge open terrace, there was a really big mob of Oldham fans more than usual but not enough to take Villa's bigger older mob on. Well surprise, surprise, just before kick off Oldham's mob of say 3/400 youths led by a gang of about twenty-five Boot Girls led by Sharon, a Skinhead bird and future wife of Slouk from the Glodwick mob. She was a hard nut, only small with short cropped feathered blonde hair with her checked shirt tight jeans and monkey boots, a lot of her mates were dressed similarly, they looked great and were really a tough crew.

Alongside Sharon was a tall Skinhead bird called Loz who married Herby, so there was a big Latics connection, as the Oldham mob approached the Chaddy End walking down the side of the pitch they were joined by loads from the paddocks, the mob grew and grew and the Villa fans did not charge down to meet them but sang "come on take your kop back ha ha ha" - it was so exciting for us hiding in the Chaddy End and there were quite a lot because as soon as the Oldham mob jumped into the Chaddy End they were joined a couple of hundred other Oldham fans. Now this was one big mob surging up the terraces led by the Oldham Boot Girls who piled right into Villa's mob wielding steel combs and other sharp instruments, the Villa fans tried groping them but were soon being attacked by the big Oldham mob from side on and below both mobs mauled and brawled and the police could not cope with so much aggression from so many people,

There was a brief stand off halfway across the Chaddy End with a ten yards no mans land, when all of a sudden a mob of around 100 lads began chanting United United from the Oldham side, and "Oldham Reds we are here whoa whoa," this wound the Villa fans up who came charging back across the terraces. It also wound a lot of Oldham fans up who didn't want United's fans help and fights broke out between Oldham and United fans, they left after while with quite a lot battered by Oldham fans, then we got about re taking back the Chaddy End which we eventually did by half time forcing the Villa mob out of our end, we matched them for numbers and after many charges finally had the better of them but it was hard, so many one to fights and mass brawls, the St John's ambulance service was very busy as were the police there were dozens of arrests and even more ejections from both sides.It was a fantastic victory for the Oldham thugs, even aided by United for a short while, that was the last time Oldham Reds ever came in the Chaddy End as a mob, they may have come many times with their Latics supporting mates but they never shouted "United! United!" again to undermine us.

That very eventful day against Villa we lost the game 6—0 as Villa marched onto win the league and their then centre forward Andy Lochead who scored a hat-trick against us actually signed for Latics a few weeks later and helped us to win the Third Division 2 seasons later. He was a big hard rugged centre forward who knocked fuck out of opposing centre halves, re taking the Chaddy End from Villa really built up our confidence in the Chaddy End and a few weeks later on January 6th 1973 we were due to play the hated Bolton Wanderers who terrorised us and indeed the town the season before. We would be ready this time, the town was up for it, slogans appeared on walls all over town "Bolton Die January 6th!" it was the talk of the town on the streets in the schools in the youth clubs in the pubs, this just wasn't football it was Oldham town defending itself...

Come the day it was a bright sunny but very cold morning and as usual I was up town with me mam mooching and having brecky in Littlewoods cafe – cheese on toast and a cup of milky coffee by 11 am there were already hundreds of Bolton youths up town but also loads of Oldham and there were several clashes and loads of cops with dogs, the tension was rising rapidly. Paul called for me at midday and we walked down Rochdale Road towards the ground and there were loads of Bolton youths marching up towards town centre chanting and being as cocky as ever. We were at the ground by 12.30pm and there were hundreds of Bolton fans outside with more and more arriving all the time in vans and buses, we both looked at each other and thought the same, there was no way of holding this lot back today there were just so many of the cunts and they seemed so up for it.

A few Oldham lads came early but got ran off by the much bigger Bolton mob, the doors opened at 1pm again and the cops let the Bolton lads into the Chaddy End but then within half a hour Bolton had well and truly taken over the Chaddy End once again and revelled in the chanting. "We took the Chaddy End" but come 2.30pm more and more Oldham fans came in from both sides and although we could not shift them like we did with Villa, we put up a very spirited fight but Bolton were too strong and aggressive, they were very tough and violent and would attack anyone, many kids my age got slapped including me who took quite a few blows and kicks. By kick off Bolton had all the top of the Chaddy End and Oldham were pushed to the bottom and sides but there were scuffles all the first half, after about twenty minutes after kick off we all noticed a huge mob in the open end and they were not Bolton and they were not Oldham, they wore sky blue scarves and were chanting City City City! It was a massive mob, bigger than what Oldham had but not quite as big as the Bolton mob but very impressive and Bolton fans were taunting them to come "across the pitch!" at half time they did that – hundreds of Man City fans came charging across the pitch it looked magnificent and we encouraged them but Bolton were made of stern stuff and charged down the terraces to meet them head on as City all jumped into the Chaddy End. It ended in a mass brawl that lasted fifteen minutes, Oldham joined in with City and forced Bolton back up the terracing but Bolton came back en masse and eventually forced the combined mobs of City and Oldham out of the Chaddy End into the paddocks. It was a fantastic effort from Bolton and by the end of the game City fans had fucked off and most of Oldham had also, Bolton Wanderers not only took the Chaddy End that day but fucked Man City off aswell and confirmed just how hard Bolton were back in the early 1970's!

The rest of the 72/73 season flew by and once again our team did us proud by finishing third and just missing out on promotion - our last game of the season saw us play Blackburn Rovers who gave us fans such a torrid time the last time we played here after the game especially on the fairground and they had also taken over the Chaddy End last season although they did not this season but still had a big mob in most of the game. This was April 1973 and Oldham took a big crowd to Blackburn which was only 28 miles away, dozens of coaches arrived between 1 and 2.30pm and Oldham's big following encamped in the Darwen End which was very much like our own Chaddy End and many ends back then, a terraced stand with a roof on behind the goals, it was opposite Blackburn's home end which was called the Blackburn End. The Darwen End soon filled up with a buoyant upbeat Oldham mob demanding to know where Blackburn's mob were, they were packed out in their home end and threats and insults were aimed at each other before the game and throughout the first half, at half time a big mob of 100 plus Blackburn fans came into the Darwen end all of them greasers with hob nailed boots loads of crude Indian ink tattoos on their knuckles and wearing leather jackets, they were a scruffy but hard looking mob and they came piling right into the Oldham's fans and it was a major battle, once more the cops showed great leniency to the Rovers thugs and arrested loads of Oldham lads. This hard core mob of Rovers thugs could not be shifted and fights were breaking out throughout the 2nd half, after the match the dreaded half mile long walk back to the coach park which once again has a fair on it and we got twatted all the way back there and once again the gypos and revellers attacked us as we boarded our coaches, most had their windows put through, we got hammered, Blackburn was back then a very rough away ground, we vowed revenge once more, we had a lot of avenging to do.

That day one of our local lads Barry Ten Bellies made his mark, Barry would be about 20 then and was a very heavily built lad, he had long curly black hair was a bit of a rocker, he had a bit of a name in the Northmoor area, after the match as both mobs were making their way to the coach park, some Blackburn lad twatted Barry from the side and nicked his scarf, well Barry was not having that and chased this youth into the Blackburn mob who engulfed him and set about him but Barry was windmilling for his life and knocked half a dozen to the deck, he got his scarf back and fair play to the cops they let him stroll back to the Oldham mob, Barry was beaming and getting loads of deserved praise, he fed off that for years and us young Northmoor boot boys were rightly proud of big Baz.

The biggest and hardest lad in our area was Big Les McKinley a huge 6 foot Northern Irish man, in the early 70's he'd be early twenties and was a teddy boy, he was massive, with a massive chest arms and shoulders, with a big quiff and huge sideburns, fortunately he was a big Oldham fan and although not part of any mob he wasn't shy at knocking away fans out, him and his mate big Chris, same build and stamp as Les but an Crossley Skinhead, together they were a top tough as fuck duo.

One night Oldham played away at Rotherham, I was with my brother, there was only 2 coach loads from Oldham at this game, near the end of the game about 40 Rotherham fans came and surrounded us, it was looking bleak, until Big Les and Big Chris came in amongst us, both stood back to back and beckoned on the Yorkies who came flying in but almost all got knocked down off Les and Chris. It was fantastic even the coppers were impressed and just dragged the stricken Yorkie boot boys out of the away end walking back to the coaches we all huddled around these two Oldham giants.

# GLAM ROCK DAYS

THIS WAS A PIVOTAL YEAR for me - it was 1973 and I was 12 and beginning to take an interest in fashion and music as well as stepping up my interest in the world of football hooliganism. I began to become influenced by certain people, like Pete Ure the cock of my school Grange Comprehensive, Pete was 15/16 and was a very strong but smartly dressed youth he was still a skinhead even though there were very few around most people were Smoothies, long blown dry hair flares and penny round shirts. Although there were still a few Crombie wearing Suedeheads who dressed like smart skins but wore their hair longer, Pete Ure was cool and was hard and looked great in highly polished brogues red socks black parallels hanging perfectly at ankle length Barathea blazer with Lancashire rose and had the best image of that time and arguably all time, the Suedehead look was so smart and he carried it off so well. I was 4 years younger but he let onto me ruffled my hair, I made him laugh cos I was a cheeky fucker.

However us younger ones were into Glam Rock - Slade, Sweet, T. Rex, Bowie, Roxy Music and Gary Glitter yes Gary Glitter and the Glitter band were brilliant aswell! It was all up beat music and stomping sounds. Another top band were Mott the Hoople - the lads at school all loved Slade they were a rough arse band loud n proud and a former Skinhead band,. The softer lads liked Bowie and T. Rex but we all secretly admired them aswell but they were seen as girly or puffy but Gary Glitters big stomping sound was a big hit with the Boot Boys who adopted the brilliant "Hello Hello it's good to be back" which become "Hello Hello Oldham aggro" or whichever team you supported. It certainly roused you up when this was chanted as we went into battle.

The first time I heard this was on Boxing Day 1973, we played Blackburn Rovers and expected those big hard tattooed Greasers would be coming in the Chaddy End again. Me and Paul were in the Chaddy by 1.30 and couldn't believe our eyes there was a mob of Blackburn fans at the top of the Chaddy End there must have been 200 of them and not one was over 15 and almost everyone of them had football cardigans on blue and white stripes (they were a big fashion item back then) and fans wore them in their team colours, but to see a full mob all wearing them was very impressive, this mob of young boot boys were all chanting "hello hello Blackburn aggro..." it sounded great but I knew these were too young and would be fucked off when Oldham's big lads came into the Chaddy which is what happened by 2.30pm these young Rovers lads had been chased out of the Chaddy End. None fought back they all scarpered, God knows were the big rough arsed Blackburn fans were that day!

The chanting of rival mobs back then was as exciting as the actually brawling and hand to hand fights, each team had their own chants and songs and they fascinated me, the timing and passion was brilliant, many a time rival fans would listen to their rivals chanting or singing then pile in a strange kind of respect, many chants of course were provocative ie: "Your gonna get your fucking head kicked in" was a hint as was "we'll see you all outside" when the cops had it boxed off and we could not get at each other, some chants both sets of fans joined and tried to out sing each other, all added to the wonderful atmospheres created on the terraces back in the 1970's, I often chanted these to myself in bed eagerly awaiting the next game home or away..

## WE WILL BE WE WILL BE CHAMPIONS OF DIVISION 3!

The 1973/74 season was one of the most exciting ones in my life as an Oldham Athletic supporter, I went to every home game and most away games including four rounds of the FA Cup... even the pre season friendlies were great as Oldham's mob grew and grew the gangs of Oldham had more boot boys than ever before as the on field successes brought in lots more support and we even began to attract large support from the Mancunian border districts like Middleton, Moston Ashton Failsworth and Stalybridge, by now many boot boys were also wearing brogues all leather shoes most had blakeys in the heel (steel clips) and they became a lethal weapon especially when kicked in the shins, face and head by them, also this season of Butcher coats being worn by many hooligans often with slogans emblazoned on them, the scarf were not worn dangling from the wrists anymore, too dangerous and too easy to grab you by and swing you by, scarves were worn around the neck tied in a knot.

In the summer of 1973 few fashionable items came out like the silk bomber jackets, white skinners, parallel denim as worn at half mast, shirt jackets, which were a thin checked cotton shirt but worn as a jacket, football jumpers, a striped cardigan worn in the colours of your team,

Birmingham bags, flared baggy trousers with large pockets at the side of the knees, platforms had been out for a while I had some cracking bottle green all leather ones at two inch but some lads wore 4 and even 6 inch platforms which looked ridiculous... the hairstyles were now centre partings and grown long.

The wearing of the baggy white skinners with shiny cherry red docs was a striking one, and was very popular until the Bay City Rollers burst onto the scene a short while later and claimed the image and then it became unpopular but for 12—18 months it was the image of the boot boy and photographs of the many pitch invasions in that era show hundreds and sometimes thousands of youths wearing them. A good example is April 1974 when thousands of Manchester United hooligans invaded the pitch when their former hero Denis Law backheeled them in to Division Two.

I bought a pair of white skinners off Taffy's stall on Oldham's huge Tommyfield market in the summer of 1973, Taffy was an old Welsh lady who sold loads of youth wear, like Skinners blue denim and white ones, two tone trousers and Ben Shermans shirts, left over from the original skinhead era... she only charged £3 for the white skinners whereas the fashionable shops were charging £5 and sometimes £7.

Pre season 73/74 saw us play at Rochdale in the annual Rose Bowl competition which saw us as per taking over the town and the Sandy Lane and though Rochdale always had a spirited little mob to have a go Oldham just swamped the place and wreaked havoc, however in the September of 73 Rochdale played Bolton Wanderers in the first round of the League cup, me Paul and Neil Wood decided to go to the game, it was a Tuesday night match and as expected Bolton took over the whole ground...all four sides of Spotland were full of Bolton fans, I did not see any Dale lads at all in the ground....we were shitting ourselves in case any Bolton fans sussed us out but we blended in and even joined in their Bolton chants etc...to be honest they were a very loud boisterous crowd but when the gates opened at three quarter time we decided to leave the ground and walk back the mile or so into the town centre to get our bus back home, as we got into the town centre all of a sudden we were surrounded by about ten lads who asked us who we supported, we noticed they were Dale fans and blurted out "we are Dale fans" so this big skinhead asked us whereabouts in Rochdale so we said near the Summit, which bordered Oldham with Rochdale, and he demanded what street, as he interrogated us. Neil said Salmon Avenue, Paul said Pike lane... well I was convulsed in laughter and said

Cod Street, by this time all three of us had cracked up laughing but the big skinhead who we found out was the legendary Rochdale leader Moggy, said, "listen I know you are from Oldham with your accents (Oldham has a very distinctive half lancs/yorkie accent) said you can join up with is tonight we are going to do Bolton! Well we cracked up laughing again, we had just seen how many Bolton fans there was and told Moggy there's fucking thousands of them and there's only ten of you lot... well he whistles and from behind all these bushes popped out about 70 Dale lads all armed with scaffold grips, bottles and bricks... nowhere near enough to take Bolton on but enough to have a go.

So Moggy tells us to arm ourselves and get ready to attack the Bolton fans, fuck me I was only 12 and a half but we had no option...it was very nerve wracking as all these Dale lads hid behind bushes etc, we could hear the massive Bolton mob marching down towards us, Moggy was running about giving the orders, "Don't cob out til I say!" he was like General Custer, and it was the same numbers! Well this Bolton mob come into sight and there were hundreds of them all across the road in one big raging mob... well the Dale lads were perched above them on this big hill and Moggy bellowed out.. "Right lad's let em have it!" and with that the Dale lads rained the scaffold grips, bottles stones and loads of other things down onto the Bolton mob, who did not know what had hit them and how many Dale there actually were. It was dark and Dale were all screaming and chanting "Dale Dale!" Bolton fled, many were hurt and Dale give chase until the cops came in their vans and with dogs. It was a major result for little Rochdale, no Bolton fans would ever admit this happened but it did and I was there. All the Dale lads were backslapping each other, congratulating each other on a job well done, I often wondered why they never took Oldham on when we took over, cos Bolton were a far bigger mob than us back then, and fair play to Moggy he walked us back to the train station telling us it would be too dangerous at the bus station as both Dale and Bolton would be hovering about and Dale hated Oldham.

I was very impressed I loved the whole underdog thing and had to laugh at the Dale lads who had no fashion sense whatsoever, they looked liked something out of Oliver!, but under the stewardship of Moggy they did some damage to Bolton that night as loads got hurt by the missiles, and we were chuffed cos Bolton up until then had took the piss out of Oldham and done some serious damage to us.

We played Bury away in the League cup that season again on a night match and Stott's tours hired about ten double decker buses to take us the short distance, ten miles, well most of the people on these buses were hooligans and it was mad, that night on our bus was a gang of greasers from Primrose Bank, the tough council estate a mile or so from Northmoor, these were rough tough scruffy fuckers, most wearing airdale black straight leg leans with bright coloured piping up the leg and coloured turn ups and hob nailed boots, they had long greasy hair and swore a lot a lot, amongst this unruly mob was Nick Baker who had gained a big reputation around Oldham for being game as fuck and never giving in and not shy to use a weapon, he'd be about 16 then, only slightly built but looked mad, then there was Donty Shearing a tall gangly lad, Loopy Morrow who had long dark red hair and was very chirpy, Danny "Eggy" Standring who was a skinny long haired youth with leather jacket and very noisy and full of mischief, throwing seats through the bus windows and ripping the light bulbs out and throwing them through the windows, another one was little Tony Diveny who only small also had a reputation, John Cunliffe who had fantastic sideburns he was really stocky and looked hard and was smartly dressed, there were a lot of them and they were rum buggers..

When we got to Bury we went straight into there end and soon took it over, the only lads in there were Bury Reds but they got fucked off and ended up in the paddock were they spent the whole first half chanting 'United, United' as if to scare us. It didn't work and at half time the Primmy lads went into the Paddock and sorted them out and also set fire to the stand and the fire brigade had to come thankfully they put it out before it became too dangerous, but it built up Oldham's growing reputation and that of the Primmy Nutters, we lost the game and after the match Oldham overturned a few cars and clashed with the cops before all the buses set off back to Oldham, but as we are leaving Bury centre a few buses had their windows put through from a few brave Bury lads hiding before running off..

We took Bury every time we played them and they always had Bury Reds with them but they were no fucking use either, and I always rated Rochdale a lot higher than Bury back then but then I had been impressed by Rochdale's ambushing of the mighty Bolton Wanderers which has gone down in Rochdale folklore and rightly so..

An early game that season was Bournemouth at home and as it was miles away wasn't expecting any trouble but as I was watching On the Ball at about 12.30pm it came on telly that a mob of Bournemouth fans had arrived in the early hours of the morning broke into Boundary Park and they had spread a load of lime on the pitch which the ground staff were desperately trying to clear before kick off, well word soon spread around Oldham and by 2pm the Chaddy End was full as we searched for these cheeky Bournemouth bastards but they were in the Ford Stand paddock, about a 100 of them all big fuckers, taunting us and lobbing bricks into us. The Oldham mobs ran down to confront them and were trying to climb into the paddock when all of a sudden a big bearded Bournemouth fan produced a double barrelled shot gun and shot it in the air, well it made such a racket and he looked a mad bastard, well we all hit the deck, hundreds of us, and the cops moved in and arrested this nut case, we all moved sharpish back to the top of the Chaddy End out of the road in case any more had guns - it was scary. At the end of the game Oldham waited in the car park for Bournemouth and hammered them and smashed both coaches to bits, every window going through...it would be a long trip back down to the south coast!

The Chaddy End in the 73/74 season was filling up much earlier now as we were sick of getting caught out by away fans who would get in before us and claim the top of the Chaddy End, one game were in early for was Halifax Town whom we had taken over the year before, we expected them to make an effort seeing as it was only 17 miles away, well this day the Chaddy End was packed and bouncing and there was no Halifax fans in the away end but all of a sudden 6 coaches pulled up onto the large car park attached to the ground we had a great view and as these coaches unloaded we saw every single one of them were boot boys and every single one of them were wearing the popular White Skinners, with their Cherry Red Docs, 300 lads. It looked great many of them sporting Rod Stewart blonde Feather cuts, we all piled down the Chaddy End to meet them as they came through the turn-styles but disappointingly they all headed toward the away end but they were very vocal and it was nailed on we were in for a major battle after the game. As the gates opened at three quarter time the Chaddy End emptied as we all marched round to the away end to take on our Yorkshire foes, we piled into the open terraces and fair play they came at us and a big brawl ensued, the cops and their dogs getting stuck in aswell, plenty were arrested.

After the game the battling continued but Oldham's greater numbers overwhelmed the game mullet headed boot boys of Halifax, one incident that stands out was one Halifax fan who got corned by about half a dozen Oldham fans, and just as they were gonna set about him he started mumbling and using sign language, indicating he was deaf and dumb, a few said. "aw leave him, he's deaf and dumb" but one Oldham lad had no sympathy and booted him in his balls, he went down clutching his groin and shouted out, "Ouch tha Oldham Twat!" in a clear Yorkshire accent, well obviously he wasn't deaf and dumb and got his justified kicking!

Early in the season we played Huddersfield Town away which was only 18 miles away from Oldham, we were also on a ten match unbeaten run and we took twenty odd coaches over the Pennines, but the coppers there were twats and they made all of us wearing Docs, take them off which was almost everyone under twenty! Hundreds of us had to take our Docs off and mine were only two weeks old, the cops just threw them all into a massive pile then forced us into that massive paddock. It wasn't just docs, all the greasers had to take off their hob nailed boots and I was panicking thinking some scruffy greasy bastard is gonna claim my cherished docs after the game, it was a great atmosphere during the game and

Huddersfield had a big mob in this paddock and there were many clashes throughout the game, just before the end of the match I went to reclaim my docs and thank fuck I got mine back because loads didn't as the scruffs claimed the best docs and left their shitty hob nailed boots behind the cops just laughed their tits off at the anguish, a few Oldham fans clashed with each other on the coaches going back as they spotted their docs on the feet of greasers who never wore docs, there were also quite a few battles after the game on the coach park, Hudders had a big crew of lads who like their neighbours Halifax were mainly feather cutted Rod the Mod look-alikes, think Rod Stewart was popular in West Yorkshire.

Early that season the club had booked the League Liners, which was a 600 seater special train especially kitted out for travelling football fans, it even had it's own disco on and the team's players travelled back on it and mingled with the fans, each week for the past 12 months one team could hire it, the first ever team to hire it was Burnley, Oldham were the second and it took them to Bournemouth, I was not on that one but my brother Pete was, and there was a photo in the Oldham Chron of Oldham fans on the station and Pete was on the pic.

The one I was on took us to Cambridge and I was buzzing to be on it, it soon sold out and even my mam, dad our Pete, uncles, an aunty and a few cousins were on it, there were loads of lads from all over town and it was great just walking up and down this long train, when we arrived in Cambridge there was no police to greet us, we just had to make our way to the ground across this massive field, it was a miserable wet day, we were ambushed by some Cambridge hooligans who bricked us but were soon chased off by this massive mob, all the gangs of Oldham were on this train, Oldham took Cambridge's end that day, they were not expecting so many lads as all the gangs were boosted because of this trip on the league Liner, we won the game and after the match walking back to the station several fights broke out as pockets of Cambridge hooligans attempted ambushes, they were a game mob to say a couple of seasons before they were non league.

On the train home a few fights broke out between rival Oldham gangs, most of the lads were pissed from the bar installed on the train, the players were on board and mingled well with us all, chatting and having photos etc, when we arrived back at Mumps station the main train station in Oldham town centre a big fight broke out with Abbeyhills and Fitton Hill who had long been rivals, it was in the subway leading out of the station and the noise levels of the roaring and screaming abuse was very loud and exciting, dad had to drag me away as I was intrigued by this mass brawl, strangely enough the next home game they are all mates again and joining up to attack/repel away fan

## FA CUP RUN

Apart from the great start we made to the 73/74 season we also had a great FA Cup run beginning in October 1973 when we were drawn to play non-league Formby Town away, Formby is a little town near Liverpool and Oldham sold their 2000 allocation in no time, Formby's ground was pitiful with no stands just three banks of terracing and behind what was going to be there end they rented a mobile stand for the day which got loads of publicity for little Formby as I believe it was the first time it had ever been used for a football game. Our coach arrived really early maybe mid day and as we got there we were met by a big Formby fan a six foot odd rocker in leather coat and hobnails boots and filthy jeans and he was offering every one out as we got off the coach, he must have been 30 years old. He stank and had a horrible scraggly beard and tattoos all over his neck and hands, no one would take him on and he clouted a few, we went into Formby's supporters club were a few locals warned us about him, he was the local nutter and always in and out of prison, well it was pissing down and he waited on the coach park for all the coaches coming in and there were loads and he was still offering every man woman and child out as they got off the coach until one of the old Glodwick mob stuck the nut on him and dropped him to the deck then loads of young Oldham fans set about him, kicked fuck out of him until he crawled away..

Most of us were in the ground for 1 30pm as it was time of power cuts and a 2pm kick off, we filled three sides of the ground, I was in the end behind the goals were most of the mob was, the Formby fans were in the opposite end in their rent a stand. Behind our end was a main road some thirty foot below us and just before kick off a Salvation army band marched by, and the Oldham fans bricked them, and the band put their drums and instruments over their heads but still marched and singing 'Onward Christian Soldiers' - legends!!

At half time hundreds of Oldham fans charged across the pitch towards the Formby fans, many of them leaping out of their stand to flee, when we reached the stand we shook it from side to side and loads of Formby fans were clinging on for dear life, it was all high jinks and soon we were marching back across the pitch to our own end, we won the game 2 −0 to go in the hat for the 2nd round, we were pleased to know it was our Yorkie neighbours Halifax so we knew we would take a great following and have a go at taking their end again - also we knew we would beat Halifax Town.

The day we played Halifax Town I woke up at 6am I couldn't sleep properly, I was so excited and I decided I was walking to Halifax, I walked everywhere and it was a nice crisp sunny morning I made myself some butties and set off through Saddleworth moors, by mid day I was a few miles outside Halifax when a van pulled up one of the lads recognised me it was full of Fitton Hill lads and they gave me a lift into Halifax town centre, where I got out and went for a mooch about, there were loads of Oldham mobs in Halifax many going on the "rob" at 2pm I entered the Shay, to see hundreds off Oldham boot boys fighting already with their Halifax foes only this time Halifax fans had come into Oldham's end, Halifax had a top mob out that day Oldham kept on coming in through the turn styles and by half time had ran Halifax out of this end, at half time there were a few scuffles on the pitch before the cops got a grip, end of the game no sign of Halifax fans, I sneaked on one of the coaches home.

Kevin Lowther was a tough youth from Fitton Hill estate one of Oldham's largest and toughest council estates, he recalls his trip to Halifax that day, he drove up with his pal and fellow Fitton Hill youth

Billy Kennedy, another tough lad, well after the match they got split from the main Oldham mob and found themselves down a dead end street when they were faced by a mob of around 30 Halifax lads, Lowie convinced Billy to act calm and just walk through them without a care in the world, Bill reluctantly agreed, the Halifax lads kicked fuck out of them and 40 years on Billy still hasn't totally forgiven Lowie!

The 3rd round of the FA Cup saw us drawn to play Cambridge United at home Jan 1974, a game we fully expected to win and see us into the 4th round and the very likely opportunity of playing a big club, this was the time of the power cuts and many games had to be played early kick offs because you were not allowed to use floodlights and midweek during the day, our original game on a Saturday was cancelled due to the bad weather so it was to be played on a Tuesday afternoon and at 1pm. Now this created two problems, people would be at work and those of us in school would or should have to be in school however the crowd was over 10,000 as hundreds of school children truanted en masse, all the schools of Oldham were represented, most still wearing their respective school uniforms and ties, there was much taunting between rival schools and a few fights broke out as tensions rose, there were loads from Grange my school which was one of the nearest to Boundary Park and had many Latics fans, loads of teachers were at the game looking out for their pupils and next day dozens of us were lined up in Assembly to get strapped for truancy including yours truly.

The game was fantastic and Cambridge surprised us and drew 3-3 taking us back down to Cambridge for the replay on the following Sunday which was *the* first ever game to be played on the Sabbath, I did not go to that game but my brother Peter did to see us draw again 1—1 with the prize of meeting Burnley in the 4th round at home, a great draw as Burnley back then were 2nd from top of Division One a great team with players like Leighton James, Steve Kindon and David Thomas in their team and was only 18 miles away from Oldham, a full house guaranteed, but Cambridge were proving bloody hard to defeat. The third game was at Nottingham Forest's City Ground, again on a Tuesday afternoon and another one I could not make, once again my brother Peter went and told me the cops put all the Oldham fans in the Trent End which was Forest's home end and a load of Forest fans decide to defend their end that day whoever was in it and Happy Harry Randall of the Sholver mob was rendered unconscious as Forest fans set about Oldham's mob. I heard it was horrendous in the Trent that day and many Oldham lads got beat up, however we managed to win the game 2—1 to set up a juicy 4th round tie against Burnley which was made all ticket and sold out within a week.

Oldham had a big mob by 1974, we had been top or near top of Div 3 all season and the Chaddy End was packed almost every game, no one had taken un since Bolton some 12 months prior and we had come a long way since then, this particular day the Chaddy End was packed to the rafters by 2pm as was the away end with Burnley fans, at 2.30pm hundreds of Burnley fans came across the pitch maybe a thousand and more, it looked brilliant and Oldham charged down the terraces to meet them head on but when Oldham saw just how many Burnley fans there was many fled back up the terraces even jumping out of the stadium. The shithouses leaving those few of us to get mauled, a couple of hundred of us still met Burnley head on, me included I was still a week short of my 13th birthday, but I plunged into the fray, swinging my fists and boots, I soon got decked and felt a sharp pain in my inner thigh and then the sight of blood seeping through my skinners, I had been slashed, I still bear a six inch scar to this day, I didn't feel any more pain and the blood soon stopped. I was more upset seeing the Chaddy End taken over for within five minutes Burnley had taken the Chaddy End and taking it in fantastic style, a proper taking over not just filling up the end before any home fans got in but coming across the pitch and fighting hand to hand and forcing their way up to the top taking many blows in the process. I was gutted but was so impressed at what was in my eyes and many others one of the best taking over of an end I have ever witnessed, the Chaddy End was a big kop and packed out and Burnley came into the unknown not knowing how many lads were in there - they were brave and gallant and I have nothing but respect for their mob that day.

Oldham tried in vain to re take the Chaddy End but were only at half strength as at least half of the original mob had left the ground or found their way to safety in the paddocks, Burnley taunted us with "We took the Chaddy End "just like Bolton and Blackburn had done, and their rendition of "No Nae Never no more" was brilliant and I've never heard fans so loud in the Chaddy End, and adding to all this misery we lost 4 fucking 1 with Leighton James the flying Welsh winger raping our full backs! Very little happened after the game Oldham did not have the will for a fight we had been humiliated both on and off the pitch... So there ended a glorious FA Cup run which took us to non league Formby, onto Halifax then we had three games to over come Cambridge before finally coming unstuck on and off the pitch against Burnley who got to the semi finals only to lose to Newcastle at Hillsborough.

That season the FA Cup final was Liverpool v Newcastle United and the day before the lads in our year the 3rd year chose Liverpool as our team and the lads in the year above chose Newcastle and we arranged a battle during the lunch time break, now in the year above there were only 2 maybe 3 hard lads, we had about half a dozen and we fancied our chances and we went into battle confident, no holds barred a pure battle with maybe twenty on each side, there were a few bust noses and black eyes but we got the better until loads of teachers came and broke it up, on the Monday we all got lined up in Assembly for the strap in front of everyone and named and shamed. I was proud of my lads, I wasn't the "cock "of my year, maybe 4th/5th but I was seen by most as the leader and already an experienced and active football hooligan with the scars to show.

Early in the 1973/74 season we played Rochdale away and me and John Hart who was a pal from Grange school decided we were gonna be Glam Rockers for the day, we sprayed our docs silver, dyed our hair bright red and wore tinsel around our foreheads ..we must have looked a right pair of cunts but on the 10.30 am train we went from Mumps (Oldhams main train station) the first train to Rochdale that day full of Oldham lads there would be another dozen trains following on, only 4 carriage trains mind but the amount of Oldham lads arriving for our usual piss taking take over of Rochdale was phenomenal, our biggest away following for ages, the town centre was full of Oldham boot boys, I tried telling as many as possible how they did Bolton but no one believed me and still don't to this day but me Paul Sykes and Neil Wood know because we saw it with our own eyes. This day no Rochdale turned up and the pubs and cafes were full of swaggering Oldham fans, at about 2pm a massive mob marched the mile or so to the ground chanting and ballooning, the heavens opened and mine and John Hart's days as Glam Rockers were numbered as all the red hair dye we had applied ran down our faces and everyone thought we had been "glassed" it streaked down our faces and onto our Levi and Wrangler jackets, loads took the piss out of us.

The game was same as ever we took the Sandy Lane and had a big mob in the opposite end but no show from Rochdale and funnily enough no sign after the game as well, I fully expected them to ambush us like they did with Bolton... the trains home got smashed up as per usual.

The run in for that season was so exciting we just knew we were going up and maybe even win the league, we were scoring loads and taking loads away. At Tranmere one Friday night we took their end and only a big mob of Scousers who came in near the end of the match put up a fight but we fucked them off, that night I was carrying a knife, God knows why maybe the thought of Scousers frightened me, well after the game there were more battles with the Scousers and one of them got stabbed apparently and the cops were searching all the 12 coaches. I panicked and threw my knife under someone else's seat and the cops found it and dragged an old feller off, I felt shit but also felt sure they would soon realise he wasn't a knife merchant and neither was I! They let him back on and let the coach go on it's merry way, I never took a knife to football again although I used all sorts of other implements.

We played Chesterfield towards the end of the season and took absolutely loads, we filled the open end and there were a couple of hundred Oldham in their end fighting all the game, and not only that a 100 had been arrested at Sheffield station en route for robbing the mail bags, this included loads of the original Glodwick mob who would all be early twenties by now but very lively, the younger Glodwick lads were known as the Glodwick jays and had a massive mob of lads and girls, a right mixed bag of rockers, boot boys teds black lads many of the white lads were of Polish and Ukraine descent, one of their main lads was a tiny feller called Mouse who was about 5 ft 2 brave as fuck he had hair like Marc Bolan and always had loads of birds hanging about him. He was one of three brothers, the Kennedys, John (Mouse) Stesh and Malc, other lads that stood out were Big Graham Hall a massive lad twenty odd stones with a baby face and snow white curly hair he was hard as fuck and banged loads of away fans, his brother Harry (R.I.P.) was the broadest lad I have ever known, he was as wide as he was tall, a one puncher who dropped loads. Gaz Tierney (R.I.P.) a real rough arse fat lad who was in and out of nick, a right character/rogue, he was prematurely bald with long black curl hair at the back, he looked 40 when he was 16... Mad Eddie Fitz a ginger haired nut case scared of nothing who wasn't shy at getting stuck in, Ste "Tat's" Taylor who wore specs but was a big strong lad, a lad called Glenn Barratt who actually came off Holts estate which was a big Man United supporting area, Glenn had great sids, great skinners the shiniest docs in town and looked every inch the boot boy but he had no bottle and would melt to the back when it kicked off, I think he got fired after a few games by Mouse, given his p45 and sent back to Holts and his United mates....a lot easier to hide within United's 10,000 strong Red Army !

The Glodwick Jays was a proper mob and the only proper mixed raced mob in Oldham with game black lads like Gus, Zoots, Twiggy, Tony Gale, Kirtley, Spider, Mamma Seale, Phil Drayton and more, plus other tough lads like the Dixon brothers, the Novak brothers, Selwyn, Yanni, Henryk, Howie, Johnny Lonsden, Crazy George (Slouk's brother) Ian and Pete Connolly, Si Brooks, John Brock and the Paki brothers Hassan and Nanu who were half castes and brought up by their white mam, both game lads, then you had the toughest boot girls in town with their monkey boots and don't give a fuck attitude girls like Dobbin, big tits Sue, Kath, Syl, Cat, Bev, Sue Hartley, Sheena - this was one big and lively mob.

The Easter of 1974 was magnificent for both the club and its fans on Good Friday we beat Southport 6-0 at home, the day after we beat our closest rivals Bristol Rovers 2 -1 at Eastville, in front of a full house on and it was on Match of the Day. I am gutted I did not go down there, my loyal brother Peter went though and said it was fantastic, Oldham fans were singing "we had joy we had fun we had Bristol on the run" all way through the game, but Bristol was a rough place and plenty of Oldham got attacked after the match and a few coaches were smashed up, but it looked great on tele as we saw the Oldham fans celebrating a monumental victory. On Easter Monday we played Southport away and what a dream fixture that was, we took ten thousand fans that day coaches were leaving Oldham from as early as 8am in the morning, one of the early coaches was one full of the old Glodwick mob, the coach was called "One of Alf's" which tickled me, I saw the coach going down Chadderton road towards the motorway, It whetted my appetite, me Paul and a load more of us were getting the train at 10.30 from Oldham which arrived in Southport a hour later, the train was rammed with Oldham boot boys all chanting and singing along.

When we arrived at Southport we headed right onto the Pleasure beach were there were hundreds of Oldham fans, a few scuffles broke out with gangs of Scousers but Oldham had too many, we were to pay the price later on that day....but pre match it was all Oldham as more and more coaches arrived and at 2pm we headed towards this little ground at Haigh Avenue, many of us just climbed over the wall, Oldham had taken all four sides of the ground and there were very few Southport fans in there or if there was they were very quiet. There were joyous scenes, me and Paul nicked a couple of blue and yellow Southport scarves but a few moments later Tony Diveny nicked them off us, he was 3 years older than us, a few later he wouldn't have stood a chance, but we were 13 and 14 then, we put it down to experience. Tony never grew in size whereas me and Paul did, we bore no grudges and he never took liberties again meanwhile there were many pitch invasions as the Oldham fans got too giddy and took the piss, there were that many from Oldham that most of my extended family were there my brother Pete me mam and dad uncles Jack Roy and Fred and a few cousins, Paul joked there were more Bardsleys (mam's maiden name) here than Southport fans. We won the game comfortably 2-0.

After the match most Oldham fan went back home on the coaches and trains but about 100 of us went back to the Pleasurebeach, big mistake, waiting for us were a load of Scousers, many of them in their twenties and real rough fuckers many carrying knives and they attacked us from all angles, Oldham ran and a few got caught and slashed, I saw one of our local heroes, Steve "Ned "Kelly hid under a car, which made me laugh because he always acted so hard and confident but we were heavily outnumbered and it was very heavy situation, most of us got away unscathed and were soon on the train back to Manchester then onto Oldham...all in all was a great day great result and another 2 points towards the inevitable promotion. Our next game was Huddersfield at home which we won 6—1 in front of 18,000 fans, these here heady times and thousands invaded the pitch as promotion was secured, we still had a good chance of winning the title, only Bristol Rovers could stop us, we had three more games left, York away, Charlton at home and Plymouth away last game of a wonderful season....

# TOMMY'S TOURS

To coincide with the 1973/74 football season I also got involved with playing football for a bloke called Tommy Sinclair, who ran a boys football team that played all over the North West, Yorkshire and even London, Tommy Sinclair was a notorious man in Oldham whom in the late 1960's got jailed for offenses against young boys whom he had set up a football team with, he came off the very rough Limeside council estate and set up football teams with rough young lads aged 12 to 16 from there, he was a huge powerfully built man well over 6 ft tall, when he came out of prison he set up another football team in the early 1970's, called Tommy's All stars, there were a flood of complaints to the police and newspaper, Tommy took it on himself to take a big advert out stating he was misunderstood and that your boys are safe with me! It caused great controversy at the time. I had absolutely no idea of all this until many years later one of my pals David O'Brien was recruited by Tommy to do some part time building work for him. Tommy did a lot of work for the pakis who were intimidated by his size.

Once Tommy had OB under his wing he began setting another football team up, OB recruited a load of us from Grange to play for Tommy's All stars, we had no idea he was a bender at first, we were just kids 13 - 16 years old and were being offered the chance of free travel allover the North West and beyond, and Tommy bought us all football kits and trainers, the kits were the then very popular Man City away kit, white with red and black diagonal stripes, very trendy, the trainers were cack plastic efforts, another thing Tommy did was to provide food for us all and brought loads of butties and often bought us all a chippy supper, he was assisted by a skinny feller called Bill, we called him Bill Chin because he had a massive chin, and we'd all chant "Bill Chinnery, Bill Chinnery, Bill chin cher roo!" he and Tommy would laugh their heads off..some of the venues we played were Moss Side Sports centre, Ardwick Green, Old Trafford and Irlam in Manchester, Bootle Kirby and Toxteth sports centres in Liverpool, Birkenhead, YMCA's in Bolton, Blackpool and Burnley and various other youth clubs, these games were always on Friday nights apart from a few trips into Yorkshire which were on Sundays plus we played one game in London before being treated to the FA Amateur cup final at Wembley....all exciting stuff for a 13 year old boy.

Tommy also had a few lads working on the jobs for him during the school holidays me included, we soon latched on that Tommy was a fruit, word soon got round but we felt safe in numbers and I can honestly say I don't know if he got a grip of any of us although he did try it on with me one day. I'd been working for him on a pakis house in Glodwick, he paid us fiver a day but most days we were done for 2pm, well this day he took me to Butterworth's chippy, the best chippy in town were you could sit down, he told me to order what I wanted, so I ordered home made cheese pie chips n gravy, it was lovely but just as I was about to finish Tommy put his big grubby hand on my thigh, and I plunged my fork into the back of his hand, it went right in and was stuck, he grimaced and pulled it out and blood spurted out, he dabbed his even grubbier hanky to stem the flow, and apologised, and begged me not to tell anyone, and slipped me another fiver, which I took, and still told all the lads, many then admitted he tried the same with them but none had crumbled...

Once we had played a few games for Tommy our confidence soon built up, we were all Latics fans as was Tommy and we got into a few scraps with rival youth teams especially when we played at Bolton YMCA, we marched in singing "Oh Wanky Wanky Wanderers!" which riled them up and the games were very aggressive, we had all our clothes and belongings robbed at Ardwick Green and clashed with the black youths at Old Trafford one night, we all came from Westwood and Werneth, which neighboured each other and we all went to Grange with a couple from St.Anselms, we travelled to most games on the train and were always causing chaos fucking about and chanting football songs, one of our favourite chants was.. "Don't bend down when Tommy's around yer might get his willy up yer arse!" he and Bill Chin would just laugh their heads off, one of Tommy's tricks was to go to the toilet and then stick his head out and say can one of you lads bring me tablets please they are in me jacket pocket, we'd all chant "fuck off Tommy! Fuck off Tommy!" he took it all in good fun.

He was a big hard bastard though and one night we were coming back home on the train from Manchester to Oldham well halfway home these three big lads about 20 years old got on at Failsworth and they spotted Tommy with us lot and began giving him grief calling him a puff and worse, he tried to ignore them, we were a bit scared because they looked really hard, all of a sudden Tommy jumps up and knocks all three of them out, all decked in a pile on the floor, we all cheered but in retrospect they were only looking after our interests, we had no idea he was a paedophile that word was never mentioned back then we just thought he was a puff and as long as we stuck together we were safe, he did look after us though in many ways and the best thing he ever did was to lay a coach on for us to take us to York for Latics 3rd game from end of the season it seemed the whole town was going and it's reckoned there was up to 10,000 made the 50 mile trip over the Pennines into Yorkshire.

Tommy booked and paid for a 52 seater coach, all free plus he provided 2 big skips full of butties pies cakes sweets and cans of booze, we were all under 17 apart from Bill Chin, Tommy's dad who was about 80 and Tommy himself, we were picked up at 10 am that Saturday morning, must have been the first of over 70 coaches to leave Oldham, yet we were the last one to arrive at just before kick off as we stopped off fucking about in Huddersfield, Leeds and York city centre, robbing everything we could including scarves off York fans. Entering York was an amazing experience as we snaked past the big hill were the grand old duke of York marched his men up and then back down again, we all sang that, we were buzzing especially seeing so many Oldham fans in the centre, it was only 1 o'clock and we begged Tommy to let us off for a bit, which he sorted with coach to pick us back up at 2.15pm, we ran wild through that wonderful historic city centre, huge gangs of Oldham fans outside all the pubs singing and chanting, we took over York that day.. We got into the ground just before kick off, we paid into the open end behind the goals which full to the brim with Oldham fans as was the paddock on the right side and half the paddock on the left which was York's end and that's were we lot made our way to help to take it over and push the York fans out, there were many clashes and York fought gallantly but before half time Oldham's much bigger mob had taken over the whole stand, it was a great taking over, me and Paul got a great view of all the scrapping from an opening at the back of the stand which we climbed up to and had a great vantage point, we also had both nicked York scarves in the town centre before the game, the atmosphere was brilliant as we all sang "Lancashire la la la, Lancashire la la la".

We drew the game 1-1 with our hero Maurice Whittle scoring yet another brilliant free kick to send three sides of the ground wild, many invaded the pitch, when the game ended most of us invaded the pitch in celebration...outside it took a hour for all the coaches to move away and snake through York city centre, we mithered Tommy to let us off when we saw a supermarket so we could rag it, robbed everything in sight, but one of the lads nicked a York scarf off a young lad walking by and he told a copper, a reet big angry looking Yorkie bastard, who told us to hand the scarf back or we'd all be arrested. Tommy snapped, "hand the fucking scarf back or I will sort you out!" All of a sudden the whole coach began singing "Don't bend down when Tommy's around yer might get his willy up yer arse!" even his best mate Bill Chin joined in until Tommy gave him a back hander, god knows what the burly Yorkie cop thought, but the scarf was eventually handed to the cop but then he demanded the names of the six lads on the back seat, they all give daft names like John Wayne, Elvis Presley, Noddy Holder John Lennon and Ted Heath which this big daft copper jotted down, but when John Hart said Raquel Welch he snapped, and said "stop tekking the piss I'm not fucking daft you know!" - the whole coach cracked up laughing, he stormed off calling us bloody idiots!

It was a fantastic trip and day out, but we didn't see much more of Tommy after that summer, think he got sent down again I never saw him again and apparently he passed away in 1994 aged 54 but we had some great times and many funny memories, funny enough I still see Bill Chin now and then at Belle Vue dogs, he must be 70 odd now...

Because of our cup run and 3 games against Cambridge, Bristol Rovers season finished on this Saturday and were top of Div 3 but we had 2 games left and needed just one point to claim the Championship and we had a home game on the Tuesday against Charlton Athletic, the ground was full by 7pm hundreds of home made flags adorned the stadium, 18,000 plus, I made one out of one my bed sheets and paint sprayed it, the atmosphere was unbelievable especially in the Chaddy End which was bouncing for over a hour before kick off, we lost 2 –0! 2 fucking 0!!! Talk about an anti climax... still thousands invaded the pitch to proclaim our heroes who had won Promotion for the second time in three years, we all then ran back to our beloved Chaddy End which we had fought for and defended so many times, and shed blood for...it took the coppers half a hour to move us on, "We shall not we shall not be moved!" we sang defiantly, eventually en masse the mob marched into the town centre overturning a few cars and smashing a few windows, random stupid vandalism, a few arrests were made.

Friday night last game of the season Plymouth Argyle away the farthest away game in the league and on a Friday night, apparently one coach made the long arduous trip, while the rest of us were glued to the radio, the game ended 0 –0, we were Champions of Division Three, fantastic. I was so proud I rushed out into the street cheering, at the end of our street the Old White Hart regulars were in full voice, "We will be we will be Champions of Division Three!" - they spilled into the streets singing, dancing, cheering, Oh I wished I was old enough to be in that pub that night celebrating with them all. It had been a fantastic roller coaster of a season... one that has stuck in my memory forever.

On the following Monday Oldham Council set up for the players to be acknowledged for their fantastic achievements by having a celebratory dinner at the town hall, prior to this they were to show off the Third Division trophy to their loyal fans, as it was thousands of Oldhamer's turned out in force, closing the town centre streets off, many climbed on roofs of pubs and shops to get a view and hundreds including me hung on for dear life on the long Victorian iron railings that faced the town hall, it was a majestic and emotional sight as we sang danced and chanted for our blue heroes, the players loved the adulation we afforded them... 'Champions! Champions! Champions!' thousands roared. When the players finally retired for their big posh meal the huge crowds dispersed, but a mob of around 200 youths took it on themselves to march the mile and half to Boundary Park, why? I do not know but I tagged along, but as we got closer we were met by dozens of police with snarling dogs and batons, and the youths me included began bricking the cops and stand off occurred, we could not break through their lines but we got close and fought with them, until too many of us got bit by the Alsatians, we then turned around rampaged through Westwood's Pakistani district, smashing windows etc, it was a mad night of mayhem, but the following night was to be much much worse, we had an end of season friendly at Rochdale of all places, whoever fixed this up must have been crazy and was gonna regret it.

Me and Paul made sure we were on the 4 o'clock train to Rochdale to make sure we didn't miss any of the fun n games, and even on such an early train there was 50 odd lads. There were 3 trains a hour leaving Oldham to Rochdale and almost everyone up until 7pm was full of Oldham hooligans, we waited in the train station cafe at Rochdale until about 6pm by this time there was hundreds of Oldham lads milling about the station, we then marched into town down Drake street smashing windows and causing havoc, there was a mob of about 50 Rochdale lads near the cenotaph but they ran off when they saw this massive mob come charging down, there were loads more Oldham in the town centre that joined up with us as we marched triumphantly towards Spotland, it was one of the biggest mobs I had seen up to date and even the coppers gave us a wide berth, we all made for the Sandy Lane as usual and chased out the twenty or so brave Dale lads who fled across the pitch... we soon filled this little kop and also filled the paddock on the left hand side where there were quite a few scuffles a tidy mob of Dale were in there but they soon got ran out to the end opposite ours, by kick off the Sandy lane was full to bursting point, you could hardly move it was that packed out, and this was only a friendly, we swayed from side to side and up and down like a mini Kop.

At 7.20 just before kick off our team captain Dick Mulvaney came onto the pitch with the Third Division trophy, hundreds of us piled on from the Sandy Lane and Paddock we had filled with lads but then a mob of fifty or lads came in from were the Rochdale lads were, only these were not Rochdale - they were a coalition of Burnley, Bolton, Man United and Man City fans, I'm guessing they were all from Rochdale, and a mass brawl broke out in the middle of the pitch, but Oldham's massive advantage fucked them back to their end, we all marched back down to the Sandy lane were we were cheered like returning heroes. I was buzzing, the game kicked off but you could feel the tension especially as the combined mobs of Rochdale grew and grew and in no time they mustered around 300 lads, nowhere near our number but the biggest mob Dale have ever had, after twenty minutes of the game two lads came running right across the pitch carrying a fucking Bolton Wanderers flag which was like a red rag to a bull for us, our most hated rivals taunting us.

Well this was my moment to prove myself, I hated Bolton I had seen how they had took the piss and hurt so many Oldhamer's and I was full of vengeance and even though I was only 13 and a half I had loads of bottle even though these two fuckers looked 18, so I dived onto the pitch to confront them as did a lad called Tanya a year older than me but looked 20. Tanya was massive, very stocky very strong and had huge sideburns even though he was only 14/15, he was a man already been boozing in pubs for years and was allegedly the "cock "of Oldham for his age, it certainly boosted any doubts I may have had having Tanya alongside me, and we went flying into them, Tanya knocking one right out with a big hay maker and me wrestling with one as we rolled about the pitch in the mud, we beat em as Tanya belted the one I was rolling about with and we nicked their flag and returned to a huge round of applause from the packed Sandy Lane end for our efforts, the cops tried in vain to catch us but we soon melted into the big mob, this incident enhanced Tanya's already growing and big reputation around town but also elevated me as to one of the lads of the future and one who already had considerable bottle.

At half-time there was another pitch invasion from Dale's end, about twenty lads came across to our end, we all surged forward and first on the pitch was Micky Dunlea, a lad 4 years older than me who also came from Northmoor, he wasn't a fighter but wanted the limelight and all his pals held back as Micky walked to the Dale lads with his arms outstretched offering them out and thinking he had hundreds with him, he glanced back and saw he was on his own everyone laughing and he walked backwards but the cops pounced on him and dragged him out of the ground, and into the meat wagon (Police van). During half time I was up near the cafe bar when we noticed a mob of Burnley fans outside lobbing bricks into us, quite a few got cut up, I picked one up and lobbed one back into them and a copper pounced on me and dragged me outside and threw me into the meat wagon which was full of Oldham lads including my pal Micky Dunlea, who took me under his wing, and said he'd look after me, Mick was 17 then and I looked up to him, the van took us to the police station in the town centre after the match and we could hear all the police and ambulance sirens going off and the hooligans rampaging, it sounded eerie but exciting, we could only hear Oldham fans though and we got word off the lads arrested after the match that Oldham had ran all the combined mobs everywhere and battered fuck out of them...

I had a mixture of emotions travelling to the cop shop in the back of that meat van, I was a bit nervous not knowing what was going to happen but felt better when Micky told me I was too young and I would only get shouted at and maybe a hour in the cells, which made me feel better until Micky said the cops would probably also beat me up as well....gulp....I was kind of proud I was in amongst hooligans in the van and they were talking with me and not down to me despite my tender age, but knew my mam would give me serious grief. I also knew that my reputation would soar at school because as far as I knew I was the only one from Grange to ever get arrested at the football at that stage, at the cop shop the cops has Micky said were very aggressive smacking the bigger lads but I just got a kick up the arse, loads of shouting and bawling etc, there were about twenty five Oldham lads arrested and about five others, who were shitting themselves as the Oldham lads were threatening them, I fell lucky again as I was thrown in a cell with Micky Dunlea. Donty Shearing from Primrose bank and a lad called Budgie from St. Marys, I knew them all.

A few more Oldham lads were arrested we could hear them chanting Oldham and being defiant as the cops set about them, we cheered them on from our cells, singing 'Hello Hello, Oldham Aggro' I felt part of the crowd and the cops threw four more Oldham lads in and they were telling us how after the match Oldham ran Rochdale and their coalition all the way back into town and caught a few and that they clashed with the cops and that a dog got snatched off a copper and thrown over a bridge into a river, I listened awe struck. Poor Mick Dunlea was unlucky, he had in his pocket a set of darts, and when he was charged with carrying offensive weapons, he claimed he played darts for his local pub, but he was only 17 so he couldn't use that in his defence, he copped for a hefty fine..

At 10.30pm the cell door opened and my name was called out and I was cautioned, the cops told me that their colleagues in Oldham had been round to my mam's and told her what I had been doing and she was going to belt me when I got in, I felt embarrassed, but they released me and told me to hurry up as the last bus to Oldham was at 11pm but there would be loads of Dale fans waiting for me... gulp... as it was I walked a few stops further on and got home in one piece and was shitting it thinking me mam would snap on me, but she was pissed up on the settee and just asked how the game had been, the cops were lying ha, thank god.

Next day I was the talk of the school for my antics on the pitch and also getting arrested which elevated my reputation, but even bigger news was that the Oldham fans had smashed Rochdale town centre up smashed the trains up on the way home causing and then smashed our own town centre up with mass looting as well..

Paul Moran was involved and here is his story :

*After the match was mad as we rampaged through the streets surrounding Spotland, smashing cars and house windows and bricking the cops, we then saw Dale's mob and chased them all the way to the town centre, we then smashed a few more shops up before marching up the big hill to the train station, there were hundreds of us, far too many for one train and I'm sure it was 3 or 4 train loads, I got on the 2nd one and as we set off I lobbed a seat through the window then every one started smashing the train up and lobbing stuff out onto the lines, when we got back to Mumps station the train was a complete wreck but so was the one before and the other 2 after, we then all ran out of the station and attacked our cops who were waiting for us, they could not cope we had at*

least 3 to 400, and we the started targeting the sports and fashion shops
in the centre, smashing the windows and looting the gear, even Halfords
cycle shop got done and a few lads cycled home on brand new bikes, Dave
Stuarts fashion shop got ragged and lads were grabbing handfuls of trousers
and jumpers, the Sports shop on Yorkshire Street got done and I got some
trackies and trainers, the cops were nowhere to be seen for ages, we had a
full run for about half a hour, it was mayhem with all the alarms going off,
I got home fast as I could once I had my loot.

So despite my very eventful night I missed this mayhem said to be
the worst outbreak of violence the town had ever seen to date, I was
gutted especially as I wanted some new clobber, there was however to
be some serious repercussions as the town hall chiefs demanded people
were arrested and brought to justice for this rioting and looting... I
hardly slept that night as my head was buzzing and also I was mightily
relieved I got let off by the cops and me mam never knew anything
about it, although I think she'd long given up on me by then.

The next day in school assembly the headmaster read out a load
of names to stay behind, the names he read out were the usual suspects,
lads always in trouble and lads suspected of being involved in last nights
trouble both at Rochdale and here in Oldham, of course my name was
called out, no surprise there... we were held back for ten minutes before
in marched the familiar but very scary figure of Jack Warner..

Jack Warner was the officer in Oldham in charge of all juvenile
crimes, he had his own way of getting the answers he demanded by
knocking fuck out of you! I had met Jack a few times already, and been
twatted by him, he was also the main copper at Boundary Park on
match days... Jack was a big powerful aggressive old skool copper, no
filling in forms for Jack, he smacked the evidence out of you usually
with his head, he was plain clothes and always wore a three quarter
cream coloured mac, and looked very imposing with his big jet black
teddy boy quiff, often blowing about in the wind, he always came down
the touchline and towards the Chaddy End just after kick off from the
halfway line/players tunnel where he had been for the last hour waiting
for fans who had been ejected so he could fill them in - in the tunnel
before lobbing them out or into a meat wagon to be dropped off on the
Moors above Oldham. As Jack and his half a dozen plain clothed cronies
strolled down the touch line the Chaddy End would all chant "Fuck
off Warner, Fuck off Warner!" but as he got closer and was rubbing his
hands the chants died down as every single one of us thought he had
clocked us and would mete out revenge. He was a big tough twat and

loved piling into the mass battles, Jack also dragged many an under-aged drinker out of the pubs around town, and gave them a slap, to say he was not popular was an understatement, but I respected him, he gave me a few clouts and he butted me once but you knew were you were with Jack.

This day he was interviewing as many as he could to get names and information or confessions about all this trouble, you could see lads visibly shaking as they entered the little room he had claimed for his interview, you could hear the crash bang wallop and the screams as Jack set about em, as soon as I walked in he winged me and said, "you must fucking know summert Spiers!" but I had the ideal alibi as I was in Rochdale cells as this trouble was unfolding or on my way back from Rochdale on the last bus... he got nowhere with me, but warned me.. "I'll be having you soon enough!" which he did - many times.

Jack had hundreds of interviews throughout Oldham's many secondary schools but didn't get much joy but he did get a breakthrough at St. Anselms a Roman Catholic school a very tough school whose pupils came off three of Oldham's worst Council estates. Limeside (Crimeside), Fitton Hill and Primrose Bank. Jack couldn't have been very confident with these hardened little rogues, but he had the bit of luck he was hoping for in the shape of Georgie Kowal aged 16, George actually came from our area of Northmoor and was the son of Polish parents, his real name was Urek, but we all called him George, he was a good lad but always acting daft and trying to get attention, he had a massive head and was very stocky but he was a bloody good sportsman, especially football, rugby and lacrosse and he was also one of the best in Oldham at "nearest to the wall" a game were you throw a coin and the nearest to the wall scoops the lot up. George won almost every time, but his yearning to be one of the lads was going to be his undoing, as soon as Jack belted him George crumbled and confessed to everything Jack threw at him!

George copped for a massive fine that took him years to pay off and he thought he was impressing everyone by confessing but he was a fool and people saw him as one. The coppers had no chance of proving anything and I'm not sure anyone else got done for all that damage and theft, it ruined George he was never the same after that and it took him years to go back to Latics and he became known as Daft George.

Coppers back then were a lot harder and most lads who got questioned for anything got walloped, and many admitted to things the didn't even do, or if they did get caught out for summert the coppers would have to have a load of TIC's (offences that they would take into consideration) just to clear the back log of crimes, the cops saying it wouldn't affect your charge and would do you a favour. Ah yeah, we fell for it as kids but as we got older and wiser we knew what they were up to.

This was the times of The Sweeney - coppers and plain clothes were really aggressive bastards, well they were in Oldham. CID like Bernard Carroll a big hard drinking womanising man about town who would walk into any night club without paying with his entourage demand free drinks and grab women at will, also known to take a back hander/bribe, and also said to have all the town's grasses in his pocket, DI Keegan a stocky horrible looking man with close set eyes fierce eye brows and a habit of punching you in your stomach to wind you and force you to admit crimes - a bully. Another bully was DC Earnshaw, a six footer and another one who'd rather use his fists than fill forms in, one day he had me in for a robbery which was nothing to do with me, as much as I denied all knowledge he would punch me in the head, I snapped picked up a chair and attacked him with it, but he took it off me and then kicked fucked out of me leaving me in a bleeding breathless heap on the floor for two hours, eventually coming back to say I could go, I limped out of the cop shop, and spewed up swearing revenge, I never got the chance, I was only fucking 14!!

But as hard as they were with is there was a begrudging respect, and saved many of us going to court every other week, they were old skool cops and in reflection I much preferred their way of justice than that of today's... It certainly toughened us up.

In April 1974 I went to the FA Cup semi-final between Liverpool and Leicester City at Old Trafford, Liverpool were clear favourites although Leicester had some good players back then like Alan Birchenall and Keith Weller, I walked to Old Trafford from the city centre about 3 miles and all along the route there were Scousers everywhere, taking advantage of their huge numbers to lord it in Manchester, they were as usual full of witty banter and singing so many songs, they were great football chanters and singers, as I got closer to the ground more and more Leicester fans were milling about in their blue and white scarves, I did not see any trouble before the game as both sets of fans mingled and there seemed to be quite a bit of banter amongst themselves.

I got a ticket for the Scoreboard end where the Leicester fans were, Liverpool had the other three sides of Old Trafford and easily outnumbered the Leicester fans, it was great seeing all the Liverpool fans in the famous Stretford End and just before kick off the three sides of Old Trafford sang the fantastic Liverpool anthem. "You'll never walk alone" it was as you can imagine, magnificent, one of the greatest sights in football, it was a lovely sunny day as well which added to this spectacle. A large mob of Leicester fans booed Liverpool's anthem and a few scuffles broke out in the Scoreboard end were some Liverpool fans had got in, the mood changed.

Liverpool as expected won the game and went on to meet Newcastle in that season's final which they also won easily 3-0... in the last ten minutes of this semi-final loads of Liverpool fans poured into the Scoreboard and began attacking the Leicester fans, many fought back and for a while Leicester were having the upper hand, but at the end of the match thousands of Scousers awaited their rivals and all hell let loose, this was football violence on a massive sale, thousands of boot boys, greasers thugs and many men in their 30's and 40's brawling, the police also came unstuck as the much bigger mob of Scousers went on the rampage, over turning cars smashing shops and destroying property in and around Old Trafford, it was exciting and I just tagged along with the rampaging Scousers who marched en masse into Manchester city centre, there were odd pockets of United fans who tried in vain to attack the big Scouse mob but were soon fucked off, this is one day United could not do the Scousers, the FA Cup allowed up to 30,000 plus Scousers and it seemed most of them were in this massive mob which snaked back twenty deep a mile or so.

The cops struggled to contain such vast numbers and when they arrived in the city centre they set about looting shops, I peeled away once back in the centre and got out of the road... young rough Scousers my age were asking lads where they came from and any non Scouse accent was met by attacks and even robbery, "wur you from lah" they were horrible vile cunts and I was glad to be back on the train back to Oldham, however it was a great day and experience, the Scousers were not as loveable as we were led to believe and 3 years later I was to find this out first hand.

Having won the league Division Three title and promotion to the Second Division we really had arrived, this was the big time for most of us who had only ever known fourth and third division football and all those small teams, now we were in with the likes of Manchester United, the biggest club in the country who had been relegated from the First Division, the country's biggest mob of hooligans the Red Army who had 10,000 lads and who had taken over so many towns and ends all over the country. Then there was Sunderland who the year before had won the FA Cup against the mighty Leeds United, Sunderland were getting 40,000 plus crowds - Sheff Wed, Aston Villa, West Brom, Notts Forest, Bristol City, Cardiff City and the feared Millwall were also due in Oldham - I suppose it may have been second tier for football but in hooligan terms, this was Division One! The country's most notorious fans and when you add in Lancashire rivals Blackpool and our hated foes Bolton Wanderers, this was going to be a very violent season, it was a very violent season, I was 13 going on 14 and I grew up fast...

Added to all these juicy potentially violent games Oldham Athletic found themselves involved in the Texaco Cup that season, which was teams from England and Scotland playing each other in a competition, it later became the Anglo Scottish cup, but the first round of games 4 English clubs played each other and likewise Scotland, we were drawn against Sheffield United and Manchester City of Division One and Blackpool who were in our league Division 2, first game was Sheff United at home and disappointingly it was a very poor crowd and not many Sheff United fans and the ones that did come took a terrible kicking off Oldham's much bigger and much more up for it numbers, they vowed revenge as every team who ever took a beating did, it took three years for them to exact revenge but they certainly did do.

Meanwhile on the Tuesday we played Blackpool away and the club put a special train on, but there were only just over a hundred on it including my mam and brother Peter, this Texaco cup was not whetting anyone's appetite it seemed, the train pulled in at the old South Shore station and it was a 10 minute stroll to Bloomfield Road, we all went into their large Spion Kop, mam went to get a seat in the main stand, thank god because as soon as we got inside we got ambushed by the Blackpool mob, who had huge numbers and were relentless in their attacks and there were no coppers, we found refuge in the top left hand corner, we were joined by another couple of coach loads but they had also all been attacked by Blackpool, about ten minutes after kick off two works vans of builders in work clobber, donkey jacket's and work boots rolled in, led by a huge powerfully built bloke late twenties with a big beard, word soon got round that this was the legendary Gill Dock, the king of the Chaddy End in the 1960's, at last I got to see this big man, who did look very hard, with him was Jimmy Bobble hat Marshall, a notoriously tough little character from Northmoor, and a few more rough looking blokes, well the Blackpool mob stayed well clear of this motley crew and we all got up close to the builders, we drew the game 1-1, at the end of the match we had the long walk to the South Shore station and every single one of us got beat up and even as we boarded the train they were coming on and smacking us, fortunately my mam had gone for a drink and missed all this and laughed at us all with bust up faces, we took a terrible beating that night and once again vowed revenge ....we only had a month to wait until Blackpool came to Boundary Park in the league, and oh revenge was oh so sweet.

The third game of the Texaco Cup was against Manchester City at Maine Road, on the Saturday, I remember it was pissing down and I went in the famous Kippax, I spotted little groups of Oldham fans but no big mob and they kept a low profile, City were a massive club with a massive following, I spotted about 15 of the old Glodwick mob so I got in near them which made me feel a bit safer, we lost the game 3 –2 and there was only a muted cheer, certainly no gloating, I was glad to get away from Moss Side and back into Manchester city centre and the bus back home, as it was Oldham went through to the next stages the quarter finals.

The first game of the 1974/75 season was a massive game. Sheffield Wednesday were one of the biggest supported clubs in the country a team with huge history and tradition and only 28 miles away from Oldham, we just knew they would bring thousands, I was not aware if they had a big hooligan following but fully expected a big crowd and whatever will be will be.

At the time I was a paperboy delivering news papers for Mrs Buckley in the town centre, my round was the new council estates of Shaw Road and St. Mary's. It was a big round but it paid well even back then I was earning £3-50 a week for 7 mornings - with a 6am start 7.30am finish, I was like Billy Whizz through them verandas, at the end of my round I would go in the brilliant greasy spoon Market Cafe which was next door to Mrs Buckley's paper shop, I always treated meself to a full English breakfast and a large cup of milky coffee, it came to just 30p.

I loved the atmosphere in the market cafe, it was always bustling and full of laughter and yapping, market traders, wheelers and dealers, lorry drivers, taxi drivers, loose women and villains, it was always covered in a smokey fog as most people smoked back then, the wise cracking and howls of laughter and the shouting of orders... it was here

I strolled in on the lovely sunny Saturday morning, I had just been paid and I was famished, all the usual suspects were in there but I also noticed a group of around twenty lads with blue and white scarves and many wearing Sheffield Wednesday team shirts, well being the cheeky nosy fucker I was I sat near them, I was wearing my tangerine bob hat so they would suss out I was Oldham, it didn't take long for them to start chatting to me, they told me they had drove through the night after coming out of a night club, and had been here since 4 am, they were all about 18—20, they were asking me questions about Oldham and it's mob etc, "I warned them not to go in the Chaddy End and that we had two massive mobs, the Crossley Skins and the Glodwick Mob, they seemed impressed, but probably wondered why there were still skinheads 4 years after the fashion had gone, they also must have known I was blagging and bigging my home town up, but they were okay with me and most shook me hand before I left the cafe, and wished me good luck, I thought "good luck" what for... Oldham will smash them..

At 1.30pm me and Paul are walking down Sheepfoot Lane to the ground and there are thousands of Wednesday fans, most wearing the team shirts, something I had never seen before, it was the second largest following I had ever seen after Burnley earlier that year in the FA Cup, of course they took the Chaddy End, it was rammed full of Wednesday fans, with pockets of Oldham dotted about but nowhere near enough to challenge our Yorkshire foes. I was gutted and hated seeing the Chaddy End taken over, but it was a magnificent spectacle and they made such an incredible noise, the Latics fans were in the other three sides of the ground, there was nothing they could do this day, I was in the Chaddy End at the bottom and at half time a few of the lads I met in the cafe that morning spotted me, and asked where the Glodwick and Crossley mobs were? I said they will be coming across the pitch at any time, they all burst out laughing... bastards !!

I have to say Sheff Weds fans were not violent and even after the match which we won 2 −1 they did not take liberties and if anything it was Oldham fans spoiling for a fight but outside the ground, Wednesday's numbers were massively in their favour, however in the town centre Oldham's hooligans were picking off smaller groups of Weds fans making their way back to the coach stations and train station, I was part of a mob of around 100 Oldham fans who waited outside our main train station to ambush any Weds fans, as we were all waiting I noticed Shane Clegg walking towards us with two big Weds fans, when Shane clocked us lot he turned and attacked these Weds fans who fled, then Shane informs us there's a mob of fifty or so Weds on the way, he told these Weds he was one of them hoping there was a mob of us in wait, he fell lucky, we hid until this mob of Weds got nearby us then we attacked from all angles and caught them whacked them many fleeing over the motorway by-pass. I got my souvenir Weds scarf to add to my collection... it was a long day but an eventful one had Weds proved themselves as one of THE biggest away followings in the country, we got off lightly.

That very same day the first football fan ever to be murdered was stabbed to death at Bloomfield Road by a Bolton fan called Bevington Williams, it happened in the very same spot were Blackpool fans had ambushed us behind their Spion Kop only ten days previously, I knew Blackpool v Bolton Wanderers would be a very violent confrontation, but I never would expect someone to die at a football match, it shocked the whole country and Bolton became THE most hated fans in the country for a while. They were labelled murderers and backstabbers by rival fans. This went beyond football violence, it was in all the following day's newspapers with the government promising to close down football grounds as per usual, now even then I wasn't that naive to think it was never going to happen, I myself had been stabbed in the thigh against Burnley only a few months prior, so it could easily have been me, but this shocked me, but not enough to put me off the aggro. Blackpool fans vowed revenge and the rivalry between these two famous Lancashire clubs went on for many years.

Meanwhile our next home game of that season was Bristol City and they brought a big mob into the Chaddy End and were very game before getting overwhelmed, there was about a hundred of them big fuckers and a few of them got arrested but the Chaddy End was packed and they got forced into the top right hand corner were they were surrounded by police but a big charge near the end of the game broke though and they got kicked down the terraces although they fought back gallantly, after the game Oldham fans attacked them on the big car park and a few coach windows got put through, Oldham also clashed with the cops and their dogs and lots of bricks and rocks were thrown, the tensions between Oldham and their own police had been high for several months.

Our next home game was well anticipated, it was Blackpool and we had heard rumours that their fans had doubled since their fan was murdered first game of the season and that they were now carrying weapons, that game the Chaddy End was packed by 2pm with Oldham fans with many of our own mobs doubled in numbers ready for what was going to be a long battle, those of us who went to Blackpool a few weeks before and got kicked to fuck wanted our revenge, we took a terrible kicking, the crowd was tense and their was a slight disappointment when we saw the away end filling up with Blackpool fans but right on cue at kick off in they came with their brilliant tangerine and white scarves chanting "Hello, Hello Seaside Aggro Seaside Aggro".

It sounded daunting but exciting, there were 200 of them and they came charging across the top of the Chaddy End, a huge gap appeared and when we realised there wasn't a 1000 as it sounded like that many, we piled into them, and mass brawls broke out and hand to hand fights, it was a major battle and Blackpool gave as good as they got but they couldn't take the Chaddy End, they would need a lot more than the 200 lads they had, but they remained in the Chaddy End all the game which has to be respected and took some serious charges and assaults, one of the front liners amongst the Blackpool fans in the Chaddy that day was none other than Billy the Kid our very own DJ from the Cats Whiskers on Monday nights, now we knew Billy was a Blackpool fan because he was always mentioning it but didn't think he was one of their lads, he got loads of personal threats but he just laughed them off and he was back behind the decks on the Monday night as if nothing had happened.

It was a great Lancashire derby with a great tense atmosphere and I'm glad to say despite the rivalry Oldham fans did not sink that low to gloat about the death of the Blackpool fan in fact we all sang "Oh wanky wanky wanky Wanderers" as one but any camaraderie was soon put to one side as at the end of the game, with some street fighting occurring on Sheepfoot Lane... Oldham soon had Blackpool on the back foot but half way down the dirt track near Westwood Park Blackpool made a stand and a no mans land appeared of say some 30 yards or so... one tall gangly Blackpool fan in dungarees and big platform boots stepped forward and in a kung fu pose began squawking like a chicken. Big fat Alan Bamborough, a huge overweight Fitton Hill nutter, ran up and just kicked him in the balls and then flattened him into the dust. Kung Fu became very popular in 1973/4 with a series of Bruce Lee Films, and everyone all of a sudden thought they were Kung Fu experts, the only good thing was people stopped taking piss out of the Chinks in the chippies because they all looked like Bruce Lee!

Oldham then gathered the momentum and gave chase to this Blackpool mob who fled, across the very dusty lane, it was a hot late summer day very dry and the dust clouds kicked up like Hiroshima, we were coughing our guts up as we gave chase and our white skinners were manky! This chase lasted half a hour as Blackpool's fleeing mob missed the Featherstall Road turn off for Werneth train station and they actually ended up running down West End street where I lived, all the neighbours were out on the front watching these two big mobs playing cat and mouse, I hid amongst the Oldham mob as we got past our house where me dad was stood talking to Harry Brierley our elderly next door neighbour... we chased Blackpool all the way down the street and eventually to Werneth station, the whole chase lasted a full 40 minutes at least, at the station there were loads of coppers so we were fucked literally.

It was frustrating and we knew we could not reach them physically but we knew we could get at them for a very high vantage point above the station, the brand new West street council estate was being built, it was perfect, we were right above the Blackpool fans many whom were lying down they were that shattered, well we rained down breeze blocks scaffold grips, steel fence poles and anything else we could get our hands on, they shit themselves many running into the train tunnel nearby, the cops also panicked with their dogs and ran out of the open plan station and tried to get to us but it was a good way round by foot and by the time they had got anywhere near we were away, quite a few Blackpool got cut up by that ambush. Our revenge was sweet but we had to go to Blackpool away - it was gonna be rough.

Three days later would see one of the most violent matches ever witnessed at Boundary Park and no–one would ever have imagined it beforehand. We were due to play Hearts of Midlothian in the Texaco cup quarter final, it was a two legged match, nobody expected any Hearts fans so it was with great surprise when during an English lesson at Grange school at 2pm that Tuesday afternoon I noticed staggering down Rochdale Road through the windows were a large group of pissed up Jocks with maroon and white scarves, there must have been 50 or so and these were blokes in their twenties, the whole class ran to the windows to see what all the excitement was, the teacher a little skinny part time student fucker grabbed me and slapped me across my face! So I slapped him back only twice as hard and decked him, I then walked out of the class room and out of the school I would face the music the next day, I had to find out where these Jocks had gone, I headed up town and saw them staggering about effin and jeffin scaring shoppers, I had never seen football fans during the day on a night game and I had never seen so many drunks in one mob, many of them were carrying whisky bottles which they were slugging from.

At 4pm I called for Paul and was telling him all about the Hearts fans and that I had slapped a teacher, we couldn't wait for the game tonight, we saw load more Hearts fans staggering down Rochdale Road towards the ground as early as 6pm, we followed them from a safe distance, outside the ground there were loads more as vans and coaches kept on arriving most of them pissed up and falling over, they all went into the Chaddy End as soon as the gates opened, they made an incredible racket with their chanting and singing, most of them still holding large whisky bottles in their hands, they were nutters and attacked any fans coming in and even the police and their dogs, they took the Chaddy End because there was no opposition but any Oldham fans coming in through the turn styles got attacked, by kick off Hearts were revelling in the taking of an English Kop our Chaddy End but more and more Oldham fans were getting in and before long we had huge numbers of lads in there as word somehow reached all the estates and districts of Oldham and beyond, we forced our way up to the top and fought these drunken thugs despite many of them brandishing and using their whisky bottles, there was much blood shed and the St johns ambulances were very busy, meanwhile our cops were taking a lot of blows from the Hearts fans and were actually allowing us to mob up and get an advantage, by half time we had taken our Chaddy End back forcing the Hearts fans across the top of the Chaddy End. Rumours that one was brandishing a double-barrelled shotgun made us wary but one of them definitely had an axe but this was snatched from him and lost under the wooden terraces, the tension was incredible the fighting relentless, much blood was shed but the drunkenness was slowly taking it's toil as Oldham got stronger and really ripped into them, by the end of the match most Hearts fans had left the Chaddy End, it was a tremendous victory against all the odds.

So many of them were men in their twenties and thirties, most of us were teenagers although a lot of our older supporters got stuck in as they were taking seriously liberties but so many of the jocks were using bottles as weapons, I've never seen so much blood shed at one match, the Oldham mob by the end of the game was massive one of the biggest mobs we have ever had and we moved towards the exit on Sheepfoot

Lane as one huge mass, me and my mates from Westwood were near the front and as we were heading towards the gates a big mob of Hearts came running in bricking us, we couldn't run if we wanted such was the packed up mass of lads behind us, many Oldham lads took bricks in their face including Phil Heeney who was stood next to me, his nose split in half as blood gushed everywhere, he had a few stitches inserted, we got outside and chased them up the road but there was loads more of them and they came charging into us but many were that pissed they just fell over and we booted fuck out of them, many got their pockets rifled as well off our more dodgier fans, the smell of whisky was horrendous... the sirens of the police and ambulances were going off all over the place adding to all this mayhem.

Oldham had the upper hand and a huge advantage in numbers and battered loads of Hearts all the way to the town centre dragging them out of pubs en route, it was a long, long night and very tiring but I saw levels of violence that night and blood shed that I never ever forget and neither did anybody else who was there also.. I also got myself a Hearts scarf to add to the collection... (not many made the trip up to Hearts for the 2nd leg.)

This game saw dozens of arrests even more ejections and the largest numbers of casualties ever seen at Boundary Park. Also my uncle Jack passed away that night after suffering a heart attack during the game, he was sat with my mam in the main stand, this huge barrel chested powerful man had gone, nothing to do with the game, just his time was up, he was a very much respected man around the Northmoor area where we brought up, also a man's man, a tap room man, with a great sense of humour and presence, he was a great uncle always full of jokes and found plenty of time for me and my family, he was just 52 years old R.I.P.

My God this season was crazy. Our next home game was Cardiff City who had a huge reputation for violence and only a few weeks previously had clashed with Man United's Red Army for several hours when they met at Ninian Park, in one of the most violent clashes ever known in Britain, they both really wound each other up Cardiff chanting Munich '58 and United chanting Aberfan (a disaster in the sixties where 60 school kids died). All fucking sick stuff and United came unstuck as it seemed the whole of South Wales turned out to take them on, we here in Oldham were very apprehensive about the visit of the crazy Welshmen, however they did not bring the large numbers expected but still brought a couple of hundred lads into the Chaddy

End and were game as fuck, and took some shifting and they lasted until half time before fleeing across the pitch to join the rest of their travelling support, but halfway through the 2nd half four of them came back onto the pitch and lay a huge Welsh Banner on the halfway line, in some kind of rebellious gesture. They got dragged off the pitch by the cops and by the end of the game we felt confident enough to go to their end and attack them and got the upper hand with our bigger numbers, but they were game for sure.

Fulham came next and they only brought a few fans and stayed in the away end but me and Paul went in their for a nosy, there was about twenty big lads in Sheepskin over coats who looked the business and when they clocked me in my skinhead haircut and gear they began singing, "hey you skinhead over there, what's it like to have no hair, you make think you make a lot of noise, but we are the Fal Ham boot boys!" Everyone laughed, it was funny, there was no trouble that day but these lads looked liked they would have a go if need be.

The next game there was loads of trouble as Aston Villa arrived in town once again in massive numbers and once again sharing the Chaddy End, it was a perfect 50/50 split with a ten yards no mans land where loads of coppers tried in vain to stop us charging into each other at every opportunity, it was fantastic and fights were breaking out every minute, at half time both mobs for some reason move back about twenty yards each when all of sudden both mobs charged into each other not one took a backward step and as we clashed all the pies fags cups of coffees and other items went skywards, the brawl lasted the whole half time period, before order was restored and loads ejected out of the ground, after the match most of Villas mob had to walk the 2 miles to Werneth train station and there were clashes all the way, one lad made his name that day Nick Baker from Primrose Bank who was a few years older than me and already had a tough rep from his days at school St.Anselms, this day he fought many times and charged in and out of the Villa fans all the way, his face was smashed in but he kept going back in, there was not much to him but he was fearless, game as fuck and inspired many of us, he was on the scene for a couple of more seasons then drifted away but he certainly made an impact between 1973-77...

The night before the Villa game Oldham's Victorian market hall burned down, it upset so many Oldhamer's it was a true landmark for generations of Oldhamer's, that Sat morning me and me mam watched the final embers smouldering and their were many people stood about in shock and many crying - people still talk about it 38 years on.

The early 1970's were very violent times no wonder we teenagers were attracted so much to violence, you had all the troubles from Northern Ireland on our tellies every night, the pickets fighting with police, cop programmes like the Sweeney, images from Vietnam, it was the best era for Heavyweight boxers with giants like Ali Norton Foreman Frazier Shavers etc knocking seven bells out of each other and then almost every week there were mass pitch invasions being shown on match of the day. I remember three in particular, Chelsea at Spurs, thousands clashing on the pitch rolling about with the flares and long centre parted hair styles and twin set jumpers, it lasted at least ten minutes, then United invading the pitch when Denis Law back heeled them in to the Second Division, thousands of United boot boys charging across to the City fans who soon melted and then the one at Newcastle when a 40 odd year old bald headed man led 4000 Geordies across the pitch to attack the Forest fans and Jimmy Hill came out with the classic line, "I hope when that young man gets home his mother will tan his backside!" - he was fucking 40 odd at least Jimmy!!

All these images inspired us - the 70's was a decade of violence on a scale never seen before or since.

This season saw the peak of the Chaddy End as we filled the end most home games, and all the Oldham mobs seemed to double in size from previous seasons, most of us were aged 13 to 18 but you still had older lads there, the old Glodwick mob were still active even though they were in their twenties by now, they were backed up by the Glodwick jays, a huge mixed raced mob, the only mixed raced mob in Oldham, with both Glodwick mobs together they were by far the biggest crew in Oldham, all the districts of Oldham had crews, Fitton Hill could pull out very big numbers for certain games, they always had a large hard core mob, it was the biggest council estate in Oldham with many large families, Fitton Hill lads and girls were always smart and street wise, lads like Tanya, Birdy, Arnie, Lowie, Kenny, Billy K, Pete Hewitt, the Badbys, the Flanagans, little Hutchie, Hendy, the Shaws, Kempy, Haggis and Clock. Sholver had a big crew although they not all lived on Sholver and would have lads from Moorside, Strinesdale and Littlemoor joining in with them, the main face of Sholver was a right character Happy Harry Randall, arguably the most famous hooligan in

Oldham during that era, mainly because he was thrown out or arrested every other game, he was a complete nut case, yet you could not find a lesser looking hooligan, Harry came off the notoriously rough Strinesdale estate, an estate so rough the cops would never even go up there alone, it housed many of Oldhams worst criminals.

Harry Randall was initially an Oldham Red but apparently lost face when he bottled out in a pitch battle at Arsenal giving the Gunners the upper hand and many United fans got badly beaten, well I was never Harry's biggest fan but over the next 6 seasons I never saw him bottle out once, he took some terrible beatings but always without fail went down fighting, he was as funny looking feller, he would be 19/20 in 74 whilst his crew were all under 16, Harry was very old fashioned with his Beatles haircut, all floppy black hair hanging into his face, he wore thick national health glasses one eye was always held together with a plaster, he never replaced the broken spectacles just held em together with a sticky plaster! He always wore an old fashioned old man's blazer and cheap flared pants and those cheap bumper baseball boots, he had to be one of the least fashionable lads I have ever seen.

Harry Randall was a bully, he was many years older than most of us and intimidated a lot of the younger lads, he had good back up with his Sholver crew and knew this, of course as we grew older wiser and stronger we stopped being intimidated by Happy fucking Harry but saw him for what he was... a joke... a fucking idiot albeit with loads of bottle but unlike many of the Sholver lads he had no class no style and no dignity he was just an out and out hooligan who didn't give a fuck about the game... Sholver had some top lads though, lads like Nicky Schuller, a swarthly looking small but compact lad, game as fuck and loyal, Nobby "blue eyes" Dixon, a pretty boy but one who would get right into the battles, he seemed to have a bloody nose every game, even when there was no fighting, the birds loved him and his blue eyes, he looked like Paul Newman, and evidence of his popularity was when I went back to this bird's flat in Oldham early 1980's and there was a 'lads to do' lists from all these different birds, they each chose the top twenty lads they wanted to have, and Nobby was top almost on all of them and top 3 of the ones he wasn't.... Happy fucking Harry didn't make any of the lists.

Another good lad was Al Lees who was a well made lad and always laughing and joking about but also got stuck in, Al Riley always trendy and brave, Tets wasn't a fighter but loyal die hard Latics fan for decades, Cooky, Hoyley, Sharky who was a United hooligan but came to Latics with his mates many times and always got stuck in, Sharky was very brave and to be a United fan and a Pakistani (half caste) made him public enemy number one wherever he went but he had great courage for such a slightly built lad, he had an apprentice called Craig a few years younger whom he showed the ropes to,

The Sholver mob soon became known as the Sholver Leathers, not that the were Greasers or Rockers, far from it they were Soul boys, Smoothies, it's just that they somehow all got hold of some leather bomber jackets which were very fashionable at the time, and they all to a man wore them and looked very smart, they were a good firm who could pull big numbers when required, their estate was high up in the Moors above Oldham, a new estate built in 1970 and were plenty of problem families from inner Oldham were shipped out, most of the problem families were shoved in two horrendous block of flats, called Pearly Bank and Wilkes Street, these were really rough, with very few having electricity and many not having running water because they would not pay their bills, to be honest the Sholver lads came from the nicer parts of the estate and were smart lads. They were mainly Oldham but had one or two United mates who tagged along with them now and then.

A rival mob of Sholver for many years were the Werneth Mob which neighboured the Westwood area I came from, like Westwood, Werneth was a mixed raced district with a large Pakistan community. Werneth was always a solid Latics area even as far back as the late 1960's when Fred Hewitt was the main man and also one of the main lads in the Chaddy End, I once witnessed Fred Hewitt and Baz Kemp of Crossley Skins squaring up after a night match on Featherstall Road, this was the clash of the titans, two big hard lads, Baz being a Skinhead and Fred being a Rocker, there were huge crowds, and Fred stuck the nut on Baz but before too long the cops were on the scene, this was 1971, and there were tit for tat incidents for months after between these rival neighbouring districts.

In the early 1970's the Werneth mob had lads like King Carl Siddall, a fearsome looking youth with his skinhead crop and large sideburns, the self proclaimed King Carl was 6 years older than me, he had a big reputation but most of it was promoted by himself, he certainly looked the part in all the Skinhead gear his swagger and the way he growled through the side of his mouth like a Chicago gangster, but he wasn't all he was cracked up to be and a lot of the lads he bullied caught up with him in later years. However when Carl made the odd appearance at

Latics it did boost us younger ones, he was charismatic, other lads from Werneth then include Les Trelfa who was very tough, only small but stocky and had a big name all over Oldham, Smish, who had a boxer's nose which affected his speech, he was called Smith but pronounced it as Smish, Neil Hart and Eric Rossy.

But it was the next generation of Werneth lads that really made their mark as one of the best and most loyal mobs in Oldham, very game lads even though many of them were small they had hearts of lions, they hung about Werneth park in the summer months and fought off many invaders but also had the bottle to go into other areas like Chadderton, Failsworth, Limeside, Sholver and Royton, they also clashed with the Glodwick blacks several times but it was at Boundary Park and Latics away games they made their name, lads like Little Johnny Murphy, although only five foot two was tough as teak and feared no one and no situation, he had a huge gob and you would think there was ten men coming round the corner when Murph began chanting, he was that tough he would wear only a vest on cold winter away games at frozen places like Sunderland, Grimsby, Workington and Carlisle, he was mad but very game.

Other well known Werneth lads were Alan "Willis" Williams, Norman Letson, Wayne Ross (RIP). who got ran over on Manchester road in 1978 aged 19 ), Checks, Snowy, Glyn and Dave Adams, Nick Naum, Carl Walsh, Norman Howarth (RIP) John "Alf "Hart, Fat Doc, Dave Greenwood, Dave Trow (RIP) Les Hilditch, Ant Hilditch (RIP).

Big Al Kenyon, cock of Oldham schools for his age 1975. Tony Miceviticz, Robbo Watson one of the most famous Chaddy Enders in the 70's for his rugged looks with broken nose flame coloured feather cut, mad sense of humour, his toughness, he used to head butt lamp posts to show off his nuttyness, and he along with the other big gob of Werneth Murphy was our "zigga zagga man". Murph had the big deep fog horn booming voice whereas Robbo would go purple in the face as he screamed out "Zigga Zgga, Zigga Zagga ATH LET IC!!" or "1—2—3 –4 listen to the Chaddy roar..." Robbo was mad as a hatter but game as fuck.

John Ugivari (Yugoslavian descent ), Willy Orr, Al Buckley, Gary Dutson, Dave, Mick Scholes, Aiden, boot girls likes Lorraine Mac, Sheena, Kathy, Chrissy & Iris,

The Werneth mob were lucky in a sense that most away fans came through the Werneth train station then had to walk the 2 miles to and back to Boundary Park...so they saw plenty of action in fact more than any other mob, they were a great mob full of characters and bottle, I hung about with them for a while in the summer of 1976 and when we were all older and going in pubs I spent many great times with them in the famous Plough Inn, which was their base, the Plough had arguably THE best pool teams in Oldham for many years, and these former boot boys were the pool players.

A few Werneth lads were Chelsea fans and most of the others had Chelsea as their second team and went to many Chelsea games if Oldham were playing miles away, this was 1975—1980 when Chelsea had the biggest mob in the country and were taking ends up and down the land, I too went to a few Chelsea games, they were truly THE best mob I have ever seen especially at taking ends...

# GRAFFITI ARTISTS

A BIG THING BACK IN the 1970's was graffiti via paint spray cans, almost every ground in he country had local walls or even their own stadium walls adorned with graffiti either by their own fans or by travelling fans, it always fascinated me, the slogans and who actually had done this illegal act of vandalism, certain names seem to appear more than others, in particular Matt and Charlie BWFC, which was the walls of every ground I had been to, Im sure they must have travelled to these grounds during the dead of the night, it was everywhere and funny enough two more names that seemed to also be on a lot of walls were Ent & Fog BWFC... I don't know if these were rivals of Matt n Charlie but you never saw Matt Charlie Ent & Fog in one slogan! The best wall in the country for graffiti was the one that runs down the side of Bloomfield Road, a long narrow alleyway known locally as "Suicide Alley "for this is were Blackpool trapped and ambushed away fans, every team in England and Scotland were on these walls, including Oldham because I sprayed it whilst on my holidays in the summer of 75, and it remained there proudly for many years, I'm sure most of these slogans were put up by holiday makers and it made great reading...

We played Millwall at home in October. They had a horrible reputation arguably the most feared fans in the country, they did not have the massive numbers of Man United, Chelsea and Leeds but at home no one ever took liberties there or if they did they came seriously unstuck, even the Red Army of Manchester United who swept most teams and towns aside during this season bottled out of going to the Den on a cold October night, they had a few but those who braved had the worst night of their lives apparently. This news soon travelled the hooligan grapevine, so we here at little Oldham were somewhat apprehensive about Millwall's visit to Boundary Park, however the Chaddy End was full to capacity by 2.30pm and Millwall's travelling fans it seemed were happy to embank in the away end... surely there must be some Millwall fans in the Chaddy, we searched and high and low but no sign, the only two possibilities were two of the biggest fattest men I have ever seen in my life, who were stood right in the middle of the Chaddy End, both were well over 30 stones, both sporting big scruffy beards and both in their thirties at least.

We eyed them with suspicion but no one dared to challenge them, they were scoffing pies and drinks with not a care in the world, come kick off they both started chanting MILL - WALL  MILL  - WALL in the really slow Cockney drawl! There they were bold as brass just the two of them, well we piled into them but they were that big and strong they just batted us away like flies, dozens attacked them many trying to get a grip round their big fat necks but they stood back to back and shrugged us, off, people were launching red hot brews, pies and anything this else but it all bounced of them, they kept on chanting MILL WALL MILL WALL, a huge gap appeared as brave hearts tried in vain to hurt them and bring em down but no one could, even up to 15 coppers struggled with them, they stood their ground for at least ten minutes, before eventually being brought to their knees by 15 cops and maybe a hundred Oldham fans. It was an incredible show of strength, they got dragged around the pitch by all these coppers some with dogs and to be fair they got a standing ovation from the Chaddy End as well as their own fans at three quarter time when the gates opened a mob of around 50 Millwall came into the Chaddy from both paddocks, these were men in their twenties and wearing donkey jackets and flat caps... we attacked them but they were game as fuck and fought back bravely, we couldn't get them back out of the Chaddy and neither could the cops... after the match Millwall came out of their away end in search of Oldham but not many if any took them on....

A week and a bit later we played Bolton Wanderers away on a Tuesday night, I was at school and persuaded two mates Paul Anderson and Dave Urey to peg off and get the Selnec trans Lancs express bus to Bolton, the bus left Oldham College at 14 mins past the hour, and we boarded the 2.14 bus which got us into Bolton at 3.14, it was a double decker and we were upstairs, as we pulled into Bolton bus station two cops got on and arrested us accusing us of vandalising the bus, ripping seats up and writing slogans on in black felt tip marker they had us in the cells, the driver said it was us, the lying twat! We could not  believe what was going and we all denied any knowledge and just told the cops we were here for the match, after a hour or so they released us but told us to get back to Oldham and if they seen us again they would arrest us again! We got a bus towards Bury but got off two bus stops on, and walked back into Bolton...we were a bit wary, me and Dave had skinhead cuts so we stood out, and Bolton fans always asked you were you came from, checking out your accents, it was a scary place back then, we kept a low one until about 7pm when the Oldham coaches began to arrive, about ten coaches arrived and the cops escorted us to the ground and put us in the Railway Embankment end, a big open concrete terrace.

At first we were all buoyant and chanting away but this end soon filled up with Bolton thugs, loads of them, we were mobbed up in the middle and they were all around us, behind us and in front of us, we just knew our kicking was coming, the cops fucked off, and so did quite a lot of Oldham fans, the Bolton fans were staring at us making throat slitting motions and telling us we were gonna die, they came closer and closer to us until they were right amongst us, and then all of a sudden they attacked us, boots and punches raining down on us, they were relentless and most of us took a beating. I was still not 14, yet lads aged 18 and more were attacking me and other lads my age, it was horrendous and these random attacks went on most of the game, the cops did fuck all but just pull a few away for a bollocking, after the match the cops didn't even give us an escort back and as we walked under that big railway bridge outside the ground the Bolton cunts once again attacked us only in much bigger numbers the screams and pleas for mercy were to haunt me for a while, Im sure every Oldham fan got beat up that night... and we three had to get the fucking bus back to Oldham! We somehow broke away and hid for half an hour down some alley way... we made the wise move to walk out of Bolton and get the bus a few stops further on, we just knew Bolton fans would be at the bus station, I tasted fear many times in my life but that was one of the most scariest experiences, we got home battered and bruised and the trip home was in silence.

Time for a break from all the aggro - ha not fucking likely - next up at Boundary Park was Nottingham Forest, yet another fallen giant from Division One not too long ago but a team with great tradition and a good support and so it proved as hundreds of Forest fans poured into the Chaddy End from 2.30pm onwards and taking over in a matter minutes these were big rough tough fuckers, many of them long haired heavily tattooed Rockers who showed no mercy to us younger boot boys and wannabe hooligans, but to our credit we kept on at Forest throughout the whole of the first half our numbers getting larger as normal supporters got involved and by half time we had re-taken our end which was no mean feat because Forest were very hard, by the 2nd half we had regained the top of the Chaddy End but Forest remained in our end the whole match and fought the whole match and continued to do so for half a hour afterwards before they boarded their vans and coaches back to the East Midlands, it was a long day for sure.

A couple of weeks later we played the second biggest club in the league and one of the best supported clubs in the country, Sunderland, who the year before shocked the football world by beating the brilliant Leeds United 1-0 at Wembley in the FA Cup final, Sunderland already had a huge following but this fairy tale success gave them even more fans and they came to Boundary Park in their thousands and took over and filled the Chaddy End to the absolute maximum, we couldn't even get in if we wanted to there was that many of them in there, and to be fair they were brilliant fans very vocal – loads of banners and scarves and the songs they sang were superb, they were so passionate and even after the game there was no trouble, we could not take them on even if we wanted to, there was just thousands of them, they were truly a massive club and that's one town and team Man United did not take liberties with at Roker Park, in fact no teams did.

# THE MIGHTY RED ARMY

In all the years of football hooliganism from the early 60's to the present day there has never been any team in England that had as many hooligans following them, and this season 1974/75 was the peak for the famous Red Army who for the last ten years or so had taken over many towns, resorts, cities and ends along the way. They had up to ten thousand boot boys, bovver boys thugs whatever you called them, they attracted hooligans from almost every town in Britain, no other team could match them for numbers back then apart from Rangers and Celtic, the numbers of ten thousand lads seem incredible but when you realise that United had mobs from over 100 towns up and down the country most having mobs of between 50-100 it soon adds up added to the massive numbers they had from Manchester, they would just take over whole town centres on their travels, very few teams could take them on in the early 1970's and when they were relegated to Division 2 in 1974 many towns boarded up their shops and house windows such was the reputation of this massive Red Army.

We were due to play Manchester United at Boundary Park on 28th December, just two days after a very long days battling with Blackpool, the Oldham Chronicle was frightening to death local residents with tales of horror about the impeding Red Army about to hit town, like many other towns in their wake; shops and houses boarded up their windows, so apart from the thousands of United thugs descending onto our town we also had the Oldham Reds, a treacherous band of bandwagon jumpers who chose to follow the biggest club in the country rather than their home town. Back then they had a tidy mob of maybe a hundred on a good day, we very rarely saw them, they only came to Boundary Park en masse once when we played Aston Villa in 1972 and did help us to retrieve our end, but their constant chanting of "United, United" got them sorted out and  booted out of the Chaddy End by Oldham loyalists, they did make a half hearted attempt of a show when we played Man City pre season 1973/74 but City soon fucked em off but the Oldham Reds did have some top lads amongst them including the very charismatic Gary Riley of Royton who had his own tasty firm. He was ten years older than me and was very much respected in Oldham and Manchester, he was seen as the main face of the Oldham Reds, Gary however always maintained that Oldham were his second team it was his home town and he always looked out for our results, he also made the odd appearance over the years with his trusted little crew.

The build up to this match was incredible the talk of the town for weeks, many people were in fear due to the reputation of United's army of hooligans who had caused mayhem at most grounds and towns they had visited, for me personally I could not wait for this peach of a game that was bound to bring mass disorder and I wanted to see just how Oldham would stand up to the giants of Manchester United's massive army.

Boxing Day 1974 took Oldham to Lancashire rivals Blackpool, Bloomfield Road the place and town were the hardy few of us who made the pre season night match trip in the Texaco Cup got kicked to fuck each and every one of us, of course we avenged this at Boundary Park in September in good style which only added more fuel to this tense "derby "with it being Boxing day the crowds of both teams would greatly increase, it had all the hallmarks of a very eventful day, this proved to be the case. Oldham took a couple thousand that day, many arriving on the hourly trains from Manchester, by 1pm many of the resort's pubs on the promenade were filling up with eager Oldham fans, most visiting Blackpool for the very first time and getting a bit giddy, ignoring the fact that Blackpool was and always was a very rough town, they were soon to find out as a mob of around 300 Oldham fans marched to the ground at 2pm, it was attacked from all angles by a much bigger mob of Blackpool fans chanting 'Tower – Tower Power!', their famous war chant, it was a classic pincer move, we were attacked from behind both sides and front, it split us up and confused us, there seemed so many more than their actually was, and many of us got beaten up, there were no cops around, or if there was they kept a low profile, we got backed up to the prom were we gathered ourselves once more, this time the march to the ground was enhanced by another couple of hundred more Oldham fans, it was a huge mob, and this time we got to the ground as one and not only that we went into the Spion Kop, up the big concrete steps at the rear, of course Blackpool were waiting for us and came down the terracing at the back of the Kop and right into us, it was a major battle of which they got the upper hand due to the advantage of being above us, the cops many wielding big sticks also ripped into us ignoring the Blackpool thugs attacking us.

We mobbed up at the turnstiles then made our way around the side of the Kop then into this great big old fashioned terrace, we were game and had very good numbers and made our way to the top and to the centre to try and take this end over, but we could not shift the Seasiders, the cops made a no man's land split halfway down the Kop and there it remained for the rest of this game, with many charges to and fro, the atmosphere was electric and both huge mobs set about out chanting each other and sing songs of war.

It was very dodgy going to the bogs which were right behind the Kop, and many scuffles broke out there, Ian Mcgeary recalls a very funny incident at half time behind the Kop, there was a bit of a stand off, when the tannoy was playing the Stylistics tune "I can't give you anything but my love" when all of a sudden this big Blackpool lad with no teeth and a long leather jacket began northern soul dancing in between both sets of fans - spinning, clapping & twisting, both sets of fans laughed their bollocks off, as did the cops, it broke the ice for a few minutes, but during the 2nd half hostilities were once again back on, many mass brawls and lots of arrests, after the match it was very dark and Blackpool had the upper hand and many Oldham lads came unstuck, and it was a long dodgy walk back to the station, but we could hold our heads up high, we went mob handed went in their Kop and attempted to take over and remained in their throughout, no mean feat, many teams came unstuck at Blackpool back in those days.

# MANCHESTER UNITED

I HARDLY SLEPT A WINK THAT NIGHT, I was full of nervous tension, so excited about the days events, I made sure I was down at the ground from mid day, the game was all ticket but that did not mean anything as thousands of United fans lived in and around Oldham and North Manchester and it would have been easy for local United fans to purchase tickets for the Oldham ends. That day I wore an Oldham silk scarf around my head like a red Indian in a show of defiance, I was just short of my 14th birthday but had no fear nor respect for United and their fans, I didn't give a fuck for them, I was too proud of my home town team, and I was not going to hide my colours nor feelings, unfortunately this was not to be the case for so many Oldham fans, many bought tartan scarves from the vendors outside the ground (in 1973 tartan scarves were very popular amongst boot boys and youths up and down the country because of Rod the Mod Stewart, but Tommy Docherty took over Manchester United and bought loads of Scottish players and their fans then began wearing tartan scarves en masse, so the rest of the country ditched them) but this day noticed loads of Oldham lads wearing them so they would not be attacked by United fans. It sickened me and I let as many of them as I could know what I thought of them, calling them wankers and shithouses, many of these were older than me and had been following Oldham for years, it was beyond my comprehension, not one of them challenged me and most just held their heads in shame and rightly so, and many of them never came back to Oldham after this game, choosing the much easier option of following United or not bothering with football again.

By 2pm the Chaddy End was half Oldham, half United but Oldham had the top of the Chaddy End although United were all over the stand in various mobs, and were chanting throughout the whole game. There were scuffles throughout the match but strangely enough it was fairly quiet, on the fighting front, United however did fill the away end the huge open ended terrace known as the Rochdale Road End, their fans made a tremendous noise, their songs were magnificent, as they sang "We shall overcome" the old protest song from the 1960's, to see thousands of United fans singing this as one was truly a fantastic sight, another great song they all sang was, "We are just one of those teams that you see now and again" back then every fan wore a scarf and many had banners it looked great... the crowd that day was 26,000 with perhaps 16,000 being United fans around the ground.

To be fair the Oldham fans in the Chaddy End sang and chanted throughout the game and it was a good atmosphere and in the 2nd half Oldham got a penalty and we just knew we were going to score as our penalty taker Maurice Whittle never missed because he always blasted it down the middle and there was a big hush around the ground as Maurice stepped up and as per usual he smashed it home and into the nets at our Chaddy End we went wild, 3 sides of the ground went wild and many scuffles around the ground broke out and the Chaddy End burst into song for the rest of the game, "Oldham Oldham Oldham" rang all around the ground apart from the away end which was silenced, the last few minutes saw thousands of United fans leaving the away end and heading towards the Chaddy End but thankfully the cops held this massive baying mob back, at the end of the match more fights broke out with Oldham and United in the Chaddy End as we headed towards the exits, outside was mayhem and thousands of United fans rampaged, overturning cars smashing windows and clashing with the cops, it was very scary but exciting, to be honest I did not see any mobs of Oldham outside.

I made my way to the paki cafe we frequented on Featherstall Road which was also close to the Werneth train station, where thousands of United fans were heading, I was still wearing my scarf but not around my head but around my neck, I was a bit nervous but no one said anything, as I went into the cafe I saw half a dozen lads I knew wearing tartan scarves, fucking wankers, I told em what I thought of them, but these hadn't even been to the game, I went home a short while later, I had a huge anti climax, I was drained, and soon fell asleep. I was buzzing we had actually beaten the mighty Manchester United, I was proud that United had not taken the Chaddy End but not daft enough to think they couldn't have done of they really wanted to do so, but they did not.

Tony O'Neil author of Red Army General and Men in Black admits to being beaten up that day in the Chaddy End and ending up in the back of the nets, confirming it was not the cake walk they experienced at most grounds that season.

For a while after that match Oldham Reds numbers swelled a bit with the traitors who swapped teams that day, but we as a firm did not need nor want that calibre of lad amongst us.

One of the biggest names and most respected United fans back in the 1970's was George Lyons of Collyhurst, many saw George as the leader of the Stretford End and the Red Army, he was hard as nails, a big burly bearded man who had been active since the mid 1960's, I became a very close friend of George from 2004 onwards, even though he was ten years older than me, George is a legend with United fans and he told me some fantastic tales, he was such a dry but funny and honest man, he told me that quite a few times him and about 15 of his mates from Collyhurst would come up to Oldham if United had no game on and get stuck into the away fans. He said they were low profile, not shouting United etc but just went for the violence, he developed a soft spot for Oldham and said they were very game for young lads, that made me proud...

There was no disputing that Man United had the biggest away following this country has ever known, it was phenomenal and from the late 60's through to the late 70's they were the best mob until Chelsea challenged them for top mob from 1975 onwards. For most of my life I hated Manchester United and what they stood for, I hated the fact that so many people from other towns supported them rather than their home town teams, it remains beyond my comprehension but over the years I have got to know many genuine Manchester Reds and they also cannot understand why so many other town's people support them and they indicate that they have more respect for lads like themselves who support their own town team...

That day December 28th 1974 Manchester's Red Army did cause a lot of trouble after the game and many houses, cars and businesses were smashed up but Oldham Police saw it as not as bad as they expected... maybe George Lyons told the lads to calm it down a bit?

# FUCK OFF WEST BROM!

*"Oh I do like to be beside the seaside,*
*Oh I do like to be beside the sea,*
*Oh I do like to walk along the prom prom prom,*
*When the brass band plays - FUCK OFF WEST BROM!!"*

IN EARLY JANUARY 1975 we travelled down to West Bromwich Albion at the Hawthorns. Albion were another fallen giant with a big ground and big crowd, they had a great recent history and had players of quality like Jeff Astle, Tony "bomber "Brown, and Len Cantello, etc, that day we took about 15 coaches which was a good following and we didn't know what to expect from the Baggies, we were going into the unknown, they did not have a big reputation so we went there fearless, we were soon brought down to earth as soon as we landed on the coach park we were attacked by West Brom fans, who piled right into us many brandishing sticks, the cops just turned a blind eye as per usual, we just had to take the kicking and it was a kicking, most of us copped a bust nose or black eyes, we somehow got into the away end at the Hawthorns which was a huge old fashioned Kop, we mobbed up and there was about 200 of us, and we made our way to the top of this end, and we were very impressed by the sight and numbers of WBA fans in their home end who made an tremendous noise.

After about 15 minutes after kick-off hundreds of Baggies began walking around the pitch from their end, no coppers stopped them and many Oldham fans melted away, it left a mob of about 70 of us and it looked very dodgy as the Baggies climbed into this away end, we all said to each other 'backs to the walls lads! we are gonna get battered lets just have a go'. All stirring stuff I was the youngest, but was amongst top lads like Kenny Jones, Herby, his brother Ray, Earl Arundale, Spazmo, Stez, Big Ste Wild and a few more tough Shaw Gawbies, plus some other loyal and brave lads, the Baggies came right up to us led by a little fat feller who had a plastic arm, a fucking horrible looking lad, bouncing up and down and screaming abuse at us, he came charging into us and wrenched his arm off using it as a weapon it was all hard plastic and metal and was a lethal weapon and he smashed it into a few Oldham lads heads cutting them up, we got stuck in as best as we could but soon got overwhelmed and took a kicking, the cops eventually deciding to help us out and force the Baggies back over the side of the pitch and back to their own end, the Oldham fans who melted came back to us to swell our numbers once again to 200. At the end of the match we feared the worst as the floodlights went out and we were plunged once more into darkness, we made our way to the coach park and we saw the hundreds of Baggies milling about, it was awful and no cops about, we ran the gauntlet to our coaches getting on any we could do, we got kicked to bits many of us crawling onto the coaches, many of those coaches had their windows smashed which meant for a cold journey home up the M6..

So far it had been a long hard season and we were only half way through, we were growing up fast and quite a few dropped out, it was hard but pride kept the likes of me and many other going and I knew we would avenge all these beatings one day as we grew up, I had still not reached my 14th birthday, but had already been stabbed and taken some terrible beatings......

On Sunday February 2nd 1975 I was 14 years old... the next Monday I was at my local youth Club, Cannon Streetreet, during the night there had been a few words said with four lads who came from the other side of town, I thought no more of this and my pals left at 10pm and I was one of last ones out after hanging back chatting a bird up, as im leaving the youth club I made my way across Middleton road when I spotted the 4 lads I had argued with earlier in the evening, I feared the worst as they made their way towards me, I picked up a bottle and smashed it on a lamp post letting them know I had a weapon, 3 held back but one lad with buck teeth long black greasy hair and Wranglers on came right into me, I lashed out with my broken bottle and it cut his fore arm up with blood spurting everywhere, I shit myself as he hit the deck screaming, I threw the broken bottle down to the floor and apologised, his mates ran off, I was there for a couple of minutes before a cop car pulled up, right away they whisked him off to hospital and one copper walked me to the nearby police station.

I was thrown in a cell for half a hour when in came Jack Warner, Oldham's juvenile police officer who knew me very well and had belted me a few times and seen me fighting many times at Latics, he was very calm and told me to tell him exactly what happened, which I did, thankfully he believed me and just cautioned me and told me to get a grip of myself as I was making a name for myself and lads will be wanting to challenge me and cops would want to nick me. He also said try and give the game against Bolton Wanderers at Boundary Park tomorrow night a miss as there would be a lot of fighting... that only whetted my appetite, I had not looked forward to a game so much in my life, I thanked Jack and told him I would keep a low profile from now on. I think we both knew that was never going to happen, the lad I stabbed had 6 stitches and did not want to press charges - respects for that.

# TUESDAY FEB 4TH 1975
# OLDHAM ATHLETIC V BOLTON WANDERERS

THE TALK ALL DAY AT SCHOOL that day was of Bolton Wanderers coming to Latics would they take our end like the last two times they had been in '71 and '73 ? How many would they bring with it being a night match? Loads from school were going to this game, it was one of THE biggest games of the season for us... I was so excited and pegged off in the afternoon looking up town to see if any had come over early, but there were none to be seen, at 4pm I called for Paul and his mam made us rag pudding, chips and peas, she said 'you will need some good stock inside you for tonight' Ha. She was a young modern mam and knew what me and Paul got up to, he could tell her anything, she laughed at us getting all giddy.

By 5pm me and Paul were heading down Rochdale Road to the bus stops facing Oldham Hospital where the 400 bus from Bolton stopped it was then a 5 minute walk down Sheepfoot Lane to the ground, the first bus pulls in at 5-45pm and about 50 Bolton fans came bouncing off, all wearing Docs and black and white scarves, I hated these cunts, they were so cocky but there was only me and Paul, the Bolton lads headed up towards town, hopefully they would get filled in up there by Oldham youths.

The next bus from Bolton arrived at 6.15 in fact four double deckers arrived and all full of lads and few boot girls, a mob of 300 then marched down Sheepfoot Lane attacking lone Oldham fans and in full voice, me and Paul walked down behind this Bolton Mob, they went right into the Chaddy as per usual, but me and Paul remained outside until about 7pm and were buzzing to see hundreds of Oldham thugs arriving in big gangs, all the estates and areas in and around Oldham were out in force many with double usual numbers, there were big queues outside the Chaddy End, and any Bolton got run on Sheepfoot Lane, most of them going into the Chaddy End from the other side of the ground, as we queued we could hear both sets of fans chanting and could tell their were running battles as it proved, as soon as were in we went right to the top of the Chaddy End and joined in the mass brawls there were several hundred in both mobs maybe up to a 1000 on each side, the Chaddy End was split right down the middle and most of the fans in the Chaddy End that night were hooligans from both teams, Bolton singing "we took the Chaddy End "and Oldham singing "You'll never take the Chaddy!" and tonight they did not despite having their biggest ever mob thus far in our end, it was just we matched them for numbers and passion that night, so many bigger lads turned out for Oldham that night.

The coppers somehow separated both massive mobs with a ten yard no man's land right down the centre of the Chaddy End but this was breached many times by both mobs in mass charges and brawls, I was right there on the front line making myself an easy enemy with my throat slitting motions and calling them wankers and signalling out certain lads, one lad about my age and size really pissed me off and we constantly threatened each other the whole game. He had a feather cut, reddish hair and wore a silk bomber and Birmingham bags and platforms making him look taller than he actually was, we clashed a few times in the mass brawls pulling each other's hair and booting each other, I was desperate to get a good grip of him and fill the cunt in, the cocky Bolton bastard - this truly was the ultimate night for me, the violence and fighting was relentless, there were loads of ejections and arrests, loads of blood shed with no side giving a inch. "We are the Wanderers, We are the Wanderers!" they kept chanting. Also "Whose that marching up the hill boys" their hooligan anthem, we chanted back "Oh wanky, wanky wanky Wanderers" and "zigger zagger zigger zagger ATH LET IC!" and "1 –2– 3 - 4 listen to the Chaddy roar" apart from all the battling the chanting and atmosphere was incredible and also relentless. We chanted "murderers" at them for them killing the Blackpool fan first game of the season and they came back with "Ol Bev Williams had a knife ee aye ee aye oh, with a stab stab here and a stab stab there!" Only Bolton fans could celebrate a murder! This really wound us up and caused even more charges into the horrible bastards.

In a brief lull in the violence I heard a few Oldham birds getting all giddy about this Bolton fan stood at the front of their mob, he was a tall half cast lad with a massive afro and really green eyes which got these Oldham birds excited, he was fully Crombied up and had a rolled up brolly which he was using to whack us with, he wasn't interested in the birds only the aggro, the girls could never match the adrenaline of football violence, during one of the many brawls that night in the Chaddy End I saw Ste Kelly from our Northmoor mob rolling about with this Bolton half cast, both got a bust nose for their efforts.

That night was the most evenly matched up hooligan battle I ever saw, same numbers, probably same numbers of arrests and same amount of injuries, it was an incredible night one I have never ever forgotten and is still talked about almost 40 years on as the greatest of all battles...

At the final whistle Bolton headed left we head right in some kind of mutual respect, but that was not to last long as both mobs soon met up on Sheepfoot Lane and more violent clashes ensued, with neither side able to gain the upper hand, a mob of twenty of us broke away as the cops were getting really heavy handed by now with their dogs and coshes, we Northmoor lads were cutting through nearby Westwood park when we came across a similar number of Bolton fans, it was perfect scenario, there was a bit of a stand off when out of the shadows a young red-haired feather cutted youth stepped forward arms outstretched saying "come on you Oldham cunts". I could not believe my luck it was my enemy from the game who I had not only clashed with but had threatened for most of the game... I stepped forward and said "let's get it on you Bolton wanker" and with that we piled into each other and began rolling about, punching kicking butting pulling each other's hair (mine had grown a bit from my early season skinhead crop) all the other lads piled into each other and rolled about the bowling green until two cops with dogs came charging into us and we got up and broke away. It was a good little mini battle, once again my nose was bust and my eyes swelled. and I'm sure the Bolton cunts was as well. Me and this Bolton fan clashed many times over the next few seasons, he was always on the front line and we always signalled each other out, he was game as fuck and one game at Oldham he was cornered in the bottom of the Chaddy End and about ten lads were moving in for the kill but by then I had enough influence to stop them and he escaped giving me the thumbs up and he clambered into the paddock... I'm not too sure he would have afforded me the same respect - different breed them Bolton fans.

Later that night we went to the 400 bus stop outside Oldham College and ambushed some more Bolton lads who were catching the last bus home, we caved them in but they did fight back but we had much bigger numbers, maybe twenty to their ten. I snatched a black, white and red scarf for my collection.

What a night that was. I was battered and bruised but fucking loved every minute of it, Oldham had finally stood up to Bolton fucking Wanderers, there would be many more clashes, cuts bruises and broken bones to come...

The ejections that night were 73 with 35 arrests with many receiving medical attention from the St. John's Ambulance crews and the Accident and Emergency at Oldham Hospital being very busy...

We played Southampton twice at home & away in the 74/75 season, twice in the league and twice in the Texaco cup semi finals, in the league game which was a Saturday afternoon match there were not many Saints fans in the away end, it was a wet miserable day very foggy and murky, half way through the game Southampton scored and we heard a muffled cheer to the far right of the Chaddy End, we went to look and were surprised to see a small mob of fifteen huge blokes most wearing Sheepskin overcoats, these were not kids but men in their twenties and thirties, and they were not budging, as first of all they were threatened which they laughed at and when they were attacked they fought us off punching us to the ground, these were experienced brawlers with their backs to the wall. They lasted a full twenty minutes before finally being dragged to the ground and toed in and even then were still fighting back, the cops eventually ejecting them from the Chaddy End and to their own end. They got great respect and admiration for their courage and strength against massive odds.

Fast forward a few months to semi final 2nd leg of Texaco cup, no one gave them a thought and once again very few Saints fans made the long journey up North, halfway through the game Saints scored and once again there was a muffled cheer and once again it's the same fifteen Saints fans were stuck in the same top corner, we couldn't believe it, the very same men, man for man, wearing the same fucking clothes, and once again they fought like fuck and took some shifting and once again lasted about twenty minutes before the cops ejected them. After the game we are walking up Sheepfoot Lane when we spotted this very same crew walking ahead of us, we charged into them and I leapt on this big fuckers back wearing a Sheepy, he had huge Mungo Jerry sideburns which I was grabbing, he grabbed me and threw me into the hospital wall at such a force it took the wind out of me, the Saints crew got wasted but everyone of them went down fighting and anyone there will have nothing but respect for them.

That south coast produced some tough teams, Brighton, Bournemouth, Saints and Pompey all hard teams with very game fans, all had their era's, and all were respected at some time.

I went to most away games that season 74/75 got some terrible beatings but visited some incredible stadiums including Hillsborough, Roker Park, and Old Trafford, each of these grounds had incredible atmospheres. Hillsborough was a magnificent stadium so huge and a massive Kop which looked fantastic and sounded fantastic in full voice, I was awe struck there, as I was at Sunderland and when their wonderful fans sang "Can't help falling in love" en masse it brought tears to my eyes, it was one of the most wondrous sights I have ever seen at a football match. We took quite a lot of fans up to Sunderland and had to park a mile away on the beach, we took about 12 coaches and all walked up together and expected the worst but Sunderland are great fans and did not attack us, there were one or two scuffles after the game but very little given their huge crowd.

Sheff Weds were similar fans, both them and Sunderland had taken the Chaddy End that season but at their home ground they did not bully nor intimidate us, both fantastic grounds clubs and support.

On Easter Monday we played Manchester United at Old Trafford, the biggest club by far in the country and also the best supported club in the country by far, there was 55,000 in Old Trafford that day with maybe 5000 from Oldham dotted about this magnificent stadium, there were no big mobs of Oldham cos we would have come seriously unstuck but many wore their scarves and hats which I did. That day I met Jimmy Rafferty in Manchester at midday, Jimmy was one of Oldham's most famous fans and was an out and out eccentric, I was 14 then Jimmy would have been around 30 but he took me under his wing when he saw me wearing my blue n white bob hat, he wore a tangerine scarf.

Jimmy was a 1960's relic, he still had a Mod haircut and wore tight fitting Mod clothes and did for ever, he actually had a strong Manc accent and came from Middleton but loved Oldham, he was hilarious and fearless, no one said nowt to him as we walked the 3 miles to Old Trafford, he didn't give a fuck anyhow, I saw loads of Oldham fans outside the ground and there was no trouble thankfully and even though we lost 3–2 to the champions we gave a good account for ourselves and it was great to see so many Oldham fans cheer when we scored and I'm sure United fans applauded us off the pitch which is big respects - indeed a week or so later United won the Division Two title.

Our final game that season was York City away, we always took thousands to York and this was no different, I and many others was supposed to be at attendance centre that day, but most of us were at the game but so was Sgt Haggerty a big rough hard bastard Scottish copper, who took us for training Saturday afternoons, we gave him a wide berth at York but he clocked us all and gave us hell the week after with circuit training etc, we took the piss at York and rampaged through this wonderful city before and after the match, that day many of us wore Butchers coats with slogans all over them it was a very short lived terrace fashion for the boot boys, but there were a couple of hundred of us dressed in them that sunny day.

What an incredible season... from Sheff Wed the first game of the season to York away last game of season... so many incredible memories.

# SUMMERTIME

THE SUMMER OF 1975 FLEW BY, there was a buzz about Oldham with Latics not only surviving their first season in Division two but also surviving facing some of the roughest/ toughest fans in the country, our Chaddy End was taken over twice, Sheff Weds and Sunderland but shared on many occasions, Hearts, Bolton, Man United, Notts Forest, Blackpool with most other teams fans coming in also, we took some terrible beatings away from home but at least we did turn up and have a go when we could, we were growing up fast a football hooligan firm, we showed on occasions that we could pull in massive mobs when needed, obviously not in the Man United - Sunderland - Sheff Wed - Cardiff league but we could more than hold our own at most home games. Quite a few lads dropped out during this season, lads who could not take the heat of battle, but thankfully most stayed loyal dusted themselves down and got wise. Man United and Sunderland won promotion so that was two giants out of the way but Chelsea came down from Division One and they were already building up a big reputation and would soon be challenging Man United as the country's biggest mob. Meanwhile Blackburn Rovers won promotion from so we had some avenging there to sort out and we still had the likes of Notts Forest, Cardiff, WBA, Bolton, Blackpool, Millwall, Southampton, both Bristol clubs, Sheff United were back down and the other usual suspects... 1975/76 was going to be another lively season for sure...

French flares were the big fashion that summer with long leather overcoats, afros also became popular with blacks and whites, and steel afro combs became weapons along with steel combs, more and more youths were wearing brogues instead of docs although I still wore doc martens for a good while, I loved them and cherished them, in the summer of 75 I was part of a local mob called the Westwood park mob which was very close to Boundary Park, we broke away from the more established and older Westwood and Northmoor mobs who by now were into drinking in local pubs, it was a great summer and we attracted a few birds from all over Oldham Royton and Chadderton, we were still mainly boot boys, and every Monday we would go to Oldham's premier disco Cat's Whiskers which 1500 teenagers would also congregate, it was here we met girls and invited them down to Westwood park. In our gang were me, Dave Turner (RIP) Martin Cook (RIP), Danny Irving, Phil Heeney, Martin "Hoof" Hurst (he had buck teeth), Dozy Dunc Butterworth, Martyn "Tut's" Tulley, Big Clive, John Lund, Alan Macmanus, Paul Ashton, Phil Burbridge, Geoff Noble. We were all Oldham fans and went home and away, we were then aged between 14-17, they were great times and we had so much fun, going to the Whiskers – local Paki cafes, Cannon Streetreet youth club and nights in the park or visiting other youth clubs in Oldham.

In the park at night we would play soccer, tennis, those who drank would drink party sevens and party fours, large cans of 7 & 4 pint beers, I did not drink but most did, we went to parties around town, we were not a fighting mob as such but would stand our ground when needed, these were good lads and I have fond memories of that era..

When we played West Browm a few weeks later all talk was about getting that fat one armed horrible bastard who did so much damage down at the Hawthorns. We knew Albion would come into the Chaddy End almost every team did and on that day the Chaddy End was packed as many sought revenge, by kick off a mob of around 150 Albion had congregated in the bottom left had corner of the Chaddy End, we remained at the top allowing them the chance to come and try and take our end, they had no chance with them numbers but respects to them just after kick off they came marching up chanting 'Albion! Albion!' they were led by the fat one armed bastard who once again began unscrewing his plastic/metal arm. The Oldham mob stepped back a bit allowing a big space for Albion to came onto us which they did and we then both charged into each other, a big brawl ensued but we soon had them on their toes and fatty got weighed in good and proper and had to be carried away by his pals, he was kicked to fuck but he came into us once again wielding his arm. The Baggies clambered out of the Chaddy End and made their way to the away end, fatty although bashed up was still waving his arm above his head giving it large, the Chaddy End chanting 'you fat spaz! You fat spaz!' He loved the attention with many of his pals back slapping him, they were game fuckers as was he, and we all looked forward to meeting them after the game on the car park..

After the game Oldham's big mob headed toward the car park to take on West Brom's mob which was about 300 strong and well up for it, but the cops had a grip of the situation with their snarling Alsatians and batons, it became a stone fight as we could not get close enough for the hand to hand fighting, a few of their coaches got smashed up like ours did, so we did avenge them although we took a far worse kicking down at their ground, like most midlands clubs they were a tough bunch.

My only regret was not getting fatty's arm, I would loved to have had that on my bedroom wall alongside my ever growing collection of away team's scarves.

During the 1970's I found that almost every Midland club was tough, whether it's because of the big industries in these places or not I don't know, but they all seemed very game and could produce big numbers; Villa, Birmingham, Forest, Leicester, West Brom, Stoke, Wolves, were all rough tough teams, strangely enough Notts County had hardly any hooligans and we took their end a few times, Mansfield were handy as were Port Vale especially in the early 70's but they seemed to fade away as the decade went on. I would say Villa had the biggest mob in the Midlands, but in my opinion Forest were the toughest of the Midland fans to come to Boundary Park, but Wolves was the roughest away ground and for many of us THE worst ever away game in the 1970's. more of that later!

Pre season friendlies in 1975/76 included Bury away, well we always took Bury just like we always took Rochdale but Bury usually had a few 'have a go' heroes, we all as per usual we took their end and Bury's little mob of about 50 or so was in the paddock to the left hiding behind half a dozen coppers, being brave chanting at us... we probably had around 300 in that day so they had no chance, at half time a gang of around ten Bury boot girls came in amongst us which made us laugh but these were rum fuckers and set about a few of us, one of them a big fat girl with cropped feather cut booted me in my balls and I went down winded. She then started raining punches on my head, well girl or no girl I got up and slapped her hard across her mush, she soon went over, her mates piled in and a few more Oldham lads booted them out until they eventually fled away, we were all laughing at how rough these birds were when Happy Harry came over and slapped me across my face calling me a wanker for hitting the fat bird back. I was only 14 then and Harry was 19 maybe 20 and a lot bigger than me, plus he had his crew of Sholver boys behind him, I told him to fuck off, and he just threatened to bash me up, before walking off, he humiliated me and I wanted to fight him but my mates held me back, he had this big rep and supposedly carried a knife. I vowed revenge on the bullying prick one day. Over the next couple of seasons I began to win over Happy Harry's respect and as I got older he began creeping around me, I never did avenge that attack by him, I never got the opportunity, he was to be fair one of the gamest lads Oldham had in the 1970's but as we got older we saw him for what he was... a knob !

After the game Oldham chased Bury off outside the ground and around the town centre, one or two took a beating but nothing bad, Oldham fans wrecked the bus back to Oldham.

First league game of that season was Bristol Rovers at home, now last season a few of them came into the Chaddy but had very little impact and their rivals Bristol City had a much bigger firm in the Chaddy and caused us more problems so we were not expecting much from Bristol Rovers, at 2pm our crew and a few Northmoor lads were walking down Sheepfoot Lane when a young copper stopped us and said "don't go in the Chaddy End, they have taken it over and they are fucking mad!" They had attacked all the coppers and many of them were carrying weapons. We could actually hear them chanting but we assumed it was Oldham fans until this copper told us the craic. We could not get down there fast enough, we were well excited, but as we got near the entrance to the Chaddy End we saw lads battered to fuck climbing out of the ground, telling us not to go in there... but we ignored them and in we went and as soon as we are in we are attacked by these Bristol loonies. They were indeed mad and attacked everybody and anybody including the cops who by now were giving them a wide berth, there was only about 400 of them, apparently 8 coach loads had arrived at midday and soon as the gates were open in they went. Now I never seen such a violent mob of nut cases in all my life, they must have emptied the Asylums in Bristol that day, amongst this raging mob was a big white haired feller with just one eye who was wielding a big stick and smashing anyone he could get near to, another bloke with crutches who also was wielding them and attacking us with them, whacking us over our heads and bodies, I saw hunch backs, deaf n dumb lads, wild women, it was like a scene from 'One Flew Over the Cuckoo's Nest', that summer's big film!

They did not let up and were chanting dancing and whooping like Indians, meat pie Fred took a terrible beating and was stretchered out of the Chaddy End as were many others, the coppers bottled out and let the Rovers fans do what they want, they took the Chaddy End and we could not shift them despite our much bigger numbers by kick off, we were all around them and charging in from all sides but we could not budge them from the top so it has to be said they took our end, we could only pick em off as they went to the bogs or cafe bar, but even then they went down fighting like fuck, many of them laughing at us as blows were rained down on them.

At the end of the game the Oldham cops had been reinforced by other police and got these nutters onto their coaches and out of town and down the motorway as quick as possible, to be honest not many Oldham bothered trying to get into them after the match, 400 is a big mob especially when everyone of them was game as fuck - quite a few Oldham fans still have nightmares about this game - another lesson learnt. Never, ever underestimate any team.

Our first away game that season was Blackburn Rovers, only 28 miles away we were sure to take loads even though we had some awful hammerings up there off their fans and their coppers, it was a rough old place Ewood Park, but we took loads and filled the away end the Darwen End, it was a great mob and we were buzzing, we must have had 25 coaches all parked near the fair ground and the walk to the ground was lively but we held our own in the many running battles, Blackburn's end was full that day and they had a big mob in the Riverside paddock to our right, it was these that we were challenging and threatening, at half-time a mob of around fifty Rovers came into our end, they were all big rockers heavily tattooed and hard looking twats but we hammered them all over the terraces, they climbed onto the pitch to get away but most of them got booted in.

What a result! Even their coppers got hammered as Oldham's mob turned on them and forced them out of the Darwen end, it was such a buzz after all those times getting battered there, of course we knew it would be mad after the game as the whole Blackburn mob would be after us, but we were well up for it, and we left the ground as one big up for it mob, right on cue as we are heading towards the car park Blackburn come piling into us launching bottles bricks beer crates, anything they could get their hands on, but we fought back and slugged it out with them, it was tremendous and I was so proud and I took many blows for the cause but also dished plenty out, we got to the car park and then we attacked the fair ground and the gypos who had always attacked us in previous seasons, the cops were very heavy handed with their dogs and batons but quite a few cops got whacked also, what a turn around. We were all buzzing like fuck as our coaches left Blackburn for the short journey home, what a difference a week makes, last Saturday we had been taken over by Bristol Rovers yet 7 days later we went to Blackburn mobbed up and got the better of them.

That was Blackburn avenged, we needed to take it to Burnley and Bolton... our day would come...

Three days after the Blackburn away game we were once again on our travels and once again to a Lancashire rival in Blackpool, we were on school holidays and at midday that Tuesday afternoon I bumped into Terry Horton, a lad aged 18 and with a big reputation as a very game lad, Terry came from the rival area of Ash Dene Chadderton who in previous years had fought with the older lads of Northmoor, but Terry had married one of the Northmoor girls Wilma Harper, so he was accepted and respected, he had been in the army a couple of years and was very fit and strong and still got stuck in at the footy, well Terry asked if I fancied hitch-hiking to Blackpool for the match, I did not need asking twice, I was going to go on the train later in the day but to be in the company of such a top lad and be in Blacky mid afternoon was too much of a good thing, I had never hitched-hiked before and was quite excited by it, so me and Terry walked the short distance to the motorway junction and soon acquired our first lift, three more lifts and a couple of hours later we arrived in Blackpool for 3pm.

We went straight to the prom where we soon bumped into loads of Oldham fans who had come on the trains, we all had a stroll on the Central Pier many playing the machines and at 5pm we went into the Foxhall pub on the front and just ten mins from Bloomfield Road, the Foxhall soon filled up with Oldham fans and Terry met a load of his pals from Chaddy and had sorted himself a lift out, he told me if I was stuck for a lift back home he would sort me one out, I was ok as I had met a few of my pals by now also, the mood was great and at 7pm we made the short move to the ground, we had a decent mob of about 150 but we knew this would not be enough and was hoping loads more had come by coach and cars, as we were heading under the bridge en route we got attacked by a stone throwing mob of Blackpool, but we soon sussed there was only about fifty of them and we gave chase to the ground but as we got near the ground a massive mob of Blackpool came at us, and it was very moody with quite a few of us getting hammered, but with the cops help we survived the onslaught.

Once again we bravely went into the Spion Kop knowing full

well it would be full of Blackpool's hooligans, the noise they made with their "seaside aggro "chanting reminding us what was in store, but in we went up the steep terracing and into the great Kop, unsurprisingly as soon as we entered the Kop we were attacked by Blackpool thugs.

We were soon fighting for our lives and were forced into the top left hand corner, as the boots and punches rained down on us, I did notice there were quite a few Jocks with them, both Rangers and Celtic fans both wearing their colours and calling us English bastards as they attacked us, this did not do our confidence any good, Blackpool were hard enough on their own but to be aided by mad drunken violent Jocks was a bit much, and many Oldham fans melted away, we did not make much impact in the Spion Kop that night and it was very dodgy, as little pockets of Blackpool boot boys sought us out for some knuckle butties! I lost Terry Horton and his crew from Chaddy but seen a good pal of mine Ali Mcmanus who was with his dad Brendan, an ex-Latics goalie and a lovely big Irishman, they offered me a lift home and I remained with them throughout the match which we won 2-0, which did any Oldham fans remaining in the Kop no favours and I witnessed many assaults as the Seaside bastards and their Jock bully pals exacted pain and anguish, I was glad to get away unscathed that night, many did not, Blackpool on a night match was an unforgiving place...

A few weeks later the mighty Chelsea came up to Boundary Park, it was a Tuesday night match and the town held it's breath Chelsea had recently became the main challengers to Manchester United's Red Army for the top mob in the country! Like United in 73/74 Chelsea also got relegated to Division two in 74/75 and saw it as a great opportunity to flex their muscles and show the country who the top dogs were, they had plenty of opportunities at teams like Wolves, West Brom, Forest, Cardiff, WBA, Sunderland, Bolton, Blackpool, Aston Villa, both Bristol clubs, Southampton - they would not have it easy but they did take over most of these teams ends which was no mean feat, in fact it was incredible given how hard most of these teams were and the numbers they had but Chelsea like United began attracting thugs from all over the UK including here in Oldham, over the next few years they took over so many ends and became THE best and biggest mob I had ever seen on their travels.

This particular night match was very tense and despite Chelsea's fast growing reputation the Chaddy End was full a hour before kick off as lads came from all around town and further beyond, I have no doubts that many United fans were there that night but thankfully they kept their big "Manchester la la la" gobs shut! But I did notice many older more experienced thugs their that night I had not seen before or since, the away end was filling up with Chelsea fans and I assumed with such large numbers that Chelsea were encamped their and maybe make an attempt later in the game, but within minutes of kick off Chelsea made their move in the Chaddy End with a classic pincer movement.,.

As soon as the Cockney drawl went up "Chel-sea Chel-sea Chel-sea!" many of the younger Oldham lads scattered, Chelsea's big reputation worked and it left a massive gap between the top of the Chaddy End which they had taken and to the sides and front, as the Chaddy End was packed many Oldham fans spilled onto the pitch, causing a few minutes delay, there wasn't that many Chelsea fans in our end to be honest maybe 300, but they were all big fuckers most of them in donkey jackets and wearing flat caps which gave them an extra sense of menace, looking like dockers, their slow cockney drawl also making them sound as confident as they looked, but once we realised their numbers were not that great and they were only humans, we soon set about them from all sides, we had shifted much bigger mobs from the Chaddy End, but we could not budge these Cockney twats, they were good, they were brave and stuck together and they took some terrible stick from all the combined mobs of Oldham that night, they showed their experienced by keeping their position and backs to the wall, as soon as some of them went down they dragged their fallen foes back then another mob would join the fray whilst their comrades recovered, the cops could not shift this Chelsea mob either the cockneys showing the cops no respect either.

That night the Werneth and Westwood mobs combined to go in search for Chelsea fans who had come by train, we headed for Werneth station, there must have been about 20 of us, now a few Werneth lads were also Chelsea fans but this was our town and any invaders were fair game, as it was there was only about twenty Chelsea fans on the station and we chased them up the tunnel, but they got away, the problem for them was the other end of the tunnel ended up on the rough Primmy Bank estate so they would have been filled in up that end... we went for a mooch on Manchester Road to the chippy when all of a sudden we spotted half a dozen Chelsea fans, one was the biggest football fan I have ever seen, he must have been 7 and half ft tall and he wore a donkey jacket and flat cap, they were heading our way but had not spotted us, little Johnny Murph who was five foot two said "I'm having that big cunt". We fell about laughing, but Murph climbed onto a bus shelter and as this crew passed he leapt onto the back of the giant, we all piled into the others and they got leathered, this giant fell to his knees and a few booted fuck out of him, for a giant he went down very easily, the cops came and we fled.

Their had been many brawls and hand to hand fights at the game but we could not move them, they were game as fuck and the most organised mob I had ever seen, we surrounded them though and took the piss out of their accents mocking them by singing. "What the fackinell was thet!" even they laughed, at three quarter time when the gates opened Chelsea were reinforced by hundreds more fans who made their take over of our Chaddy End complete, it was no shame we took on the countries best mob, outside we got a bit of revenge as we picked a few of them off but Chelsea had the upper hand on the night... respect.

Next game was Notts Forest at home and this fixture was guaranteed trouble they took the Chaddy End the season before but we got it back and eventually sorted them out but we knew they would be back in again only this time with bigger numbers, we were ready for them and the Chaddy End was full by 2.30pm, right on cue at kick off up they marched bold as brass big numbers maybe 4-500 many of them greasers who always looked hard with their leather jackets long greasy hair and many of them sporting crude Indian ink tattoos across their knuckles, they soon fought their way to the top to take us on and the brawling mauling and violence unfolded, it was exciting though and I was sat on a crash barrier to get a good view when a big Forest greebo was stood right next to me he was twatting random Oldham fans who passed him, well that day I was wearing steel toe cap boots and I positioned myself perfectly as I held the barrier with one hand and swung my steelie right into his mush, down he went spitting teeth and blood out, loads saw it and I got loads of back slaps for it, he was a bully and deserved it. I had began wearing steelies for the game now as they caused much more damage. I was revelling in the violence and getting a buzz from it, I even enjoyed the regular bloody noses and black eyes I was receiving on a regular basis, which was crazy, I had been sucked in by all this aggro and was beginning to make a name for myself, which made me want to impress more and receive the respect that comes with that.

Ironically that game one bloke I did not impress was Keith Partridge one of the original Glodwick mob, who then would be in his early twenties but still active, well he did not like the amount of respect and praise I was receiving and slapped me across the face saying I bumped into his wife, it was a load of bollocks, he was bullying me and putting me in my place, I was just short of my 15th birthday, I took the slap and vowed revenge which never occurred because I ended up being a good pal of Keith's later on in life and he gave me the respect my efforts, loyalty and courage deserved within a season or two - all part of the game I suppose.

Meanwhile the Forest mob tried in vain once again to take our end but our greater numbers held them off plus we were getting more and more experienced and bigger, but we could never make a dint on their Trent End, for when we went down there with ten coaches we got twatted everywhere outside the ground throughout the whole game and after the match, they were not very forgiving for coming unstuck at Boundary Park, they had huge numbers at home and were hard as nails, it was an awful ground to go to as were so many in the Midlands!

I think everyone respected Forest, they were game and even the massive clubs like Chelsea, United Spurs West Ham etc knew they were in for a major battle at the City Ground Nottingham back then..

Boxing Day 1975 promised to be one of the most eventful days in Oldham Athletic's history with the visit of Lancashire rivals Bolton Wanderers, the game was sold out weeks before 25,000. it could have sold another 10,000 such was the interest in the "derby "game.

Bolton sold 15,000 tickets, an incredible following. Oldham sold their own allocation of 10,000 with many missing out. I as so many was so looking forward to this game as were so many others, it was our chance to take on Bolton as we did the last time we met 10 months previously on that Feb 4th night match when we shared the Chaddy End. I was hoping it was to be shared once more and hoping for as much violence as that fixture, the crowd was double so I expected the level of violence to be twice as much - no such luck ha.

I and many others were in the Chaddy End as soon as the turnstiles opened at 1pm, desperately searching for the inevitable thousands of Bolton fans who would invade our end, we assumed they had come over the short distance of 14 miles to snap up tickets for our end as Man United fans did, it was so easy to obtain tickets for home ends back then, all you had to do was mention a local district, by 2pm the away end was almost full of Bolton fans and it was one of the greatest sights

I have ever seen at any football match as 15,000 Bolton fans all waved 12 inch x 12 inch flags on sticks which vendors were selling outside, it seemed as if every single Bolton fan had one and it was such an amazing sight to behold, it was a freezing foggy day but the blue floodlights lit up this old fashioned typical northern ground, we ourselves in the Chaddy End were creating a great atmosphere with our "Oh wanky Wanderers" proving very popular. By 2.30pm we could not locate a single Bolton fan in our end, not one! Trust me we had more than enough scouting for them as well... I was gutted, I really thought this would be the mother of all terrace battles. Just before kick off half a dozen Bolton fans came into the Chaddy End at the bottom but by time we got to them they had been twatted and crawled onto the safety of the pitch, the players were having their pre match kickabout and one of the Bolton fans nicked a ball off one of our players, and began dribbling the ball all the way up the pitch towards the massed Bolton fans in the away end. All 15,000 Bolton fans cheered him on, as all 10,000 home fans booed him, he looked the part as he dribbled his way confidently to the edge of the penalty area, and then pulled back his right Doc Marten and shot towards goal, and missed - not only that, he fell on his arse! Every single fan in the ground howled with laughter, 25,000 people all laughing at this silly Bolton twat! And "Wanky, wanky wanky Wanderers" has never been sang with such gusto - it was a beautiful light hearted moment in a very tense atmosphere.

At kick off for the first time in 4 meetings at Boundary Park there was not one Bolton fan in the Chaddy End... not one... they had taken the Chaddy End twice and shared it once but today not a peep... hopefully after the match we would clash... on this dark murky freezing Boxing Day.

It proved a great Boxing Day match which we won 2 – 1, which had us taunting our hated rivals, as the whistle blew we made our way to the exit in a huge mass of swaying aggressive up for it youths and young men, it took twenty minutes for us to leave the Chaddy End such was the numbers, as we spilled onto Sheepfoot Lane already there were hundreds of Bolton thugs waiting for us, we pitched into battle and this very dark evening, it seemed every single person was swapping blows and kicking and butting each other, many falling into the gardens facing the ground the cops also waded in with truncheons and snarling dogs. It was pure mayhem, and a mob around fifty of us back tracked toward the Clayton playing fields behind the Chaddy End, we knew thousands of Bolton fans would have to go this way their hundreds of coaches parked down Broadway, we had to fight our way through brawling youths/men to get onto the football pitches, it was pitch black on their and we made or way across these very muddy football pitches in search of our enemy, we did not have to wait long as we heard the chanting Bolton fans heading towards us, it was so dark and we could not make up how far away they were and just how many there was of them, we were soon to find out.

Leading our mob that day was Terry Horton, the Soldier boy from Chadderton. This super fit, hard as nails local hero, was bouncing up and down fists clenched neck muscles bulging he looked what he was, a very determined strong as fuck aggressive young man, he piled right into the oncoming Bolton hordes, as did me, Spazmo, Tony Kirton, Paddy Costello, Johnny Cleworth, Frankie Wright, Tommy Nolan, Shaun Bowskill, Clive Rushworth, Panos the Greek, Ned Kelly, Phil Heeny, Andy Nuttall, Sean Gagan and Micky Dunlea amongst others. This combined Northmoor/Ashdene mob who clashed in the summer months were now stuck together as we faced Bolton's huge mob, we were slipping all over the show as the mob facing us got bigger and bigger , we were soon surrounded and outnumbered ten to one and were taking a serious kicking, we got split up and broke away, I found myself with Micky Dunlea and as we were walking down the fields a crew of ten Bolton bastards all sporting taches and sids, jumped me, Mick tried to pull me away but they swamped me, thankfully Micky got away, I don't blame him, he was game but him diving in would only had made things worse, he like me assumed I'd just get a bit of a shoe-ing given my tender age, still not 15, but this was Bolton Wanderers and their fans were evil as I was about to find out, I took my beating and tried getting up but was smashed back down again boots and punches raining down on me, I tried in vain telling them I had enough and I was only 14 but they laughed and booted me to fucking bits! They were now jumping up and down on me. I thought I was being kicked to death!

Not only was I tasting fear, I was tasting blood and mud, I was rendered unconscious by this baying mob, who showed no sympathy, I don't know how long they kicked fuck out of me for but it seemed forever, I came round in the car park of the Rifle Range pub some 300 yards away, I was awoken by a young couple, who soon phoned an ambulance from the pub and I spent the next three days in Oldham Hospital and was treated for a broken arm, broken wrist, broken fingers, broken nose, broken cheekbone, chipped teeth black eyes and multiple bruises...I personally vowed revenge but especially on Bolton fans a few years older than me as these cunts were - over the next few years I got my revenge over and over.

I became a man after that, a very young man but a very violent man.

We played Blackpool at home a few weeks later (I had recovered enough to want to get back into the battling, I had lost the fear and became even more violent, I did not learn my lesson as many thought I must do, it made me worse) and we were expecting a big mob from them and hopefully they would come into the Chaddy End again but like Bolton they chose to embark in the big open end reserved for away fans, they brought a few thousand but nowhere near as many as Bolton but what they did do was just before kick off they came across the pitch but what we did was to meet them half way only they bottled out and retreated which surprised and disappointed me, not one punch was thrown and not one Blackpool fan had a go, they all turned en masse and got back into their own end, we carried on the chase but the cops got to us before we could go get in amongst them, we received a heroes return to the Chaddy End, there must have been 200 of us, it was a great feeling.

After the game the Chaddy End emptied to the left and onto the huge car park where over thirty Blackpool coaches were parked up, and even then they were not too keen to play, a few had a go but most ran off or sought refuge on their coaches, a few coaches got smashed up and overall it was a big let down from Blackpool who were a tough firm but that particular day just didn't want to know... I did however manage yet another scarf for my big collection, lovely tangerine and white silk scarf... the lad actually swung a punch at me I ducked he fell over and I just booted him in the balls and snatched his scarf from him.

Towards the end of the season we played the dreaded Bolton Wanderers away, I was desperate for my revenge but we knew we'd get overwhelmed and battered here, we just did not have the numbers to take on Bolton away and many Oldham fans bottled out going to Burnden back then, it was an awful place to go to but I went with a few other brave hearts, we had nothing to play for in the league but Bolton had a very good chance of promotion to Division One and they were getting huge crowds of 25-30,000, and they made an incredible amount of noise in this old decrepit old stadium, it sounded like 100,000 when they began chanting "Oh when the whites, go marching in". This day our ten coaches arrived at around 2.30pm and we had to run the gauntlet on the car park to the Railway embankment end, as ever it was rough as fuck and the fists and boots piled into us, the few cops there turning a blind eye, once in the ground we were surprised to find very few Bolton thugs, normally this end would be crawling with them, we got a bit brave and our mob of 200 or so chanted for our boys in blue.

At half-time I went for a Bovril and as I made my way back to the middle of the embankment end, we spotted the Bolton bully boys making their way towards us. A few melted away, the rest of us took deep breaths and prepared for the usual kicking, as they got nearer one big noisy bastard with a blonde feather cut crap 'tache and Birmingham bags halfway up his legs and a cheese cloth shirt began threatening us and telling us what he was going to do to us. He looked about 19 and that was enough for me, he could easily have been one of those who almost kicked me to death, so I casually strode towards him, and poured my Bovril down his chest, he screamed like a stuck pig and ran off, yelping, his pals came piling into us and we got twatted but we were getting twatted anyhow and the Oldham fans told me it was worth it seeing me pour the red hot Bovril over this cunt, the kicking didn't last long as at last the Bolton cops actually came in and got the cunts off us... outside we got attacked again on the car park, but that was one down in my revenge mission. Many more to go...

The final game of the 1975/6 season proved to be one of the greatest spectacles I have ever witnessed, it was a lovely sunny May day, the last game of an eventful season well off the pitch, our team finished about 7th/8th but on the terraces and on the streets the battles raged. Our final game was against champions elect West Bromwich Albion managed by the legendary ex-Leeds and Irish International Johnny Giles. WBA needed to win to be certain of winning Division Two, but if we somehow beat them and Bolton won at Charlton, Bolton would win Promotion, so there was a lot to play for, there were rumours all week WBA were bringing around ten thousand fans, the club decided not to make it all ticket assuming that with our home crowd the gate would be around 18,000, officially the ground held 28,000 and we had 26,000 against Man United 18 months previously but there were gaps in the big open end, so we all knew we could cram more in.

The night before on the Friday there were rumours that West Brom fans were already arriving, I did not believe this but early that

Saturday morning when I was in the town centre at about 9.30am I saw hundreds of their fans milling about, so maybe they had travelled over night, by dinner time mid day there were thousands of West Brom fans all over town. I could not believe it, I had never seen so many away fans in Oldham town centre, they looked resplendent in their green pale blue and yellow away scarves which most of them were wearing, on the way to the ground they were inside and outside every single pub and there were loads of pubs toward the ground in those days - there was no tensions and they did not attack any Oldham fans but just seemed in a carnival spirit.

We got into the Chaddy End at 2pm and it was already almost full of Oldham fans, but the massive open end was packed with thousands of West Brom fans, by 2.30pm it was full to bursting point with many standing on the roofs and half way up the floodlights and now they were spilling into both paddocks, it was a much bigger crowd than the game against Man United, the whole ground was packed to the rafters, the official gate was 22,000 ha ha ha - we all knew it was so much more than that and Harry Wood the groundsman at the time told me many years later that there was actually over 32,000 in Boundary Park that day. It was a massive tax fiddle, this meant there were well over 20,000 West Brom fans and incredible support and it looked fantastic, awesome, a sea of green, yellow and dark blue, so many wonderful banners and so much noise and vibrancy, a mob of 100 West Brom came in the Chaddy End but were soon fucked off, it was also one of the biggest Oldham mobs that season and the Chaddy End was impregnable that day... however at half time when the tannoy announced that Bolton were actually winning at Charlton a roar went up from the bottom corner of the Chaddy End, a mob of around 50 Bolton fans were jumping up and down, by the time we got there they had been twatted and climbed out of the Chaddy End the cheeky fuckers......

West Brom got their away goal and won 1 −0 and won the league, at the end of the match hundreds of us ran onto the pitch like we do every last game of the season but thousands of West Brom poured onto the pitch but they were great - swapping scarves and just celebrating... phew! However outside their were many running battles deep into the night as they stayed in Oldham celebrating, I managed to swipe three scarves that night as well as a few one to one scraps - it was a long hot memorable day. Massive respect to WBA.

The classic Boot Boy look of the early 1970's which most of us teenagers adopted, check out the half mast "skinners" and highly polished Doc Martens. By 1975 this look had almost disappeared.

Me & Slouk, the first ever hooligan I saw in action at Stockport County 1969. He was only small but very stocky and very game, a leading member of Oldham's top mob, the Glodwick mob. Slouk has lived in Spain for many years and at one time ran a pub, Churchills in Benalmadena, Costa del Sol with fellow Oldhamers and Glodwick lads Steve Ramsden and Keith Partridge.

Carol and Skip  two of many Oldham Boot Girls who followed Latics in the 70's
and were not shy at getting stuck in.

A collection of well known and highly respected football hooligan from the 70's & 80'
plus me..  Left to right...George Lyons MUFC...RIP.
Mark "Jasper" Chester (Stoke) author of Naughty Forty and Sex, drugs and
football thugs,
Colin "Beaner" Blaney (MUFC) and author of Grafters.
my goodself..OAFC
Andy Nicholls (Everton) author Scally, 30 years of Hurt, A-Z Football hooligans..et
Venue — Trap Inn Oldham - 2007

Big Pete Buckley giving chase to a few of Rochdale's "Chosen Few" mob who had the cheek to come to the Star Inn one of Oldham's main pubs in 1982, they were soon back in Rochdale.
Pete was in the generation that followed our lot and was a top lad.

The much respected Hollins crew with special guest...
Left-right  Ronnie "yap yap" Davies...Si Boss.. Iain Kennedy (Hibs)
Alan Rhodes and Gary "Hammy " Hamilton..

Jimmy Mush and Sean McCann two of the original "Chosen Few" of Rochdale a small but very game crew who made their name in the 80's/90's following Dale and England, both great pals of mine.

Alan "Dally" Daley of Limeside (crimeside) made his name in early 80's one of Oldham's "Jack Russells" Small but game as fuck lads. Dally was one of the Oldham Nine sent down in the infamous Race riots of 2001..

Me and Jimbo Tupman of Abbeyhills but one o the Glodwick mob. Jim is a very much respecte man about town and w one of very few Mods i the Glodwick mob wh were mainly Greasers Jimbo is now 56.

Me and my lifelong pal from boyhood Paul Sykes, here we are in 1984 retired and discussing our exploits on the terraces and up and down the country.

The original cover from my debut book "We Are the Famous Football Hooligans" self published in 1996. It was the first ever book to be written wholly by a former hooligan, the book was banned by most shops but still sold out within 3 months..

King Kenny Jones now aged 59 and arguably Oldham's top lad of all time and holder of the most charge sheets last count 24!

Kenny Wild, the pocket sized former bouncer of the Boundary Club, OAFC's social club which in the 70's saw many mass brawls. Kenny worked alone and was that tough that one day he sparked out seven Sunderland fans and laid 'em all out at the entrance. He was a former lightweight champion.

Liverpool v Oldham first game of season in Division One 1990/91 season.

Oldham fans were warned not to go in any pubs close to the ground, no one tells the Werneth/West St mob where they can or cannot go...

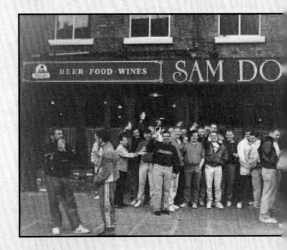

Mark Kelly of the Werneth M
Kelly was not a big lad but ga
as fuck and loved a brawl o
seeking out a one to one, he h
loads and despite being a tre
cool dude was very violent.
lived in Spain for many yea
currently in Ibiza..

Little Johnny Murph, "five foot two eyes of blue Johnny Murphy's after you". A small all action battler who feared no man or foe.. Also has the biggest gob in the north and when you heard Murphy chanting you d swear there was a mob of fifty!

Colin Norton of Abbeyhills one of Oldham's longest serving lads. over 35 years active service, if he had been in the Army he'd be a major by now! Like a few of Oldham's top lads he ended up being a doorman, a great lad well respected by all generations.. now aged 50

Me n Robbo Watson our zigga zagga man in the 70's. Robbo was a really rough tough lad and to prove it would had butt lamp posts, he was a great character and another Werneth lad. Sadly he has fought drug addiction for many years but it's still great to see him.

Mad Mick Carolan and me in 1980, Mick was a big punching giant who knocked so many lads out in his short but very productive hooligan career 1980-1985, before taking up boxing and rugby league.
Mick is now aged 51...

Me & Ste Badby central pier Blackpool prior to our first game of the 1977/78 season. Badby was a great character who had been a mod/skinhead/punk/rocker/teddyboy/biker/afroman in his short life.
He sadly passed away in 1983 aged just 24 years, he had a massive turn out for his funeral.
RIP.

Me, Carlton Leach and my son Jack when I promoted 'An Audience with Carlton Leach' in 2009. He was a te man with great manners an everyone loved him, big respects..he is a business partner of a pal of mine Ra from Glossop..

# FIGHTING AND DANCING

THIS WAS ONE OF THE greatest years in my life. It was 1976 and I was 15 but so much was going on and happening in my life; the footy, the fights, the birds, the music, the fashions, the long hot summer, the youth clubs, the discos. I moved into my pal's flat that summer and spent a week in Blackpool with my pal Hoof, I grew up fast that year and loved every minute.

This was the height of Disco... our local nightclub Cat's Whiskers was huge and 1500 teenagers would meet each Monday night to listen to Billy the kid and Pete Jurgens spinning the latest tunes and soul and reggae. I absolutely loved it at the Whiskers, we all did, the atmosphere was fantastic, the music was brilliant, so many birds and making so many new friends. It was the University of Oldham youth where you met people learned to dance fight and grew up fast, it made such an impact on so many Oldham teenagers in the 1970's. Also so many of us were Oldham fans and we planned and plotted from here, tunes like Tina Charles 'I Love to Love', The Real Things 'You to Me are Everything' and 'Can't get by without you', Disco Tex and the Sexolettes 'I wanna dance Witchoo', Billy Ocean's 'Love Really Hurts Without You', and the Manhattans had us smooching and getting semi-ons to 'Hurt' and 'Kiss and Say Goodbye'. The Stylistics churned out hit after hit, Northern Soul was big that year finally becoming mainstream so we could all enjoy it without having to go to members only all nighters like Wigan Casino and Blackpool's Mecca club, Tiffany's.

The fashions that year were Birmingham bags, cap sleeved tee shirts, stack heeled shoes, hair was longer and centre parted, Wranglers and Levi jackets were still popular, there were still a few Doc Marten wearing boot boys about, long leather over coats were for the lads who were working and could afford the £40 quid ha, perms were coming in demi waves blown waved hair, very poncey, wide lapelled jackets, shirt collars spread across the collars, the fashions were awful and I yearned for the Skinhead days when youths were so smart but they were long gone although within 12 months I started a mini revival here in Oldham to combat the awful punk scene which came about down in the summer of 76. The times they were a changing.

My mam had lost control of me that summer I was spending

more and more time at my pal's nearby council flat, he was 17 but his mam had gone working down Great Yarmouth for the summer season and left him the flat, we used it as party central. There were loads of us dossing there, we just dossed about playing tunes all night and getting birds back, my mate was called Hoof, a nickname he hated but he had buck teeth, his older brother Steve gave him the nickname, Ste was one of the original Skinheads and he was one of the most respected lads around Northmoor, he worked the holiday camps but came back every few weeks for a weekend, he was great really funny with loads of tales. He had a bird called Sylvia from Basildon, another original skin girl and I loved her tales and she loved telling them, me and Hoof went to Blackpool for a week at the end of June Saturday—Saturday but we had blown our money by the Monday and ate scraps all week from cafes until the coach took us back to Oldham.

Even in 1976 Oldham was still embroiled in summer gang wars between the districts and council estates, the most infamous inter estate battles were the Fitton Hill v Abbeyhills wars more often than not fought on the land that separated these two rough council estates, they were about half a mile apart and for many years these two estates fought against each even going back as far as the teddy boy days in the 1950's, this lot were the sons and daughters of the teddy boys and still waging war. Abbeyhills was not a big estate but was arguably the roughest estate in Oldham with many large families, many mixed raced families west Indians/white, huge families of up to 15, most of the estate ended up related to each other as neighbours married each other. The Abbeyhills lot were mainly greasers, well the whites were, very scruffy with long hair and hob nail boots, the half castes were a bit more cool with their afros and long leathers, Fitton Hill was THE largest council estate in Oldham and also had some very large rough families, mainly Irish Catholics, but a lot of the Fitton Hill lads were trendy, ex Skins. Suedeheads/Crombie boys, and boot boys of course, quite a few had scooters whereas the Abbeyhills lot stole cars or nicked bikes. There was a huge contrast in the rival estates, but none could ever take each others estates and it was all about who gained the middle ground on the fields separating them, Fitton Hill had the bigger numbers but Abbeyhills were rougher, many of them however joined forces at Boundary Park during the football season or Old Trafford or Maine Road.

In 1976 we were still hanging about Westwood Park and had a bit of trouble with the Shed lads of Royton who were our age, Royton was a big market town on the outskirts of Oldham and thought themselves independent of Oldham although most supported Oldham and all spoke in an Oldham accent, it was a new town and most of the houses were new built ones in the 60's and 70's, it was mainly a nice area and Oldhamer's who made money moved their families into Royton although there were a few rough council estates their as well, there were several gangs in and around Royton, the Shed lads hung about on the entrance into Royton from Oldham, it was a bus shelter attached to a park, there had been gangs hanging about their from the 60's, some of the lads in '76 included Andy Wright, Mark Chambers, Brian Howells, Skosh, Ged Flynn, Pete "milky bar "Wild, Foxy, Lizard Greaves, Mcginty, plus a good few more, a few of us clashed with them as our respective schools played each other. we were Grange they were mainly Our Ladies RC school.

However they had good back up with the other gangs from Royton so you had to be careful on their patch, but one summer's night a large gang of Werneth lads were marching towards Royton to take the Shed lads on, we joined forces and together we had about 30 lads and a few birds with us, our lot that night consisted of Me, Phil Heeney, Hoof, Dozy Dunc, Danny Irving, Dave Turner, John Lund, Paul Ashton, Dave Urey, Big Clive, Paul Sykes and Geoff Noble. It was a mile walk from Westwood and 2 miles from Werneth, as we approached the Shed we could see their mob but as we got within yards they fled down Broadway, they ran into the Royton Catholic club whereupon a load of bigger Royton lads came out with glasses and pool cues, we clashed in the middle of Broadway but they battered us and a few of us got a kicking, there were too many of them and too many blokes from Royton joined in, no one was seriously hurt but there were tit for tat reprisals over the next few months even in the Chaddy End in the footy season where normally all inter rivalries were put to one side... Royton had many rivals around Oldham including Shaw, Fitton Hill, Chadderton, Middleton and Werneth/Westwood.

Apart from being a mercenary in search of violence I was involved all summer in violent clashes at the discos and youth clubs around Oldham at school and all this was in the break from the football season, I even attacked two school teachers as I lost all respect for them - one day in class I was fucking about and our form teacher threatened me, he was called Mike Russell, a very big powerfully built man who wore thick glasses which gave me the wrong impression that he was a soft touch. I told him I would fight him anytime which raised a few laughs in the class, Mr Russell ordered the whole class into the corridor and locked the class room door, he then told me to do my best, which I did as I ran to him and butted him in his chest which took a bit of wind out of him but then he laid a few punches into my stomach and took all the wind out of me and I sank to my knees gasping for breath, he lifted me up and said, take a breather so it doesn't make you look so bad, he then let the class back in and normality was resumed. I had nothing but respect for him after that and I am proud to say we became life-long friends once I left school, a truly great man.

I also came unstuck with another teacher Mr Hill, our woodwork teacher who had the biggest and strongest fore-arms I have ever seen, he was only about 5 ft 8 inches but very stocky. Anyhow this one day I am running through the corridors when he bellowed out "Spiers you moron, stop now!" I told him to "fuck off!" he was not a happy bunny and grabbed me around my throat and lifted me off the ground, I butted him in his face but he did not flinch only to exert more pressure with his strong grip, so much so that when he released me I dropped to the ground like a stone, gasping for breath, fair play to him he just walked away and did not report me... I was losing control and that summer I was suspended from school twice for 2 weeks before finally getting expelled!

Because the school and my mam had lost control I was put under a child psychologist one Dr. Maden. This cunt was exposed in the 1990's for abusing young boys over decades who were put in his trust and he got ten years. He ruined so many young lives, he didn't molest me though maybe my violent tendencies made him wary, I would have ripped his head off and stabbed the vile cunt if he tried anything on with me, however I do recall him asking suggestive questions like if I masturbated etc, but my temper was raging and he soon changed subject. I saw the cunt only a few times and he got nowhere with me, I still yearned for violence especially football violence although by this stage I was fighting regularly against other gangs and lads and even men.

In July 1976 I took my school on strike... the weather for several weeks was in the 90's, it was sweltering hot and the teachers made us wear full uniform of shirt tie jumper jacket and trousers, yet they swanned about in shorts and tee shirts! I called the strike one lunch time in the top playground and had over 100 captivated by my rousing speech, I got the cheers as I raged on, all of a sudden half a dozen teachers came to break up the strike, we all ran towards the school gates but only six got through, so many bottled out, the six were myself, Loyd Scantlebury, Steven Oats, Malc and Peter Stewart and Jimmy Standring (RIP) heroes one and all, we went to the education offices at Chadderton Town Hall and demanded to see the top man, who to be fair came out and listened to our grievances for half a hour or so, when we came out the fucking press were there already, God knows who informed them! they interviewed me as the spokesman and took our photograph, it was then we noticed a few teachers from Grange heading towards us, we bolted.

This story made the late edition of the *Oldham Chronicle* complete with photo of us six rebels with me named and quoted as the leader and spokesman, I was chuffed to fuck as was my dad but mam was not one bit happy and neither was the headmaster next day. As I went into school that morning I an the other rebels were treated as heroes by everyone even some teachers were saying well done, some of the lefty ones were hoping I'd be the next Arthur Scargill! However in Assembly we were all named and shamed and made to stand up in front of everyone we were then publicly strapped six times!

I was then ordered to the Head of the whole schools office, Mr Ernest Dowson OBE, a dour man who loved to parade about in his long flowing black gown. As I entered his office he threw the newspaper at me and told me I was a disgrace to the good name of Grange, he then suspended me for two weeks, I was well happy with that, when I came back there was only a week to go before the big six weeks holidays, I spent that week in isolation in the library, because I was seen as a bad influence. It did not bother me, I loved reading books, but the good news was that the uniform rules had been relaxed, and schoolkids were now wearing short sleeved shirts with top button undone, I was seen as hero to the kids so many thanked me.

Earlier on in 1976 Bolton Wanderers drew Newcastle United at home at Burnden Park in the FA Cup 5th round, five of us from Grange school decided we were going to this massive game, and for a chance to see Bolton taken over by the thousands of Geordies. Me, Nicky Dixon, Phil Harper, John Lund and Dave Hibbert got the 400 bus to Bolton that Saturday lunch, we arrived in Bolton at 1pm, already there were thousands of Geordies all over the town centre almost to a man wearing the black and white stripes shirts of their heroes, many of them were pissed up and chanting away, we didn't see many Bolton fans bar the odd pockets of youths, it seemed most of Bolton's town centre pubs were full of Geordies both inside and out. It was a carnival atmosphere.

We made our way down Manny road to Burnden park along with thousands of Geordies, it was the first time I had ever felt safe in Bolton, as we arrived at Bolton's ground around 2pm we witnessed loads of scuffles as Bolton's thugs clashed with the Geordies, Bolton were in and outside the King Bill pub facing the ground, it was very tense but there were just too many Geordies, the cops could not cope with the extraordinary large numbers, they were lawless, they all seemed like giants and did not give a fuck for the cops,

We tried in vain to pay into the ground but it was sold out with thousands still outside, Im sure the crowd was over 50,000 that day, with over 30,000 Geordies inside and loads still outside, an incredible following, we just soaked the atmosphere up and revelled in the Geordies taking the piss, it was a sea of black and white everywhere.

We could hear the singing in the ground and it was brilliant, we were gutted we were not inside but we all of a sudden had an incredible stroke of luck when one of them old Christians with an orange placard saying "Jesus will save you" asked if we had any tickets, "no" we all said as one, well amazingly he pulled FIVE tickets out and gave them to us, all for the Embankment end where the Geordies were encamped in their thousands, he didn't want a penny and we offered him good money, he just said you must thank the good lord above, which we did... yippee! God knows how he got hold of these but we were soon making our way into the Railway Embankment end..

What we witnessed and was a part of was one of the greatest games ever, Bolton 3 Newcastle 3, I think Malcolm McDonald got a hat-trick. It was end-to-end stuff and possibly one of the best atmospheres I have ever come across, 50,000 plus roaring their teams on, it was proper hairs on the neck job. An amazing exciting wonderful match, and when the Geordies to a man all sang Blaydon Races in unison well I was gobsmacked. I knew I would remember this moment forever, it was so loud and so clear, and I have never seen such passionate and emotional fans as them Geordies, many of them with tears streaming down their faces.

There were scuffles breaking out in the other three sides of the ground each time a team scored and at the end of this pulsating match loads of Geordies invade the pitch, outside was mayhem as the Geordies clashed with the cops and the Bolton fans all the way into the town centre, it was so exciting and a day none of us would ever forget.

As well as going to every home game at Oldham and quite a few aways I often went to other high profile matches especially if I thought there would be trouble, this was the case when I went to Manchester City v Manchester United in the League Cup in the Autumn of 1975, this was a Wednesday night game and one I was really looking forward to, I got the train into Manchester at 5pm and was in Victoria Station for 5 -30pm, I took it on myself to wear a Glasgow Rangers scarf, blue red and white, in the forlorn hope City nor United wouldn't see me as the foe, back then many fans wore Rangers or Celtic scarves, however City fans were far more likely to wear Rangers scarves as United were seen as the Catholic club. The train down into Manc was full off lads mostly United, but there was no trouble on the train, but it was tense.

From the station I decided to walk the 2/3 miles to Maine Road, which was very dodgy as it was kicking off all over the place en route, I was glad to get to the ground and by 7pm I was in the Kippax amongst all the City fans, United got a third of the Kippax that night, the tension was incredible as was the atmosphere, the ground was full, United had fans all around the ground as well as in the Kippax, me being the nosy bastard got right to the front of the City mob, and got caught up in all the mouthing off etc... Loads of United's fans signalled me out but I was lost in all this and thought nothing of it and felt safe being twenty yards and dozens of coppers in between.

However at half time a big mob of United fans came into City's mob from behind and City ran, and within ten minutes United now had most of the top of the Kippax, and revelled in the taking of the famous Kippax, United's thugs were relentless and piled into any City fans and now it was very dodgy and I got a safe distance away, it didn't help matters that City win 4 - 0 and Colin Bell ( City's best player ) had his leg broken, creating even more tensions in this already very volatile match.

At the end of the game I got on a bus back into the town centre and even on the bus City and United fans were scrapping like fuck, I kept a low profile, once back in the city centre I made my way back to Victoria station and on the train back to Oldham, the train was packed out but at each stop loads of United fans got off, Miles Platting, Dean court, Failsworth and Hollinwood, next stop was Werneth were I was getting off, by now there are about twenty odd United fans on the train the so called Oldham Reds, I recognised a few of them even though they were all older than me, as the train pulls into Werneth station, they jump me, well at least six of them did, they battered me, nicked my Rangers scarf and I got a bloody nose and black eye, nothing new there, as I scrambled off the train battered and bruised, I told em I'd get them back, they laughed at me..

Over the next few years I made a lot of Oldham Reds' lives uncomfortable to say the least, well me and my pals did, often meeting them as they came back from United games and attacking them with loads of other Oldham fans, the twats could have given me the a walk away, they knew I wasn't a City fan, a couple of them actually became very good pals of mine but deny they joined in the assault on me but they did, and even today 37 years on I still see a few of them who filled me in and they can't look me in the face.

On reflection I now realise why I was so violent, there are many combining reasons, I never received any love nor affection from my mother, she was cold and hard with me, never acknowledging anything good I ever did, she did not beat me, just blanked me and made me feel worthless. Mam had a hard life, losing her eye at 10 years old, which back then set her apart, it toughened her up, so much so she was "cock" (toughest kid) of a large council school, boys and girls, she was always fighting, rebelling and hated her own father, who like many men back then ruled with an iron fist. Mam left home at 15 to work on the hop farms in Kent before spending several years in Blackpool where she had two boys from two different men, which back in the 1950's was deemed shocking, very shocking and her father was disgusted with her and never spoke to her again and half of her large family snubbed her for the shame she brought on them, the elder brother was adopted by her wealthy elder brother. This haunted her for many years, my father took on Peter and mam and dad had three more kids; me, Christina and Karen. Mam was very independent and just did her own thing, which was mainly drinking and singing in local pubs every night.

My father was the opposite, he just gave me anything I wanted, anything for an easy life, I adored dad but he was not a traditional dad, teaching me football, learning me the ropes etc, but we were very close and had many great times together, but the lack of love and attention from mam hurt me, so I sought attention and soon learned by fighting having courage and making people laugh I would gain the attention I craved. Added to all this my older brother Peter whom I loved and admired was very quiet and never stood up for me when I got bullied, he was not a fighter. So I was on my own, and I did get bullied as kid but did avenge it.

My first heroes as a teenager were the so called hard men about town; the club owners, car dealers and scrap dealers, men who in the 1970's, now in their thirties who made their names as young men in the 1960's, men like Len Withey, an ex-rugby player, boxer and wrestler, a big strong no nonsense man, who ran his night club Dreamers with a zero tolerance policy, if you crossed him he knocked you down the steep stairs. His best pal was the charismatic Tommy Wood a huge handsome man, always suited and booted he had his own demolition firm, he was an ex-professional wrestler and boxer who fought for the British title in the 1960's losing to Bunny Johnson. Bernard Dronsfield, another demolition man, premature bald but hard as iron, he lived next door to us, an ex merchant sea man who had been around the world several times, heavily tattooed and a big ladies man. Then there was Terry English a short but very stocky man, with a flat nose given to him by the only man to beat him, Jimmy Burns, a rag tatter, who looked like he was made of granite, he back handed people to defeat, he was that hard that during a spell in Strangeways in the 50's he beat the so called "cock" of the prison in a brawl that lasted 45 minutes, and then you had Eddy Alexander a good friend of my mam's, a Scouser only 5 ft 9, Eddy was a good looking man and another boxer of note in his youth. He came to Oldham aged 21 in 1962 an within three years was reputedly THE hardest man in Oldham, he fought all the so called hard men, beating most of them, those he didn't it was stopped, no one ever claimed to beat Eddy, there were so many others, these were the men I respected and looked up to and hopefully one day impress.

During that 6 week period from August to mid September 1976 known as the big school holidays, I was involved and witnessed some of the very worst football violence.

Early August saw a trip to nearby Bury on a Saturday, I actually walked the 12 miles setting off at 10am arriving by 1pm, the town centre already filling up with Oldham hooligans many arriving by bus, by 2pm the big march to Gigg Lane, a good mob of over 300 youths chanting away looking for Bury fans, none were seen, not even the cheeky few who usually made an appearance before scarpering, we all piled into the ground and into their end for the annual take over again.

Halfway through the first half a mob of fifty or so Bury fans aided by their Bury Reds made a vain attempt to regain this shitty little end, amongst this lot was about 15 Oldham Reds! Not a wise move, and even though a lot of us knew them we were very angry that they would join up and go against their neighbours, schoolmates and work mates and we set about them and the Bury mob, they all got hammered most climbing out of the ground, it just enhanced the attacks by Oldham fans on Oldham Reds over the next few seasons.

Second half we all walked around the pitch to the away end mainly out of boredom, during the 2nd half, half a dozen Bury lads came in and one big fucker asked if any of us fancied a one on one behind the end, Pete Matthews from Werneth obliged. Pete was a big fit lad, he was 3 years older than me and had been to Grange school, he was also a body builder – he and this lad went round the back and 5 mins later Pete returned smirking, he had beaten this Bury lad who was now being tended to by the St. John's Ambulance crew, Good lad Pete – after the game usual piss taking rampage through nearby Bury town centre looking in pubs for Bury Reds, none to be found then it was the busses back home.

Our next match the week after would not be so easy. Bradford City away in the first round of the League Cup, this was a 2 legged game, about 15 of us from Northmoor met in the Spinners Arms on Chadderton Road, most of us were under age but Walter the landlord served us, he opened at 11 am, we were getting coach from Barlow's at 1pm, amongst us that day were the Scantlebury brothers Loyd and Vic, Vic was the elder by 12 months and cock of our school last year, he was a great sportsman a big athletic lad who excelled at football, athletics, basketball, cricket and anything else he fancied, he was over 6 ft and very well built. Loyd was stocky very fit and very strong, about five feet ten, and another top footballer and runner, they were both half castes, their dad Vic senior was originally from Barbados. Others that day were Jimmy Harper, Dozy Dunc Butterworth, Danny Irving, Martin 'Hoof' Hurst, Paul Ashton, Phil Heeney, Paul Sykes, John Lund, Dave Turner, (RIP) Big Clive, Geoff Noble and Pete Logan, we were all aged 15 to 18 years old. We drank about 6 pints of lager, I was on lager shandy, I was never a big drinker.

At midday a bloke came into the pub with long scraggly hair, a wide lapelled jacket big beer belly and flared trousers, he looked a right piss pot, he began warning us about Bradford fans saying how rough they were and sneaky etc, we laughed him off and dismissed his advice, this man was Jimmy Kirton an original thug from the 1960's one of the very first Oldham hooligans and one of the most respected Oldham fans of all time although we did not know this then, he would be about 28 then, at 1pm we boarded our coaches at Barlow's and headed the 20 miles or so to Bradford, all ten coaches pulling it at Valley Parade at the same time, 2pm.

Happy Harry talked us all into entering Bradford's end, a small low roofed Kop behind the goals, there must have been 2/300 of us and we all followed our specky four eyed leader. We soon ran out the much smaller Bradford mob and for ten minutes we were revelling in taking over the feared Bradford's end. Happy Harry then leads us into the big paddock where the Bradford mob were now congregating only with much bigger numbers. The Bradford mob was now aided by much older men and came piling into us and despite our brave attempts we got twatted and made our way into the big open end terrace behind the goals which was were the away fans went, we thought we were now safe from the very aggressive older and harder Bradford mob, the hot weather taking it's toll, we were all sweating buckets.

Just before kick-off a huge mob of big Bradford thugs came charging down the terraces into us, most of these were men in their 20's, fists and boots swinging and showing no mercy, the whole Oldham mob ended up on the pitch to get away, (on Match of the Day that night it showed us clambering onto the pitch) it stated that Oldham fans invade the pitch at Valley Parade, this did our reputation no harm but the truth was we were fighting for our lives!

We finally found refuge in the last place we had not been in, a long paddock, we were fucked, knackered, most of us sat down and some falling asleep, three lads had been stabbed, many had their noses and faces smashed in, we were a defeated army, out of our depth, for half a hour nothing happened, but slowly but surely more and more Bradford thugs began coming in amongst us, threatening us and bullying us, taking the piss. That day I was wearing my steel toe cap boots and had my hair cropped, I had the skinhead look and stood out, three big Bradford lads were really dishing the verbals out but no Oldham lad was reacting, one focused on me saying. "Hey tha Oldham bone head, ah bet tha can't lift yer feet up tha little Oldham prick!" I tried to ignore him by looking away, but he kept on with his mates laughing, I thought to myself, your having it yer Yorkie cunt, a bit later he sat down amongst the Oldham fans and grabbing Oldham's bird's tit's and arses, still going on at me trying to goad me, I was seething, and I bit. I ran at him and as he tried to get up I booted him right under his chin, he spat some teeth out and blood spurted from his mouth. He was knocked out twitching, his mates ran off and the cops dived in right away, I melted into the crowd, the St John's came with a stretcher for Yorkie who was still semi-conscious, mumbling and moaning, his distorted face a total mess, as they are carrying the cunt out he looked up towards me and I winked at him - he won't be forgetting this Oldham prick for a while... the feeling I got from doing him was immense and it further built my fast growing reputation.

It was very dodgy after the match but the cops had it sorted and we were soon back over the Pennines back to God's county.

That night we returned back to Oldham defeated exhausted from the days events and hopefully a lesson learnt, never under estimate anyone especially big City clubs, we all went round the local pubs in Northmoor and at 10 bells landed in the Westhulme on Featherstall Road which had been closed for a couple of weeks for renovation, this was the re opening night so we knew it would be busy, as it proved, but what we saw we were not happy with, this new landlord was from Altrincham in Cheshire and had adorned the walls with Man United memorabilia ! this pub was one of the nearest to Boundary Park and would not last long, we settled down when in burst Jimmy Kirton his face all mashed up as was his younger brother's Tony who was a right hard nut about five years older than me but had a rep for one not to upset, he was one of those loonies who bit his tongue to get himself fired up for fighting and would fight by any means possible, with the Kirton brothers were half a dozen more older Oldham fans all sporting cuts n bruises.

Jimmy came running over, "what did I tell you about Bradford!" we said "we know Jimmy most of us got filled in aswell", one of the lads bought him a pint then he spent the next hour regaling us with the 1960's music and early football hooligan days mentioning his best pal and hero Gill Docker every 5 minutes, he made Gill sound like a monster but we were impressed and Jimmy was very entertaining, at last orders Jimmy warned the landlord to get this fucking United shit off the walls otherwise the pub would be trashed! The landlord promised he would and next time we were in he had done... fair play to him.

We could not wait for the 2nd leg match against Bradford, we had to exact revenge or as much as we could do, Bradford were one of the roughest mobs we had ever come across and we fully expected our Chaddy End to be taken that night, but the Chaddy End was full to the rafters by 7pm, no team could take this tonight it was physically impossible you could hardly move, half a dozen Bradford fans were spotted and dealt with and they end a really big mob in the away end, they kept on coming and coming, it was a great following for such a low profile cup game, the tension was incredible as we built ourselves up into a frenzy to take these Yorkshire cunts on after the game, we drew the first leg 1-1 and won the 2nd leg 3–1 and we were ecstatic and just before the end of the game a massive mob of Oldham surged onto the streets surrounding the ground and made their way to avenge these Bradford fuckers, the cops were out in force with their dogs and batons but could not hold us back and as soon as the away end steel gates opened we charged into Bradford's mob, of course being the hard bastards they were fought back gallantly and it was a major free for all, us the cops and Bradford all swinging fists and booting fuck out of each other.

The cops finally got a grip and separated both mobs who were both as keen as each other to get into each other a proper "War of the Roses". Our mob marched up Sheepfoot Lane towards the town centre railway and coach stations. The mob was at least 500 strong if not bigger and when we reached the Rochdale Road/Featherstall Road junction half the mob went down to Werneth station which was the traditional station for away fans but the other half included me went into the town centre where we had the options of bus, coaches and the main train station, as it was most Bradford fans went to Werneth station and were attacked all along the mile and half route...

A small mob of about twenty of us peeled off from the main mob who seemed hell bent on smashing shops up and having running battles with the police, we spotted four transit vans parked near the main station and we hung about knowing they were for the Bradford lads, we didn't have to wait long when out of the shadows came a crew of around forty Bradford, big fuckers aswell, we sent Yogi our spotter off to recruit some more Oldham lads, and within minutes another 30 or so joined us and we waited till all the Bradford lads were getting into their transit vans then we attacked them with bricks, bottles and sticks. It was a classic ambush and even though a few had a go but we hammered them and smashed their van windows and even overturned one of their vans, it was hard to sympathise cos these were the same kind of bullies who gave us such a torrid time at Bradford, these were out and out hooligans, no cops came for ages so we really set about these Bradford thugs, who were moaning and groaning, not nice but football violence wasn't nice and I and indeed all of us had come unstuck many times.

We got our revenge and many Bradford fans got attacked that night at both train stations, we do not kid ourselves, Bradford were a top mob and became even more notorious over the next twenty years with their Ointment Squad but that night was ours and the revenge was oh so sweet.

Yogi was Oldham's spotter, not the brightest of lads, his real name was Graham Ogden and he came from Chadderton and was a few years older than me, he had really thick black hair and the biggest yard brush tache in town, he looked like a Mexican bandit, he always wanted to be one of the gang and had been a spotter for several mobs for years, he was also very fit and fast, his war cry was 'they're here!' alerting whoever he was running with, every now and then he got caught and beat up but it did not deter him from his risky job. He was very well known and everyone took pity on him and he was always into the latest fashions and styles... it seemed every team had a spotter similar to Yogi back then.

Having such a massive mob turn out to avenge Bradford really built up our confidence we felt we could now take on all comers and eagerly awaited the game at Wolves two weeks later. Wolves were a famous old team with big crowds and a proud history, they had just been relegated from Division One and like other fallen giants Manchester United, Chelsea and Aston Villa etc would want to be flexing their muscles no doubts, this was one test I and many other were looking forward to.

By September 1976 we were sweltering under the hottest summer on record temperatures were still in the high 80's. One Friday afternoon me and Dozy Dunc were just dossing about on the local estate when we bumped into a lad called Ste Whitehead who was a few years older than us and a right rogue, in and out of borstal and prison. He originally came from Salford and had the slight Manc accent, he was sound though and we were telling him we were going to hitch hike to Wolverhampton at midnight for the game tomorrow, he said I will meet you at motorway junction at midnight and drive you down there, he was not a football fan but it was a nice gesture and we agreed to meet him at motorway junction.

At midnight me and Dozy Dunc were stood at the junction, it was still warm and we were wearing shorts and tee shirts in this incredible weather, right on cue Ste turns up in a big jag! We got in and I said " fuck me Ste this is a nice motor, " he said, "aye it is Ive just nicked it!" fuck me this wasn't in the plan, we did not argue and just hoped we got to Wolves in one piece. I say one piece because he drove like a loony at 100 mph! I was shitting it and asked Ste to pull into Keele Services as I needed the bog, he did and we went in and had a brew and nicked loads of sweets as you do... as we are getting back into the car two cop cars swoop on us and dragged us out of the jag - we were arrested and taken to a local nick. What a nightmare! But Ste said to us that he'll take the rap and just say that we are hitch-hikers and don't know him, fair play to Ste and this is what we said, after a couple of hours in this local cop shop two Oldham coppers turned up to take me and Dozy Dunc back to Oldham. They let us off but kept Ste in custody, the Oldham cops dropped us off in Oldham town centre, it was by now 5 am, and we made our way back to the motorway junction to hitch-hike once again to Wolves.

Within three lifts we were in Wolverhampton and it was only 9am, the sun was shining brightly as it had done forever it seemed, we found a cafe and had some breakfast, I had never seen so many darkies as I had that day in Wolverhampton, it was like being in a Tarzan film! All added to the vibrancy of this city, this cafe was facing Wolverhampton train station and at 10.30 am we spotted three familiar faces from Oldham we knew Tommy Nolan, Sean Bowskill from Chadderton and Ian 'Max' McGeary from Royton. All good game lads as we were to find out within minutes of them arriving in Wolves, as we were strolling away from the station a group of six Wolves youths attacked us but we soon had them off on their toes, us five were all up for it and we clipped and booted them as they scarpered, we feared though that they would be back with more numbers, this was the case and we spent the next 2/3 hours avoiding marauding mobs of Wolves hooligans, at 1pm another train came in from Manchester with around 100 Oldham lads on it, we joined up with them and made our way to the ground walking through the town centre chanting. Fortunately we had a police escort because big mobs of Wolves fans were following us making threats and throat slitting motions, they had a lot of black lads with them which looked scary as their big Afros made them seemed like giants!

As we approached this famous old stadium Molineaux, we spotted hundreds of Wolves fans on every street corner and on hills were the by pass was, it was like Zulu, and I'm not on about just all the black lads but the massive numbers, it was daunting but even more so when the cops said to us "right lads just make you way through that subway and you will be at the ground". This subway was a long dark tunnel that snaked under the motorway for about 150 yards, it did not help matters that emblazoned at the entrance in crude graffiti were the words, "Welcome to Suicide Subway...your gonna die!" fuck me it looked scary, it was so dark and we could see Wolves fan on the other side making their way towards this hell hole... it was gulp time, but in we go into this pitch dark abyss. All the lights had been smashed so it was total darkness and even some of the cops were smirking. We began chanting in the forlorn hope it would make it sound as if there were hundreds of us but these Wolves lads had followed us from the town and knew just how many there were of us, what made it worse was that back then the Black lads in the cities were renowned for carrying weapons, these were tense times and only a couple of weeks prior there were major riots at the Notting Hill Carnival with loads stabbed up..

It's a strange feeling knowing your going to get filled in, all hooligans get this feeling at some stage but this was particularly scary given the circumstances and the amount of Wolves thugs around, because not only were they coming in from the opposite end they were now behind us aswell, taunting us, all of sudden up goes the chant "We are Wolves, We are Wolves!" and they charge into us from both sides. To cut a long story short we got kicked to fuck everyone of us it seemed got busted noses and black eyes, we crawled out of that hell hole subway on our knees heading for the light at the end of the tunnel as the Wolves thugs laughed at us booting us for good measure, when we eventually got to the other end the cops suddenly appeared, many of them laughing at us, they then guided us towards the massive Kop on the South Bank, reserved for away supporters only, so the sign said above the turn styles. Yeah right... in we go and make our way to the top of the massive old fashioned terraced kop, it was one of the largest in the country, we were buzzing when we saw a mob of 3-400 Oldham fans congregated at the top of this end and they were telling us there were loads more to come as there was a lot of coaches broke down on the M6. Some fault or other, by kick off we are all chanting away and our confidence restored but that was soon shattered as this away supporters only end began filling up with hundreds and hundreds of Wolves thugs coming up the terracing from both sides and up the middle. Oh for fucks sake here we go again! And so it was they attacked us from all sides many of these much older than us youths but very violent, loads of them wearing bib n braces dungarees, the cops took ages to restore any kind of order but by this time we are right at the bottom encamped under the floodlights near the entrance.

Many Oldham fans chose to leave the ground such was the level of violence, those of us who remained took some terrible stick throughout the whole game off these Wolves thugs surrounding us, gobbing on us and making random assaults. You dare not go to the bogs, horror stories of them slashing lads up put paid to that, whether they were true or not the thought was there and no one doubted it the way these mad fuckers were acting, it did not help matters to see the late comers from the broken down coaches in the adjoining paddock, all buoyant and waving at us, many of us did not want to be seen as we tried in vain to melt into the crowd... the sound of noses jaws and cheek bones being smashed put even more fear into us and haunted me for years, the sneaky bastards would just whack unsuspecting Oldham fans, our pleas to the coppers fell on deaf ears as they came out with the boring old "you should know better than to come down here chanting" blah blah fucking blah! You dirty horrible cunts, you are supposed to protect the public...

It was a long horrible day the very hot sticky weather not helping and the only respite was Wolves thrashing us 5-0! Ah not fucking likely, every goal they scored they celebrated by piling right into us fists and boots flailing, our best player the enigmatic Alan Groves got sent off as well. So it was a nightmare on and off the pitch!

We were praying for the final whistle but then realising we were going back by train filled us with even more horror, as the final whistle eventually blew the Wolves thugs made one more big final charge into us, the cops once more stood back laughing at our plight. Outside the Wolves fans made their way to the coach park, to attack the main mob, and those on the train got an escort, but about 14 of us hung back in the forlorn hope of getting a lift back on the player's coach, it was a long shot, I had had lifts back on the players coach a couple of times but only 2 or 3 of us, now there were 14 of us! The players began boarding the coach and the driver told us he couldn't take us back and then all of a sudden a mob of Wolves come piling into us, and amazingly Alan Groves our star striker came bouncing off the coach and piled into the Wolves thugs, Groves was a very powerfully built man with a boxer's face and the Wolves fans scattered, Grovesy was already our hero he was even more so now..

So there we were all alone outside Molineux, it's now 6pm on a balmy evening and we did not have a clue what to do, we were all skint so could not go home by train unless we jumped it but none of us fancied the long walk through the town centre. We then decided to hitch-hike back home, the motorway was close by so we staggered ourselves and began hitching, half of us got home the other half got lifted by the cops outside Stafford and arrested for jay walking! I was amongst those arrested, what a fucking nightmare, but finally we came across decent coppers who allowed us to stay in the cells overnight they plied us with bacon butties and cups of coffee and next morning a black maria (cop van) turned up from Oldham and took us back home, the Oldham coppers laughing at our stories, we arrived back home at 10.30am absolutely fucking shattered I had hardly any kip since Thursday night, 60 hours! I slept til Monday afternoon.

A lot of lessons were learned at Wolves, the main one knowing our place especially away from home, teams like Wolves were big time and had five times as many lads as the likes of Oldham, of course we could handle most teams at home but we were very naive thinking we could swan about a rough city like Wolverhampton, this was many Oldham fans worst ever experience at a football match it certainly was mine. I was kicked to fuck and several times, and still not yet 16, we all vowed revenge as we always did when we got twatted, and to our credit we did avenge this terrible beating we took for several hours, but our revenge was in one major charge and over in two minutes, hardly on par with the sustained savage attacks we took that hot late summers day..

The terrible beating we took at Wolves on and off the pitch and inside and outside the ground seemed to toughen many of us, we thought surely we could never come across so much violence at one game especially 95% towards us but our next home game at Boundary Park was none other than our hated Lancashire rivals Bolton Wanderers.

# THE GREATEST DAY

Saturday October 6th 1976 will stay in every Oldham hooligan's memory. Those who were that day and many will recall the level of violence that very hot Autumn day was incredible to say the least. All of us carrying bruised cuts, wounds and aches from Wolverhampton had only just recovered just in time for this bloodbath and this was a bloodbath, I for one was seeking revenge and I was hell bent on really hurting as many Bolton fans as possible due to the way over top beating I had taken just 10 months before on Boxing Day 1975 when grown men pulverised me and put me into hospital for a few days.

Again I wore my lethal weapons - the steel toe cap boots a size too small so they were pinching my feet but were so tight they gave me extra spring in my step, I polished the outer steel toe cap that morning knowing damn well they would be sinking into some Bolton hooligans shins stomach and head! I had it in mind to target lads with taches and sideburns as that is what I recall the cunts who savaged me having, the mood around Oldham that morning was one of confidence and trepidation, for most Oldham fans did not see any violence on the previous Boxing Day fixture as no Bolton came into the Chaddy End for once, only those of us foolish enough to go hunting them after the match knew and felt the force of these bastards. I just knew they would attempt to take the Chaddy End this time, this game was not all ticket so there was nothing to stop them coming into our end as per. The town centre was full of Oldham lads that sunny morning, all the usual suspects marauding about in various gangs from the tough estates of Oldham, a big mob of about fifty lads were lying in wait at the 400 bus stop that brought the hourly bus in from Bolton, every hour from as early as 9.30am Bolton fans came in by bus on the 400, and they all got ambushed up until 1.30pm, after mid day many getting off near Boundary Park, but those who ventured into the town centre got filled in.

Me and ten of my pals caught ten Bolton fans going into the Snipe pub in Oldham centre, this was a real rough pub frequented by shop lifters, thieves and ex-teddy boy thugs all tattooed up with their greasy quiffs, who were not happy about outsiders coming into their pub, we hung about outside the Snipe knowing damn well the locals would set about these Bolton fans which they duly did, we heard the sound of glasses being broken and thrown and lo and behold out came the Bolton fans many of them cut to run into our young but tough firm, we piled right into them aided by half a dozen teds and kicked fuck out of them, even a couple of the women shoplifters booted them about the bodies as they crawled away, I had no sympathy these were rough looking lads and I knew they were Bolton hooligans they just thought they could take the piss like in previous years, we set off the mile or so down to the ground at 1pm a mob of 100 plus, all buoyant and chanting away, we were buzzing for the most guaranteed day of violence we could wish for, we were not to be disappointed.

Halfway down to the ground down the Rochdale Road we spotted three transit vans unloading around 30/40 Bolton lads, this was facing the Queens pub, which would be full of Oldham fans aswell, we broke off into three groups of 30 plus each and set the ambush up from three sides and sent Yogi our spotter to go to the Queens and tell the lads in there, It was a classic pincer manoeuvre we hit Bolton from every angle many of us picking broken branches up beer crates and anything else we could get our hands on, they fought back but go the justified kicking until a cop on his bike came screeching across the croft were they were parked but by then most of them had been twatted, a few gobbing off that they were gonna take the fucking Chaddy End again! We laughed at them but deep down we knew they would be in the Chaddy, these would want revenge for the hammering they just got, the last section down to the ground as very lively especially down Sheepfoot Lane a long snaking steep hill that saw so much bloodbath over the years, one side a 150 yard long high stone hospital wall the other side various car parks and crofts, scenes of many running battles, it was no different today.

It was chaotic down Sheepfoot Lane as running battles ensued with more and more Bolton fans getting involved as we neared the ground, many running up from the ground to join in the scrapping, I got a few smacks and kicks and a thick ear but gave plenty out, the cops were out in force and made quite a few arrests, we finally get to the turn styles of the Chaddy End and we could hear the Bolton fans chanting loud as fuck "We took the Chaddy End, We took the Chaddy End" but we could also hear Oldham fans chanting, "Oh wanky wanky wanky Wanderers!", just as loud, the rush I was having was incredible we knew there was loads of battling going on you could sense it and hear it.

I was desperate to get amongst this fighting and defend our Chaddy End against these Bolton bastards! There were hundreds of Oldham hooligans outside as equally as keen to get into our end, as soon as I am in I run right up to the top of the Chaddy End and joined in the mass brawling across the top, both massive mobs charging at each other the coppers breaking it up briefly before more charges occurred, the cops managed to get the ten  yards no mans gap between both mobs which stretched right down the middle of the Chaddy End which was a big steep terrace, the chanting and atmosphere was so intense, I spotted my Bolton rival with the ginger feather cut and we threatened each other with throat slitting motions both calling each other wankers etc, I actually began to recognise quite a few Bolton lads seeing as we fought each other so many times.

It was a perfect even split right down the Chaddy End, both mobs with same very big numbers, Oldham had one of its very best ever turn outs as all the usual mobs doubled and even trebled in numbers, we needed to be as Bolton brought their biggest ever firm into the Chaddy, there was a brief lull in the battling when all of a sudden a skirmish was happening at the top of our mob where a mob of about 15 big Bolton bastards had got in behind us and were giving it the big one, lashing out and bullying, well they soon got sorted as the mob engulfed them, I fought my way through the angry Oldham lads to get into them when I saw a bloke who I am sure was one of the cunts who beat me up on that Boxing day on Clayton playing fields, he was on his knees trying to get back up when I ran at him and booted him right in his face, with my steel toe caps! I heard the awful sound of steel connecting with bone, amongst all that noise I heard him scream before his mates dragged him into the main Bolton mob to get away, they all got caved in.

That day a lad passed me an afro wig which I put on as two coppers saw me booting the Bolton fan and came for me, I set off down the no man's gap between both fans, everyone could see what was happening and one of the coppers grabbed my wig which came off and he went flying, both sets of fans howling with laughter, but I got caught at the bottom of the Chaddy End by three more coppers who pounced on me and dragged me onto the pitch then dragged me around the pitch booting me along the way, the game had been going for over 20 minutes, the normal fans in the paddocks booing me, demanding I get the birch. As I got to the player's tunnel where the cops took you up, I spotted Jack Warner the big CID hooligan cop, he was punching arrested fans in the stomach as they passed him, winding them, I tensed my stomach as I was being dragged by Jack, who sussed it and kicked me in my bollocks winding me even further. But respects to Jack, he told the coppers "just throw the bloody idiot out!" and winked at me, thanks Jack.

When I'm outside the ground, there were loads of lads there being thrown in back of police vans both Oldham and Bolton and a few ambulances which were also filling up, I spotted that big fucker I had booted he was on a stretcher just like the Bradford bully I sorted out a couple of months prior, he looked to be in his early twenties, a big blonde tache and long centre parted hair, I told him it was me who did him, but he was cabbaged he didn't even reply, just moaning and groaning, his face was horribly swelled up, a copper told me to get home or he would arrest me, so I nipped home which was only ten minutes away, had a quick swill got changed and headed back to Boundary Park to get back into the Chaddy.

I had to wait outside the ground for a few minutes before they opened the gates to let out people who wanted to leave early, this was called threequarter time, and there was always loads of people who came to see the last twenty minutes of the game for free, we called these the threequarter time mob, sometimes there could be a couple of hundred and there was this day for what was a big game, soon as the gates opened we all pile in and things were as when I had been lifted, still an even split. Bolton, despite all their big numbers, could not and did not take the Chaddy End that day despite chanting it every 2 minutes, to take an end you surely have to clear the end of home supporters or at least most of it, this day was 50/50, with both mobs taking as many hits and injuries as each othe.

It was an incredible day's battling, much blood was shed and the arrests figures were 65 with 135 ejections such was the level of violence, more and more police came in between us as the game neared the end, so much so that they had it boxed off by the end of the match, where Bolton headed left out of the ground and we headed right, although there were scuffles up Sheepfoot Lane with rival fans, our massive mob headed towards the town centre hoping Bolton would make their way their but very few did do, we picked a few off here and there at the bus stops and train station but the coppers won the day by keeping both mobs apart at the end of the game, I was absolutely shattered by 7pm, drained but it was one of THE most exciting and eventful days in my football hooligan career, I had exacted some kind of revenge for the terrible beating I had take the season before but once again had took many blows to my head face and body and I ached all over, and was in bed for 9pm.

This was a hard game this football violence but I loved it, thrived on it, I was still not 16 but had built up a good name and reputation and played up to it showing great courage and determination, the big hard Oldham lad's were now acknowledging me by my name.

Another fallen giant appeared in Division Two that season West Ham United - this great club who only a few seasons earlier had had the likes of Geoff Hurst, Martin Peters and England's greatest ever captain Bobby

Moore playing for them. By '76 though they had all gone, although Bobby Moore was playing at Fulham and it was a honour to watch him on Boundary Park and even more of a honour seeing him score a diving header, into our goals. The best own goal I've ever seen.

West Ham fans had already secured a big reputation with a big away following much like Chelsea, and it was no shock to see hundreds of them enter the Chaddy End just before kick off and try and take our end but we stood firm against this very organised and tough looking mob, most of them wearing donkey jackets and flat caps adding more menace to their fearful reputation, they had half of the Chaddy End, and there were a few mass charges but it was nowhere near as bad as Bolton Wanderers, there was not the level of hatred and it seemed West Ham were happy just to be in our end, they did look and sound impressive though especially when they sang their "Pretty Bubbles" anthem, there were only a handful arrests during the game but after the game it really kicked off, 500 West Ham fans had come by train and had to do the long walk back to Werneth train station, the road they took ran above a sports field Westwood running track and we all headed across there to head them off and they did not need much encouragement to break away from their police escort and they came charging down into us, it was an almighty clash as we had equal numbers and it was a good scrap and lasted ages or seemed to, the cops and their dogs eventually restoring order and making a few more arrests, we were well pleased with ourselves taking on such a hard firm as the Hammers, we did not claim victory but the fact we took them on was great credit to how far we had come in such a short time.

Funny enough our next game was another team in claret and blue, Burnley away, only twenty miles away and another team who had recently been relegated form Division One. Now the last time we played Burnley two and half years prior they had taken the Chaddy End in the FA Cup, and taken it in great style, the best ever taking of our end, so it was with trepidation we set off to Burnley, back in 1974 they had a massive mob, but they were tumbling down the leagues now and their gates were also tumbling, a load of us went up there on the bus via Rochdale an were in Burnley town centre by 11.30am, there were no Burnley lads about and even more and more Oldham fans began pouring into Burnley off buses and vans etc. By 1.30pm we had a big mob of 200 plus and walked unchallenged down to Turf Moor, only half a mile of so from the town centre, as we get near the ground we noticed a number of pubs and a lots of Burnley fans outside these pubs who were soon out throwing pots and ashtrays at us, we threw stuff back and there was a big stand off in the middle of the road as we swapped missiles, we didn't get close enough for close contact, at least we now knew Burnley still had a firm, and a tasty firm it seemed, the cops got a grip and escorted us towards Turf Moor and shoved us into this huge Paddock called the Longside. It was very similar to Man City's Kippax stand and like City this was Burnley's home end, the coppers separated us with a no mans land and it was very tense in there Burnley had massive numbers still and the atmosphere was red hot and their rendition of "No nae Never" as still as impressive as when we last heard them singing this when they took our Chaddy End January 1974, Oldham to be fair also had a great mob in there that day and Burnley must have been surprised, and we were game as fuck and quite a few Oldham got arrested breaking police lines and getting into Burnley's mob..

Burnley were very passionate and aggressive fans and they made many attempts to break the police lines to get into us, it was very tricky going to the cafe or bogs behind the stand because there was no segregation there and Burnley fans were following us into the bogs and attacking us at random, the coppers seemingly turning a blind eye to this, that game an Oldham fan got a dart stuck in his forehead thrown from Burnley fans, he was escorted around the pitch and this image was in all the Sunday newspapers, it looked horrific and could easily have taken his eye out but this was how violent it was back then, many missiles were thrown to and fro between both sets of fans and the st john's ambulances were very busy - this lad who got the dart in his head ended up being a Man City fan, I think he thought it was too dodgy supporting little Oldham.

After the match was very rough, there is a long narrow alleyway at the back of the Longside end and as we are walking away from the ground Burnley fans engulfed and ambushed us, and quite a lot of us got done it, we still had to get to the town centre to the bus station and that was also very dodgy and many of us got filled in although we still fought back but Burnley's much bigger numbers giving them the advantage, and we were glad to be back on the buses and back over the hills back to Rochdale, to change buses, and when we got to Rochdale bus station at about 6.30pm lo and behold a mob of around fifty Rochdale lads were waiting for us with their leader Moggy at the thick of things, there were running battles for half a hour or so but more and more buses began arriving back from Burnley and we soon had the upper hand and chased Rochdale and their cheeky little firm out of the bus station and through the town centre, this scenario happened every time we played Burnley away.

The dreaded Millwall came up to Boundary Park next, it was a really miserable day and they had a big mob in the away end, but at about twenty minutes after kick off a mob of around 100 of them came into the Chaddy End but we soon sussed them out and were right into them, it was a good scrap with lots of ejections/arrests, the cops let them stay at the bottom right hand corner of the Chaddy End, and insults and threats were being swapped. One half case Millwall fan was really giving it out, and he offered Shane Clegg out into the bogs behind the stand, Shane was game as fuck and followed the lad into the bogs and came out first wiping blood from his face but triumphant, the Millwall lad came out a bit later mashed in, nose and lips bleeding heavily and he was very groggy... yes! Get in Shane – Shane Clegg was one of the top lads in Oldham in the 1970's, he was a striking sight with his maroon long leather over coat, and the best Afro in town, not bad to say he was blonde and white, but he had naturally curly hair and it looked great, he was 5 years older than me and a pal of my older brother Pete so Shane knew me, he was also one of the Oldham Smoothies a crew of lads who hung about the town centre all trendy and all into Northern Soul being regulars at Wigan Casino, he was one of the best known lads in town.

At half-time this Millwall mob was escorted around the pitch to the away end to joining the rest of their supporter, they had tried in vain to take our end but as hard as they undoubtedly were there was no way 100 fans could take the Chaddy End but they had a good go and respects for that, outside would be a bit different because they had a big mob up that day.

After the match Millwall came charging down Sheepfoot Lane into our mob as we left the Chaddy End, they over ran us and even attacked the coppers, they were nuts, so many blokes in their 20's/30's and even 40's, these were not youths and boot boys but fully grown and angry men, they did us outside, a crew of around 30 of us peeled off and headed towards Werneth trains station hoping to pick some of them off, we were walking up Chadderton road when we spotted a transit van stuck in the traffic, it had a sign on the side of the van saying

South London on it, one of our lads wrenched open the back doors but they were ready and about 15 big mad fuckers came out all carrying hammers, shovels and pick axe staffs and came right into us, a few of us got hurt there, a few got cut up most scattered, these Millwall thugs were really violent, by the time the cops had come they were on their way, job done, we did not bother carrying on to the train station. We were out of our depth.

The FA Cup in 1976/77 gave us a kind draw in the 3rd round when we were drawn to play non-league Northwich Victoria away in January 1977, we were only allowed 1500 tickets as Northwich's ground only held 6000, the queues on the Monday night tickets went on sale were incredible and never mind 1500 there was at least 5000 all around the ground desperate for tickets, we soon sussed out we had no chance of getting tickets so we set off in a van to Northwich which was only 20 miles away in leafy Cheshire, the only problem was hundreds more Oldham fans sussed this out and it was like Wacky Races as we all headed down the motorway to Northwich, it was hilarious as we all gave each other the vees pipping our horns as we made the mad twenty mile dash, we were soon there and joined the snaking queues of Northwich and Oldham fans queuing for tickets, we got ours in fact over 2000 Oldham fans purchase tickets from Northwich and the police and the FA decided to take the tie to Maine Road, home of Manchester City FC. This was a dream come true, the chance to take over the magnificent Kippax stand, I just knew we would take at least ten thousand as it was there was over twenty thousand from Oldham at Maine Road that day in the 28,000 crowd with maybe 5/6 thousand Northwich fans and rest neutrals.

Manchester is that close many walked the 7 miles all downhill from Oldham, me and my crew were in Manchester around 10 30am, dossing about in the Arndale shopping centre before heading to Maine road at mid day, we expected City's lads to be out in force as they were playing away at Newcastle and not many of them would fancy that on a cold January winters day, as it was the weather was fine and sunny in Manchester, we did not have to wait long for trouble as we bumped into 20 City youths and set about them, they were soon aided by more City lads and we had to retreat but then a couple of van loads of Oldham thugs turned up and not just Oldham thugs but Abbeyhill's lads, the roughest toughest estate in Oldham! Talk about the cavalry arriving, hard lads like George Cragg, Tony Cragg, Col Norton, Derek Meggy, Spider, Egg head, Jacko, Clint, Black Alf, big Joe, Jimbo and so many more, most of these lads were in and out of Borstal and fearless and they piled right into these City lads who soon fled, more and more Oldham fans came every few minutes and soon there were thousands outside the Kippax on that huge car park waiting for the gates to open, it was so exciting, proper cup fever.

Oldham were allocated the large section of the Kippax and Northwich were given a quarter of it, and surprisingly they brought a big firm of lads aided by Man City fans who were not best pleased at the " Yonners " from Oldham taking over their beloved Kippax end, Northwich played in green and white like Celtic and many of us were desperate to get our hands on these scarves for our collection, although there was a large police presence there was loads of fighting in the Kippax for half a hour before the game and throughout the first half, with many ejections, at half time a crew of about 30 big City hooligans came in amongst us lashing out and trying to bully us, they soon went down and I got lifted as I was setting about one big ginger haired horrible looking fucker, with huge sideburns like Noddy Holder, he was wearing bleached denims cherry red docs and stank of cider and BO!

Two giant coppers grabbed me and then dragged me down those really big steep concretes steps at the back of the Kippax bouncing my head off the steel barriers on the way down and when I got to the bottom a big sgt whacked me over the head with them big long truncheons, they opened the gates and I was hoping I would just get thrown out but they shoved me into one of those big hooli vans, static police cells, it was a tiny cell and very claustrophobic, these cells were full of mainly Oldham fans, effin an jeffin and chanting 'Oldham'.

I was gutted because I could hear the Oldham fans singing and celebrating after scoring 3 goals to Northwich's one, near the end of the game my cell door opened when a copper asks "is there any room in this one?" the other copper said "yeah shove the fat cunt in here!" Fuck me there was hardly any room with just me in but when they shoved big Graham Hall in aswell who happened to be Oldham's largest fan and at least 24 stones and I honestly thought I was gonna suffocate to death! Graham was a legendary Oldham hooligan, a huge man, about 6 ft and 20 odd stones he had a baby face and blonde curls and did not look a like a hooligan but was very aggressive and many away fans felt his power and wrath for many years, big Graham s as everyone knew him was from Glodwick Oldham's hardest mob, he had a brother Harry smaller but somehow stockier he was as wide as he was tall and had a knock out punch and dropped so many away fans they were a formidable pair, best mates aswell as brothers, both game as fuck.

At about 6pm they released all those arrested some 30 odd, every five minutes or so we could not be together, handed over our charge sheets and told us to fuck off, which was okay apart from the gangs of Cool Cats hanging about on the car park, the Cool Cats were a very large gang of mixed raced lads who followed Man City, led by Donald Francis and his brother Mickey, they had a fearsome reputation around Manchester, rumoured to carry Stanley knives. I tried to avoid the gaze but a few of them started following me in this god forsaken hovel that is Moss Side, I set off running up and down back alleys, I was running out of breath and could hear them within yards with their taunts and threats, I saw a green wire mesh fence which was at the end of this back alley and led into a primary school, I made a mad desperate dash for this fence and clambered up it, these twats were grabbing my ankles to pull me back down for my kicking, I felt the sharp pain as something was stabbing the back of my legs, but fear can give you great strength and I somehow got away from their grips and over this fence landing heavily on the concrete play ground of this school yard, jarring my ankles.

I carried on running for my life, fortunately these City cunts did not carry on chasing me, after another five minutes I collapsed on some spare land, spewing my guts up totally exhausted, I lay there for about 10 minutes before composing myself and finding a bus stop that took me into Manchester City centre, I was reflecting on the nightmare I had just been through, when I got into Piccadilly gardens in Manchester to change buses, I noticed loads of Man United fans milling about. They had played QPR that day in the FA Cup, my scarves were already tucked under my jumper and I kept my head down and found the bus to take me back home, I foolishly went upstairs to the back seat, I say foolishly because at the next stop 6 Manchester United lads got on and came and sat next to me, asking me where I was from I told them Oldham thinking they would have no problem with that, how wrong could I be? They began spitting at me, slapping me about the head, throwing sneaky punches into my face, it was horrendous, these twats were from Failsworth which was on the border of Oldham and Manchester, I had 4 miles of this or I thought I did until a few bus stops later ten of my Oldham pals got on the bus and came upstairs, they recognised me, "hey Carl how yer doing pal". I could hear these Failsworth/Mancs crumbling, shitting themselves some even trying to apologise to me, but I had grob all over me and my face red from the slaps and punches, my mates soon sussed out what had been happening and set about these wankers.

It was poetic justice as they begged and pleaded for mercy, saying things like "we are all Oldhamers" in their false fucking Manc accents, they got battered every single one of them all ending up on the deck and yes I put the boot into them especially those who had give me most grief, they pleaded to be let off at Failsworth, we dragged them off in Oldham town centre when we got off and gave them a few more slaps, half of them were crying and they were not kids but youths 16 -20, we had mates from Failsworth who were Oldham, fans there was a good crew led by one of Oldham's top lads Kenny Jones from Failsworth and one of these lads kept saying he knew Kenny blah blah blah, but they got their justified kicking.. There had always been bad blood with Failsworth and Oldham due to many of them claiming to be Mancs and speaking in fake Manc accents.

Another long long hard day but what a day, I was very lucky that I only received a caution through the post, a lot of lads got heavy fines, I was a week off my 16th birthday.

If we thought that was a dream FA Cup draw the next round would take us to the best team in the land and soon to be the best team in Europe, the mighty Liverpool FC at Anfield, this brilliant team with its fantastic and friendly fans, the most welcoming fans in the country we were to take ten thousand fans the 40 miles to Merseyside for what for most of us was the biggest game of our lives so far, the whole town was buzzing and everyone was looking forward to going, whole families were making the trip, of course no one gave us a hope but that did not matter the day out at this fantastic ground was what we was all excited about - we were about to be brought crashing down to earth.

It was a bright crisp winter morning but more like spring that February 1977, I could not sleep the night before as we were going to Anfield home of the champions and the best team in the country and Europe, this was a dream for most football fans, I was going as fan not a hooligan it did not enter my head there would be any trouble, Oldham offered no threat to the Kop and I was not aware of any attempts on it, this was just going to be a great day out supporting my home town team and I was going to cheer my team on despite not having any feasible chance.

I boarded one of over 100 coaches that made the short trip down the East Lancs road that that at mid day, we were one of the first coaches to leave Boundary Park and we arrived in Liverpool within the hour and parked up on a long road at the bottom of the huge Stanley Park which separated Anfield from Everton's Goodison's ground, as we get off the coach we spotted a few young Scouse kids, scruffy snotty nosed little urchins, they were really cheeky saying things like " hey yer fuckin woolyback, yer gonna get yer fuckin heads kicked in lah" (woolyback was what Scousers called all non Scousers from Lancashire), we just laughed them off although I wanted to clip the cheeky little cunts, as we walked through the park up the big hill these little rats were following us still taunting us, we told them to fuck off home and have a wash, but they were relentless and fearless getting in amongst us demanding money etc, they were really getting on my tits but they were only about 12/13.

As we are walking into this entry at the top of the park with Anfield in sight a load of Scousers came piling into us, they had us surrounded and we had to run the gauntlet taking kicks and punches as we headed towards the ground these little rats jumping on our backs aswell swinging from our necks, spitting in our faces, fortunately a big copper appeared with a huge stick and started whacking the Scousers, he was a big man with a big black beard that made him look like a pirate, and these Scousers shit themselves, he knew a few by name and told them he would deal with them later, they melted and fucked off, the cop then told us to get inside the ground into the Anfield road end facing the Kop, which we did.

Once inside the magnificent stadium we relaxed and admired the surroundings, we were the first Oldham fans in but over the next hour and half thousands more poured into Anfield, many bleeding and bruised regaling horror stories about the walk through Stanley Park, not only had many been assaulted beaten up and battered but loads had been mugged, had money taken off them, watches scarves and even clothes! Yes fucking clothes, a mate of mine had his trainers taken from him and was in his stocking feet! He wasn't the only one... there were even rumours of women and children getting battered and mugged also.

By 2.30pm Anfield was full as was most of the ground the Kop looking as magnificent as ever especially when the sang. " You'll never walk alone". It was an incredible atmosphere and the 10,000 Oldham fans in three sides of the ground madethemselves heard, just before kick off fights were breaking out all around us, hundreds of Scouse thugs had infiltrated the away end/Anfield road end and were just lashing out at anyone, we fought back mainly out of fear because they were coming from every angle even from under our legs jumping up like Viet Cong, a few Oldham fans climbed onto the pitch to get away, I saw total fear in people's eyes, they felt trapped, the crowd was that big it was very difficult to move anywhere, I just butted any Scouse cunt within range.

The cops with the big sticks came wading in and soon began to sort things out and these Scouse Rats just seem to disappear into thin air, many Oldham fans were bleeding and the St John's crew were busy as fuck and a couple came up the terraces with a stretchers over their head. Two minutes later this stretcher comes by as everyone parts to let it through and it's none other than Happy Harry Randall, his face caved in, his national health glasses smashed to smithereens, he was semi conscious, his loyal band of followers from Sholver chanting "Happy Harry Happy Happy Harry" he gave a feeble wave with a clenched fist, ha the mad bastard would have gone down fighting for sure he actually got a standing ovation from not only the Oldham fans but Liverpool fans in the main stand unless they were taking the piss..

Throughout the game Oldham fans were getting assaulted and mugged still whenever they went to the toilets, these Scouse cunts just hung about the bogs picking people off, we were so disorganised and couldn't mob up, such was the density of the crowd, on the pitch it was a great game and we did ourselves proud before going down 3-1, the magnificent Kop giving us a rousing round of applause at the end of the match - very touching, these were the genuine loving welcoming fans we were told about. At the end of the game we were not looking forward to the long walk through Stanley Park to the coaches, as we are leaving the ground gangs of Scousers were stood on the pavement making throat slitting motions laughing at our trepidation, I just wished I could have got fifty or so lads together and get stuck into them but we were all over the show, I will be honest, after the match I walked through the park and got away with just a few clips and kicks up the arse and got on our coach pretty intact if not fucking angry, but many came soldiering back on like wounded animals, many bloody noses thick lips, many without the wrangler and levi jackets they came with, many minus their scarves and bob hats many shaking, all saying the Scousers are the biggest set of cunts in Great Britain, horrific tales of lads being told to get down on their knees to beg mercy whilst the Scousers laughed at them and then kicked fuck out of them, as soon as our coach was full we were away and glad to get away from this fucking hell hole and even on the way out of Liverpool our coach and I'm sure all the coaches were pelted with missiles.

My older brother Pete and 12 of his mates went to Anfield that day on a mini bus from their local pub the Old White Hart, half of them still dressing up like Boot Boys in their half mast skinners and cherry red docs, they stood out like sore thumbs in trendy Liverpool who hadn't seen Boot Boys since 1973! They also got ambushed in Stanley Park with one Jimmy Yaw taking a full house brick over the head, he missed the game and was in hospital, one of the lads Sean Gagan an Irish lad and one of the most violent lads in Oldham back then picked the brick up and whacked a Scouser with it, but he scuttled away, Jimmy was kept in hospital overnight, but was surprised when at 8pm he received a visit off the very same Scouser who had bricked him! He apologised which Jimmy being the man he was accepted, ironically Jimmy and his brother were big Man United fans and Jimmy often wonders if the Scouse bastard would have been so apologetic knowing that?

In March 77 I made three trips to Burnden Park, I was becoming obsessive in my hatred towards Bolton Wanderers, the first game was when Oldham played there and we made the very foolish decision to actually go into their Lever End, their so called fortress, two coach loads of us arrived at Bolton at 2 o' clock all lads and we made our way to the feared Lever End in a do or die mission, surprisingly when we got in there was very little opposition, maybe around fifty young Bolton lads whom we soon chased off, we took the Lever End very briefly for about 5 minutes and chanted " We took the Lever End" just like they always chanted "We took the Chaddy End" but we were soon getting escorted around the pitch towards the away end the Railway Embankment, but we had made our mark and it was on tele the Big match on Sunday afternoon showing us being escorted out of the Lever End and around the pitch, so it cannot be denied, but the truth was the vast majority of Bolton lads went into the Embankment to confront us not thinking for one minute we would have the bottle to go into their beloved Lever End, we were to pay for this act or bravado.

As we are getting closer to the Embankment we could see Oldham fans getting absolutely twatted by huge numbers of Bolton thugs who outnumbered them ten to one at least, theywere also surging down the steep terracing to welcome us cheeky fuckers chanting "you're gonna get your fucking heads kicked in!" We just knew we were about to, within seconds of been thrown into the lions den by the Bolton cops were swamped and attacked, I didn't mind this, I loved a good brawl and a few of us fought in vain and took the beating, Bolton surrounded us for the rest of the first half, at half time fifteen of us made our way to the bogs and got into a scrap outside the bogs the cops broke it up then took us fifteen and shoved us into main stand paddock alongside the embankment end, well it wasn't long before we were getting attacked in there by normal fans, middle aged blokes, we got right into them cunts, the cops then dragging us out walking us down the pitch and up the halfway tunnel, this was also seen on tele, more glory ha..we were just lobbed out..

Once outside we made our way to the coach park to await the end of the match there was still half a hour to go, we were just dossing about when three blokes in their twenties came towards us, gobbing off calling us Oldham wankers, big mistake, amongst our little crew that day were the Hall brothers Big Graham all twenty odd stones of him and his brother Harry the stockiest lad whoever walked gods earth, big Kenny Davies, a tall well made Manc lad who followed Oldham, hard as fuck and game as fuck, he ended up being one of Oldham's top doormen in the 80's. George Cragg a big heavy hitting lad from Abbeyhills, Oldham's roughest estate with a few of his pals, a few Shaw Gawbies one of the biggest and best mobs in Oldham me and a couple of my pals, it was a hard little crew and certainly not going to take shit of these three pissed up bully boys, we could not believe our luck, as they walked right amongst us trying to intimidate us, bang Harry Hall knocks the first one out, bang Kenny Davies knocks out number two, the third one realises the situation and tries to run but is tripped up and booted all over the car park and Big Graham jumps all over him all twenty odd stones of him, he must have smashed his body to fuck, from nowhere the cops arrived and arrested a big blonde lad called Wisey from Shaw they caught him attacking one of them, Wisey got done for that and sent down for 6 months, at the end of the game we clashed with more Bolton fans under the Railway bridge were they always ambushed away fans, before getting overwhelmed by their big mob.

Two weeks later I am back at Burnden Park for the visit of Chelsea who by 1977 were THE top mob in the country taking most ends they went in, they had such big numbers and so many mobs from all over the country very much like Man United earlier in the 1970's, only where United were great wreckers of towns rampaging and taking over whole town centres with their massive numbers, Chelsea seemed more interested in taking ends and the fighting. Chelsea in the 76/77 season either took or got into ends like Wolves, Cardiff, Blackpool, Burnley, Oldham, Spurs, Birmingham, Notts Forest, Preston - the six of us from Oldham were looking forward to them taking over Bolton's Lever End, with me that day were John Lund, Nicky Dixon, Tony Blood, Phil Harper and John Hart, we were all 16 apart from Tony who was 17, we arrived in Bolton off the 400 bus at mid day and just dossed about the cafes in the market hall, we were not wearing scarves so were not sussed out by the groups of Bolton lads milling about. At 2pm we walked the mile or so down to Burnden Park and Chelsea were everywhere and we all bought Chelsea scarves off a vendor on the Manchester road, id never seen so many lads, thousands of them.

There were not many Bolton about on the sunny day even the pubs near the ground had been taken over by Chelsea, we paid into the Railway Embankment end were the thousands of Chelsea fans were, the Lever End was also full with Bolton fans making a great noise, it was a great atmosphere, we were stood behind the goals and next to us was this black man with one arm and his one arm was the biggest arm I had ever seen, he was wearing a cap sleeved tee shirt, his bald head shiny as a pool ball, he looked such a mean hombre, he had a big crew with him and they called him Babs. He fascinated me, he was telling anyone who would listen, "just after kick off - it's gonna kick off in their end then we all go across the pitch, you got it?" everyone agreeing like nodding dogs, including us six Oldhamer's, fuck me I was excited, I hoped they did invade the pitch and take the Lever End, this was a dream come true for me, then the whistle blows for the kick off, and Babs and his crew make their way to the perimeter , and we all follow, I glanced over to the Lever End and right on cue it kicks off, hundreds of Chelsea fans surge across the terraces and a mass brawl breaks out. Babs is on the pitch urging the Chelsea fans to join him, and they did hundreds of them including us and across the pitch we went and into the Lever End, Bolton to be fair fought like fuck but Chelsea's numbers and aggression was too much even for these hard bastards and Chelsea took the Lever End, it was an incredible manoeuvre, very well organised and it was one of my top moments as football hooligan albeit with another team.

There were sporadic fights throughout the game in the Lever End but by the end of the match Chelsea had the whole end, and after the match they rampaged outside, fighting the cops and smashing shops etc, we found a few of the Werneth lads from Oldham who had came over in a van, half of them followed Chelsea and they gave us a lift back in their tranny van, we were all buzzing at the ultimate show of football hooliganism, I would love Oldham to have been as good as this mob but then again no other mob in the country were anywhere as good as Chelsea back then.

A couple of weeks later I was back at Burnden park for the visit of Notts Forest whom had always came into our Chaddy End the three times we had played them, Forest were a tough mob and I assumed they would attempt to take the Bolton end, I went with Phil Harper and once again we arrived in Bolton via the 400 bus and was there for 1pm, we walked to the ground but there were not many Forest about certainly not as many as Chelsea, but there lots and lots of Bolton lads about. and they were angry looking bastards obviously upset at being humiliated by Chelsea, it was very dodgy for me and Phil even though we were not wearing scarves they viewed us with suspicion and don't forget I had made many personal enemies with Bolton over the past few seasons, we wisely decided to go into the away end and in here it soon filled up with Forest fans who brought a very good following but not enough to take over Bolton, in fact quite a few Bolton lads came in and a few scraps broke out.

At the end of the game all the Forest fans went towards their coaches on the big car park, me and Phil walked onto Manchester road were all the Bolton fans poured out of the Lever End, there were hundreds of them making their way under the big Railway bridge to get to the Forest fans, it was at that moment I did something that I can never explain a pure moment of madness, stupidity craziness whatever, I climbed half way up this bridge that overlooked the hundreds of Bolton fans some twenty feet below me, I then began lobbing rocks down onto them, and as they looked up I shouted at them "Fuck off you Bolton wankers, I am from Oldham!" My pal Phil set off running up the side of the bridge and I followed him, as almost every Bolton fan followed and chased us, over the railway lines, now Phil was okay he was the Oldham schools 400 meters champion and was well ahead of me, I was struggling a bit and could hear them getting closer, I looked over my shoulders to see the biggest mob of lads chasing one lad I have ever known and that one lad was me, big gob me from Oldham, I rolled down this grassy verge when I heard Phil whisper, "Carl, get in here quick!" It was an old disused shed and we threw a load of tarpaulin over us, we were trying to stifle our nervous giggles, Phil as not happy with me and who could blame him, we stayed there for at least half a hour.

We eventually crawled out and thankfully no one as about, and we made or way away from the town centre were we knew loads would still be milling about, we walked about a mile or so then saw a bus going to Bury, we got on it and sat at the back downstairs, we both sighed heavily and began relaxing a bit. Fuck me three stops later half a dozen Bolton fans get on and right away clocked us, and made their way towards us, we pulled the emergency exit open and climbed out of the window and set off, but these fuckers gave chase, Phil was off like a hare again with me in pursuit, they concentrated on me as me and Phil went different ways, they were catching me up and I vaulted a garden fence and actually ran right through someone's house, they were having their tea, I did apologise, I ended up on this posh estate and finally shrugged my pursuers off. I walked a couple of miles before getting on another bus to Bury, this time it was peaceful, when I got to Bury bus station Phil was there shaking his head. We burst out laughing and got the next bus to Rochdale and then the bus back home to Oldham, I asked Phil if he fancied Bolton v Millwall, he told me to "fuck off!"

The last game of the 76/77 season was Luton Town at home, we did not expect much from them, they had no reputation as such, but was very surprised and pleased when at 1.30pm a mob of 200 of them turned up outside the ground and not only that almost everyone of them was a Skinhead! I had been a fully fledged Skin for a good few months now I had been reading all the music press *NME*, *Sounds* and *Record Mirror* about the Skinhead revival down in London to counteract the outbreak of Punk Rock. The Punks were seen as middle class posers playing at it whereas the Skins were traditionalists and very smartly turned out, this appealed to me. I had read the Skinhead bible "Skinhead" by Richard Allen a few years previously and it really influenced me and many others no doubts. So I was buzzing when I read about this revival, and loved the pics – I always loved the music of the original era reggae ska and Motown and there was an upsurge of this aswell on the horizon, unfortunately there were not many Skinheads in Oldham in 1977. Maybe ten of us, me, Loyd Scan one of my best pals a half caste lad, Ste and Mick Yearn, Pete Jackson, Tom Brown, Ste Walsh, Gary Smith, Ste Badby, a Skin bird called Tank who had been an original Skin in 1969 and another original Skin called Rob who stayed a Skin throughout even though like Tank was in his early twenties in '77 and a local girl called Sue who wore the crombie and monkey boots.

We all looked the part in our Crombies, Ben Shermans, Harringtons Stay Prest trousers and more of us wore brogues and loafers rather than docs, we were more into looking smart rather than the cruder looking bovver boy look. We had no pubs though and many would not even serve us, and the only acts I saw was Desmond Decker at the notorious Tower Club a disused church on the edge of Oldham town centre, the ultimate dive run by a 6 ft 6 inch black gangster called Big John, big bad John... I also saw Sham 69 at Manchester Uni but they were crap and not even Skins!

So when I saw all the Skins from Luton in May 1977 I was buzzing, and so many fit skin birds, but they did not want to know me and we were soon battling with each other outside the ground, about 50 of them actually came into the Chaddy End but soon got fucked off to the away end, but they did bring a big following it looked very impressive. At 3/4 time the Chaddy End emptied as we headed to the away end to take on Luton's impressive mob of skinheads, they may have looked the part but as we piled into them down the terraces very few fought back and many clambered onto the pitch to get away. I was disappointed in them, and as it was the last game of the season was looking forward to a good scrap once I knew they had a big firm. We did however have it on the car park with our own cops a long running battle with us bricking them all the dust on this hot dry day kicking up adding effect, the Luton skins all watched us as we fought the police and even cheered as one four lads boots one off his motorbike and the bike was skidding around sending sparks into the air, eventually the cops got the upper hand with their dogs and a few got lifted.

This ended the most violent football season I have ever known, I needed the three month break, my hands were fucked and brittle from the amount of heads I had punched, I had bruises and cuts from day one at Bradford August 1976 that never recovered as every week or two I was fighting again and taking more and more blows, but I was addicted to violence and took to the streets fighting in the summer of 1977 there were many more enemies locally to fight; rockers, teddy boys, punks, blacks, pakis, piss heads, bully boys and bouncers......plus fighting over birds!

Apart from my craving for violence I did in my defence target the bullies or make it so I would be picked on, mainly because of my skinhead appearance, people did not appreciate this image apart from the ex-skins who would tell us that they dressed like that once and it was the best days of their lives, but in general people wanted to have a go at any skinheads, I think we all got some stick but me and Loyd in particular sought confrontation as did me and Paul my best pal from childhood, Loyd Scan was my age, an excellent footballer and athlete, he was naturally fit and strong and game as they come, he was target number one for any rival hooligans cos he was black, well half caste and though we had a few black and half caste lads Loyd was always at the front alongside me - "get the nigger!" they would shout and point him out. Loyd would laugh at them and welcome them to try, he punched many to the ground, for a couple of years we were inseparable, and for a while he even dressed as a skinhead and looked the bizzo in his Crombie, when we were 16/17 we would venture into the town centre on Friday and Saturday nights in the hope we would get picked on which was more than likely given that we were skins and the fact Loyd was black, these were very racist times and a lot of the beer swilling piss pots in their twenties and thirties would abuse Loyd, this suited him and his aggressive ways, whilst most of our pals were bothered about under aged drinking me and Loyd do not drink, we were fighters, street fighters and football hooligans.

Many times that summer we would go up into the nearby town centre hoping but knowing someone would have a pop at us, we thrived on it - it was ideal if it was some twenty odd year old Man United fan, challenging us for wearing Oldham colours in our home fucking town! We would entice them down a back alley then set about them, we never lost a battle, one night two older lads we knew were giving us some grief. Paul Heap a Northmoor lad 5 years older than us and right hooligan but one whom always seem to get a second prize, he was always being battered and thrown out, he was like a poor man's Happy Harry, loads of bottle but as much use as a chocolate fireguard, well this night up town he was with a right big hard bloke called Big Al, an ex Army lad 6ft tall heavily built but in a powerful way, he ended up being a bouncer for years on the clubs doors, him and Heapy were calling me and Loyd wankers, so we offered them out two on two behind the Mess House pub, we knew Heapy would be no problem but big Al would be, Loyd picked up a broken branch, we then piled into them, as we knew Heapy went down right away in a foetus position, we set about big Al with Loyd whacking him about the head and body with the branch I was punching and kicking for all my worth, we all fell down in a ball on the deck, and rolled about, he was a tough fucker and gave me an Loyd some good punches but he ran out of steam and gave up, we let him up and go, Heapy had fucked off leaving his pal. I've no doubts big Al would have sorted Heapy out for that when he caught up with him, Heapy ended up being a good pal of ours over the next few years, he just thought we were still kids, he learnt his lesson.

Sadly both these well known Oldham lads passed away well before their time, Paul Heap died a lonely man in a hostel for Alcoholics down Manchester in 2002 aged just 45 and Big Al died in a hit and run in 2006 aged just 50, this big very much respected good man mown down by a coward who sped off. Ironically an hour before big Al was killed he had called into the wake/funeral of Loyd's dad Victor at Shaw Road Con Club to pay his respects. RIP Heapy and Big Al.

My other partner in crime was Paul Sykes my boyhood pal, who wasn't naturally tough but loved a scrap, we were often searching out and putting ourselves up for the piss pots, men in their twenties, we'd bump into them then apologise offer our hands then when they brushed us aside and told us to fuck off they would get it, we did however come unstuck one night or Paul did. We were walking through the centre at about 2 am, and two big blokes were coming towards us they looked pissed and were singing, Paul bumped into the biggest one who had a pock marked face and looked hard and he was hard, he nutted Paul and dropped him, I swung for him and he bent my arm up my back so I could not move, eventually letting me off with a warning, telling me and Paul who had by now got up all groggy with his nose bust to get ourselves home and stop picking fights! Thankfully his pal seemed okay and just said "listen lads you were lucky this is Jeff Munford" a well known hard man from Oldham several years older than us, we moved on rapidly.

Another time me and Paul were walking along Union Street in the town centre at about 10 30pm one Saturday night, we heard this lad whistle at us, he was up a back alley having a piss, we looked towards him and he beckoned me forward, he said "hey skinhead come here I want a word with you?" Paul said "go Carl, we'll do the cunt," so I walked up towards him and he zipped up and grabbed my arm, and said listen I want you, let's walk to Oldham edge ( a local beauty spot about half a mile walk away ). I froze, my initial reaction was to nut him, he was a big strong fucker a few years older than me, dressed in Levi's jacket and jeans with big boots on, he had thick long blonde curly shoulder length hair and looked more like a heavy rocker, I said to him "let me just have a quick word with my pal," he said ok, I told Paul, "he's a bender and he wants me to go up to Oldham edge with him" Paul said "tell him you will, I will walk behind and then up there we will jump the cunt!" I told the puff I will come but my mate is gonna follow us up, he actually agreed to that, I felt better, I knew Paul would not let me down and this puff was gonna get hammered.

The 15 minute walk through a very busy Oldham town centre was horrendous for me, this big puff was holding my hand with a big silly smirk on his face but not as big as my so called pal Paul walking ten yards behind us creased up laughing his tits off, I was so glad to get through the centre and heading towards the dark moors of Oldham edge, this puffs grip on me tightened as we got nearer the barren fields lit up only by the moon, I beckoned Paul with my free hand to come on get stuck in! But by now he's doubled over crying with laughter, all this going over the puffs head who was focused and by now breathing heavily, what a fucking nightmare! All of a sudden the big puff kicks my legs and spins me round the forces me to the ground, then lies on top of me wrenching my brand new yellow and blue adidas tee shirt to shreds, then licking my chest, telling me he fucking loves me! "Come on Paul for fucks sake hit the cunt!" I screamed but by now Paul is convulsed.

I begged him to attack this cunt, the puff meanwhile is in a frenzy licking me up and down my belly and chest, I could not get him off me, he was that big and strong, I was being fucking raped! Paul ran off but came back within seconds and handed me an old antique two pronged fork with a wooden handle, well I slammed this into the puffs head several times, he's now screaming that he loves it! "I fucking love it!" he 's bellowing out as the blood pisses out of his napper, he's still on top of me forcing me down as I thrashed about, I was losing my strength and he was grinning like a Cheshire cat when all of a sudden I heard a heavy thud as Paul wrapped a scaffold tube around his head and then his back, this took the wind out of him and I was able to free myself,

Paul ran one way I ran the other and all we could hear was this big mad bender screaming "I fucking love it!" me and Paul met up a hour later at his mams, both covered in blood, the puff's blood! We told his mam about it who cried with laughter also, as she made us a brew and butty, I've had a few nightmares about this scenario since.

That summer of 77 was a big one in my life apart from all the aggro there was loads of birds night clubs disco music was peaking. Punk Rock exploded, the Queens Jubilee, me and Paul robbed the biggest Union Jack in town off a local mill roof tower, it was 30 ft x 20 ft. We risked life n limb for it and it was that heavy we had to roll it off the mill roof were it crashed to the floor some 60 feet below then get 4 more pals to help carry it to my house nearby, it was a great summer great weather not as hot as '76 but still sunny for most of it, there were lots of parties throughout town, we had a few days out in Blackpool and Southport, life was good, I had more or less moved into my pal Hoof's flat on Clarkwell estate and we hardly slept a wink playing tunes til we dropped off in the early hours, I had several jobs in the first 12 months since leaving school, jobs were aplenty and there was no need to take any shit which I did not and just walked out of so many jobs and was back in work within a day or two.

The last week of June was the week when the football fixtures came out, same day every year, the last Thursday in June, I eagerly awaited the *Oldham Chronicle* to come out and was absolutely thrilled to see our first game of the season, Blackpool away - the ultimate first day fixture for almost every club in the country. But so much so for Oldham we would take thousands, only a hour away and we had already built up a big rivalry with the Seasiders over these last few seasons, everyone was on about it, everyone saying they were going for the weekend, everyone saying we are gonna take the Spion Kop this time, we had always gone in but always came unstuck, Blackpool were very tough at home...

Pre season friendlies saw us away at York which was another great fixture for Oldham fans even though it was over 60 miles away we always took loads and always took over their lovely little city centre and Bootham Cresent, and even though this was a friendly we still took loads up and took over again, many of us going by train in fact several trains from Manchester to York arrived with Oldham hooligans on board, there was very little action from York fans, and I was lucky not to get arrested as I had invaded the pitch before kick off with cops in pursuit, but I leapt into the paddock and Oldham fans in there hid me, I swapped shirts with some kid and got away, daft bastard I was.. There was as usual some Leeds fans there, game fuckers who came I amongst us but paid the price, why do fans of big clubs think they can bully fans of smaller clubs ? very disrespectful, after the match a couple of hundred of us rampaged through York en route to the train station, my good pal Dozy Dunc Butterworth got arrested as did quite a few, Dunc got charged and released in time to catch the service train back to Manchester with us, it left York at 6.30pm.

As the train left Leeds station  few lads began throwing seats out of the train doors onto the tracks, and then started smashing the train up, running through carriages and just causing mayhem I didn't get involved in that I was not a vandal but I did pull the emergency cord just as we were pulling into Huddersfield train station, for I knew the cops would be waiting for us and would just arrest lads at will because of all the damage, the rain screeched to a halt, and around fifty of us jumped off the train and fled the chasing cops with their dogs, they chased us for ages and we ended up in the moors on a country lane, a few lads hailed taxis but there was still about twenty of us who decided to march home over the hills, Oldham was 18 miles away, so we worked out we would be home about 1 am in the morning, as it was we got back in Oldham at gone 2am absolutely shattered but proud that we had walked so far, we had a right laugh, telling jokes singing songs, it was a lovely summers night very clear, there were some great views..

One week later was our first game of the season at Blackpool, loads went for the weekend, me and Ste Badby went on the Friday night on the train arriving in Blackpool at 9pm, we got in a shitty bed n brecky near the prom, and then went for a mooch down to the pleasure beach, Blackpool was very busy, this was the height of the season, loads of gangs of birds and lads come to that, Me and Badby had all the Skinhead gear including pork pie hats, ha we thought we looked so cool, there was quite a few Skins in Blackpool but loads of punks aswell, at around midnight me and Badby are having a burger facing Central Pier when we heard a commotion in the subway below us, being nosy bastards we went down to see what was going on, and was shocked to see big Graham Hall his brother Harry and big John Manning scrapping with half a dozen Mancs, who were chanting "United aggro" Graham, Harry and big John were knocking fuck out of them, they were three of the biggest lads in Oldham, these skinny gobby Mancs were were getting knocked down every time they charged in and me and Badby set about them aswell and within a minute they were all crawling about the floor moaning and groaning, they had picked on the wrong lads, Big Graham told me they kept asking them were they were from, he said we tried ignoring them but they followed us into the subway so we battered the cheeky cunts!

Me and Badby went back to our digs but were up for breakfast at 9am and looking forward to the days events, after brecky we went on the prom for a mooch and saw loads of Oldham fans who had come Friday night, by mid day there were hundreds of Oldham fans on the prom many heading for the Foxhall Tavern which was near the ground but still on the promenade, it was a really busy lively pub with bouncers on, by 1pm it was packed out with Oldham fans and a few holiday makers, it was great in here, all the main lads seem to be in here, we were all singing our heads off stood on tables and chairs, the bouncers couldn't do anything about it, it was boiling in there so I went outside for some fresh air, there were some young Oldham kids outside, far too young to get in the pub maybe 12/13, they were chanting Oldham songs being all giddy and excitable when these three big Barnsley thugs aged early 20's set about them, well big Colin Shaw who was not a hooligan but very tough, he was one of the heavy Rockers who followed Oldham every game home and away, Col walked over and knocked the biggest one out, clean out big thud he hit the deck, his two mates ran off leaving him writhing about the floor, a few of us wanted to fill him in once he came round, but Colin let him get away and go and find his shithouse mates who ran off on him, the Yorkshire bully boy looked very groggy, mumbling apologies etc.

At 2.30pm we vacated the Foxhall and marched to Bloomfield Road which was only a few hundred yards away, we had a big mob and it was getting bigger as we neared the ground as more and more Oldham fans tagged onto us, Blackpool were waiting on the car park outside the ground and we charged into each other, but the Blackpool cops are very good and very tough and came wading in, they are used to brawls in Britain's busiest seaside resort so these football hooligans were no problems to them, amazingly they allowed us into the Spion Kop again, where there was bound to be even more trouble, maybe their philosophy was keep the hooligans in one end so they could administer some kind of control, well it suited lads like me who thrived on the confrontation, the chanting and intense rivalry, this was our biggest following to Blackpool and even half an hour after kick off Oldham fans were arriving many of them pissed up, we didn't take the Kop despite many attempts, but we could not break the huge and disciplined police lines separating both sets of fans, but we had as many as Blackpool and the atmosphere was truly electric, it was a fantastic end this Spion Kop, the acoustics were brilliant and the noise created by both sets of fans was incredible.

There the usual scuffles in the bogs and at half time but all in all the cops seemed to have control, but outside after the match would be tasty and the chanting by both sets of fans singing " we'l see you all outside " fired us all up for what we knew was gonna be a massive brawl, and so it proved, as the final whistle went we all pile down the big steep concrete steps at the back of the Kop onto the massive car park, and now the cops struggled with such numbers of youths and young men trying to get into each other, missiles flew overhead, many were cut loads of hand to hand brawls, people rolling about punching and kicking for all there worth, it was relentless until the cops and their dogs did finally managed to separate both mobs, a mob of fifty of us decided to break away from the main mob and head back to the Foxhall, this proved a mistake as a much bigger mob of Blackpool sussed us out and followed us, and when the bouncers would not allow us in the Foxhall the Blackpool mob pounced on us, and we assumed there was many more than there actually was and fled down the prom, I had on me a full can of coke which I had in my pocket, and it came in handy as the Blackpool fan got me in a bear hug, I slammed the coke can into the bridge of his nose which open up and blood spurted everywhere. He soon let go of me, we were getting overwhelmed with many of us splitting up, I was alongside a big lad called Al Campbell, a tough lad from Ashton Under Lyne, Al was a few years older than me an original Skinhead who still wore his docs every game, and he was game as fuck, me and Al clambered onto the balcony of one of those big fancy hotels on the Prom with about ten Blackpool lads in pursuit, there were some people having their tea there and we had to take their plates off them to smash into their heads and also launch cups n saucers at them, it bought us a bit of time to get away through the hotel, we then had to negoiate a way back to the train station which was very dodgy as there was loads of Blackpool lads milling about but we got back in one piece and were pleased to see hundreds of Oldham lads there, Blackpool came onto the station but we ran them back out catching a few and kicking them in, we then filled the train back home, loads got lifted that day including Dozy Dunc, twice on the trot.

Three days later Bury away on a Tuesday night in the League cup, same old script we took over them as per took the piss and clobbered any Bury Reds who turned up to fight foe their town, the only highlight of this game was Dozy Dunc getting arrested for the third game on the trot, resulting in him getting 3 months Detention Centre and there ended Duncan Butterworths hooligan career aged 18. when he came out he chose the life of a hippy and we are all Mods/Skins so we saw very little of Dunc and he became a world traveller especially India to fulfil his Hippy dreams, the odd time we saw him his hair was down to his waist, he told us he found peace at last ha ha..what a beauty he was.

It was in 1977 that a small group of us from various districts of Oldham began to knock about together especially at the match, me, Loyd Scan, Paul Sykes, Eddy Benedek, Dennis Wright and Dave Clarkson, Loyd and Paul were from Northmoor like me and went to Grange with me, Loyd was game as fuck and fit and strong and revelled in the hand to hand fighting, he had boxing skills and streetwise skills, Paul was always my right hand man and game and loyal, we had been side by side since we were snotty nosed 8 year old kids, Eddy Benedek came off the tough Limeside council estate, Eddy was very stocky and possessed the biggest punch I had ever seen, he knocked absolutely loads out at the footy, breaking many jaws cheekbones noses and smashing teeth along the way, not a brawler but a one punch man, which to be fair was a great weapon and he very rarely got hurt unlike those of who loved a brawl and maul, Dennis Wright came off another rough estate at the opposite end of town Holts estate which was a big Man United supporting area because of its large Irish Catholic community.

Dennis was a Proddy a proud protestant who had been to Oldham's prestigious Church of England school Bluecoat, he spoke well and dressed well with good manners and easy way about him, but he loved a scrap and loved the footy violence and was also game, Dave Clarkson came from Royton and hung about us for a while, he was built very much like Eddy very stocky and loved a ruck but he got done too many times and ended up sent down like Dozy Dunc then slowed down after that, we didn't drink like most of the lads apart from Dennis, and we peeled off from the main mob in search of little gangs like ourselves, we'd be at it from morning til evening searching out what we considered our rivals " top boys" over the next few seasons we battered loads of away lads and always one's who deserved it, we were not into rampaging through towns although we got caught up in that kind of things many times, but we targeted "main lads " especially lads older and harder looking than us, we loved the challenge, we saw ourselves as a bit of an elitist little crew and were proud of ourselves.By '77 Oldham has a hooligan firm had many mobs and some great lads coming through making a name for themselves, lads like Ian McGrath, a small but stocky lad with no front teeth but fearless and would not take any shit from away fans, not scared to take a beating and had a good set of lads with him..

# 1977

THE '77/78 SEASON PROVED another very lively one as we progressed as a very tough firm at home and even taking big mobs away to grounds we once feared, an early game that season was Tottenham Hotspur, the mighty Spurs one of the countries great football clubs, like Chelsea and West Ham they had been relegated but their massive fan base did not diminish and Spurs also had a top reputation to uphold and it was no surprise when a couple of hundred them came into the Chaddy End and stayed there the whole game despite being attacked every few minutes from the much larger Oldham mob, the Spurs fans were trendy bastards with their blown wave hair, gold chains and pringle golf jumpers, they also wore trainers, the first fans I had seen in large numbers to do so although a lot of Scousers did at Anfield in February, the forerunners to the Casuals, it's just that Scousers always seemed to look scruffy no matter what they wore, they had that haunted hungry look as did the Mancs a bit later. Cockney's looked bigger stronger and healthier and certainly more confident in their brash way.

They held their own that day and gave us a good scrap on Westwood running track close to the ground after the game as they returned back to the train station at Werneth, along the way they were ambushed as were all fans going down that route, another early game around September was the visit of Stoke City another fallen giant and did they come up in big numbers, smashing up several pubs before the game, they also came into the Chaddy End and it is to our credit we held the Chaddy that sunny day, Stoke were tough and game as fuck and would not lie down, they kept on coming until we eventually forced them into the top right hand corner by sheer numbers, outside aided by their huge support in the away end they ran amok and ran Oldham, smashing cars and attacking the cops in the process. Stoke did a lot of damage that day and thank god all their fans did not get into the Chaddy End that day.

Another team to attempt to take the Chaddy End was Millwall, this was the third time we had played them but this was their biggest assault on our end, on the previous Monday night there was a television documentary that followed Millwall's notorious fans to a few games interviewing a few of their more livelier followers, one of these called himself Harry the dog, a big loud cocky fucker who wore a flat cap, he was part of a mob calling themselves the F- Troop, another mob was called the surgical mob and wore surgical masks, this Harry was shown fighting at Bristol Rovers and was a nut case, it was the very first TV programme about football violence and it seemed everybody watched it and were talking about it, well would you believe it Millwall's next game after this programme was going to be Oldham Athletic away at Boundary Park. Well Millwall had now put themselves as the top mob in the country and everyone wanted to measure themselves against them including little Oldham, well everyone was going to this game, all the usual mobs doubled and trebled in numbers and the Chaddy End was rocking from 2pm, chanting "Millwall where are you?" the away end was showing a big mob of Millwall but we were disappointed none seemed to be in the Chaddy End, but jsut before kick off up went the roar. 'MILL-WALL MILL-WALL' as a big appeared around this 100 strong mob, many Oldham fans melting away as this angry hard looking mob in their donkey jackets and flat caps braced themselves, there was a very brief lull and one big lad stepped forward arms outstretched announcing that he was "Harry the Facking Dog! and who want's a facking go? " well cometh the hour cometh them man.

This was a great opportunity to cement my reputation and I stepped forward and announced "I'm Carl the fucking Cat!" and with that I gave him a diving head butt and we rolled over, the big mass brawl ensued, until somehow the cops and their dogs separated the warring mobs, many Oldham fans were backslapping me although quite a few thought my best pal Paul had done Harry cos he was wearing Harry's flat cap like a trophy haha... Millwall were tough though and remained in the Chaddy End the whole game and Oldham fans would not walk through them to get to the bogs, they chose the longer option to the left, at half time a big surge occurred in the away end as a large combined Manc mob of United and City piled into the Millwall fans, it was hard to tell who had the upper hand cos there was lot's of fights breaking out, both mobs claimed victory, however the main Millwall mob were encamped in the Chaddy End so we come out with most credit holding them off, outside Millwall were everywhere and bossing the streets, but once again we held on to our Chaddy End.

Forest came next with their annual attempt to take the Chaddy

End once again not quite managing it but a very good attempt, same with Wolves and West Ham both of whom remained in the whole game with sporadic out breaks of brawling. It seemed the Chaddy End was finally impregnable, we had defended it against some of the countries top mobs, we were now into the winter months of 1977 and at the end of November we played Sheffield United away, Bramhall lane a cold horrible place surrounded by back alleys and dark unforgiving streets, Oldham did not take to many maybe cos Christmas was coming up and the 300 or so of us in the away end got some terrible stick by the Blades thugs, who outnumbered us and attacked us at every opportunity, the cops did fuck all, me and my pals from Westwood were surrounded by about twenty Blades, there was about 12 of us, and one big fat trebled chinned fucker in particular was picking on me, kicking the back of my legs and calling me a Lancashire cunt. I told my pals I'm gonna do this fat cunt, they pleaded with me not to as we'd all get a kicking, well we all had a kicking anyhow and were bound to get filled in again so I decided fatty was having it next time he kicked me, right on cue he kicked the back of my legs making them buckle as his mates laughed out loud at this bullying cunt, I bent forward and then slammed the back of my head right into his fat fucking mush, he dropped like a small sherry, his face spurting blood and as my pals feared his mates piled into us and we got booted all over the show, but I was happy to have dropped the fat wanker.

After the game my pals deserted me as I was being targeted by loads of Sheffield lads, but one lad stood by me telling me he would back me no matter what, it was Johnny Murphy from the Werneth mob who only stood five feet nothing but had the courage of a Belle Vue tiger, outside it was pitch black drizzling and very moody as the Yorkies moved in, they spotted me and Murph and we agreed it's do or die and just dived in knowing full well we were getting hammered, so we did and they did batter us, we somehow both clambered on top of a parked car and ran across a few more as they closed in, eventually getting dragged to the ground for another kicking before the cops rescued us and got us onto our coach, battered bruised and aching, vowing revenge which was only two weeks later as they came to Boundary Park in what turned out to be one of THE maddest games ever in the 1970's and that is saying something.

Revenge was in the air that freezing foggy murky December 1977, I had taken a terrible amount of stick two weeks prior at Bramhall lane and someone was going to feel my wrath, in fact a lot of Oldham were out for revenge and the Chaddy End had a very good mob in by 2pm, at 2.30pm a mob of 200 Sheff United fans came in the Chaddy and challenged us, a huge fight ensued and we ran them to the bottom of the Chaddy End and many clambered onto the pitch, this was the sign for hundreds more of them to come charging across the pitch from the way end, we ran down to meet them on the pitch, unfortunately many Oldham fans fled to the main stand paddock when they saw how many of them there was coming towards us, added to this there were 200 blades still in the Chaddy End and on the pitch fights were breaking out everywhere it seemed, I was in my element, I was not alone around 100 Oldham fans slugged it out on the pitch in the goalmouth with our Yorkie foes, I clocked one big silly fucker galloping towards me just in front of the goals, I caught him flush in his bollocks with my size 9 Docs, and down he went skidding into the back of the nets, I ran about arms aloft as I if had scored the winning goal at Wembley.

Fights were breaking put all over the pitch I was booting and slapping as many as I could before being rugby tackled by a copper, then dragged around the pitch, I glanced back to see that Sheffield United had taken the Chaddy End most of our lads holed up in the paddock, to be fair they were on the pitch at the half way line attacking stray Yorkies but should have been in the Chaddy End defending it, funny enough photos the next day show these Oldham fans attacking the Sheff lads on the pitch and they were all buzzing cos they were in the *News of the World* - pity they had fled first though. I got lobbed out and told to fuck off home, I fucked off right back into the Chaddy End to try and re take our end, by now its almost kick off and more and more Oldham fans were piling into the Chaddy End, but we could not budge Sheffield who had taken us good and proper, we were all crowded around the floodlights but we attacked any Blades who came anywhere near us, two big fuckers in Sheepskins came in the Chaddy through the turn styles with their birds, they were swaggering about pushing Oldham fans about when me and Herby set about them, we got arrested as did the Yorkie lads, and we were dragged up the side of the pitch again past the Oldham fans who had fled and they were all laughing cos it was the second time in twenty minutes I was being dragged by them by the coppers, this time we were put into the back of a cop van, all four of us, we were soon joined by 4 more Oldham and 2 more Sheffield who were not so gobby now....trying to talk to us but we fucked them off and told them as soon as we are out of the van they were having it.

I kept having flashbacks two weeks prior of the bullying bastards, we Oldham lads were relieved to see the van going up towards the Moors above Oldham which meant we were not getting charged but dumped in the middle of the Moors, which is were Oldham cops dumped hooligans they did not charge, as soon as we are dumped from the cop van the two cops said "right fight it out here, see ya lads ", happy days, we set about them , two ran off tripping up over the hills, the other four fought in vain, we hammered them, then set about walking back towards Oldham, hitch-hiking. Me and Herby got a lift straight away and were dropped off at Boundary Park for half past four, still twenty mins left and the gates were just about to open for three quarter time when 200 plus Oldham lads charged back in after being safe in the paddocks, but respects they got right into the Chaddy End to attempt to get our kop back of these Yorkshire cunts!

We had our work cut out Sheffield United brought one of the gamest and best firms for years to Boundary Park, there "ee aye ee aye yo" chant sounded brilliant, a big war cry, they controlled most of the Chaddy End right across the top and half way down our big end, Oldham were half way up in a mob of about 500 and pushing and probing trying to get our end back, there was plenty of brawling still on the front line but no real impact could be made well that was until the last 5 minutes when Oldham's hard man midfielder Ronnie Blair got sent off for knocking out their big centre half, who was flat out in the muddy pitch just like many Oldham and Sheffield fans before kick off. Well this gave us Oldham fans a big surge of adrenalin and with one big last charge we regained half of our end back which was a moral victory at least if only for last five minutes, as the final whistle blew, Sheff fans were chanting "on the pitch" and many of us did clamber onto the pitch and once more were slugging out with our Yorkshire foes once more, slipping all over the greasy pitch lit only by the fading floodlights, I was once more arrested and unbelievably for the third time only ejected. I had got away with not being charged for the third time!

I was so lucky and got away from the ground and into the town centre. In the town I met up with Oldham lads maybe twenty of us and we set about looking for Sheffield lads, we were told a few were at the Yelloways coach station, and we were chuffed to see about ten of them waiting outside the coach station, we split up and then ambushed them, I heard this almighty crash as one of our young but very game lads Gumbie nutted a lad through the huge plate glass window, the other Sheffield United fans ran off leaving their mate on his arse through this smashed window and I was delighted to see it was none other than my big fat tormentor from Bramhall lane two weeks previous, only now he s not so brave and wimpering and pleading mercy, he looked pitiful and we left him all crumpled up in the shop window.

It was a very long and eventful day one I was so lucky to not have been done for, but I had exacted my revenge and this was the last team any team took over the Chaddy End although a few more attempts were made.

Boxing Day 1977 saw us at Hull City which was 90 miles away but we always took loads there for some reason today would be no exception and a 600 seater "special train " most of these were lads, we arrived in Hull for 1.30pm which gave us time to run amok and turn over a couple of pubs, there wasn't many Hull lads about to say it was a big City, by 2.45pm we were all the ground in the side paddock although a few Oldham fans got in their end before getting lobbed back into our end, one of these was Jeff Hurdus, a big tough looking blonde haired lad from Royton who had a big broken nose and always wore a sheepskin adding effect, he went in nearly every teams end sometimes with his little crew but often on his own, he was fearless, and we used to try and spot him in home kops up and down the country, he was easy to spot given his size, blonde hair and sheepie.

The Hull end that day was packed and they looked to have a top mob that day for a change, towards the end of the game the word went round we were gonna invade the pitch and attack their end, a couple of hundred of us made our way toward the pitch, I don't know who was calling the shots but the word was as soon as the final whistle blew on we go, I had my eyes on the ref for the last five minutes urging him to blow up, the whistle went and on I go with my good pal Gary alongside me, after a few seconds Gary gives me the dreaded news, "Carl there is only me and you here". Fuck me we are now halfway across this mudbath and hundreds of Hull are pouring onto the pitch from their Kop, Gary turned back and I don't blame him one bit, but I was daft as a brush and kept on running towards the huge Hull mob, at the front of this Hull mob was a big bald headed bloke with a sheepskin overcoat on he must have been 40 odd which I found strange but he was making a bee line for me, we clashed and both hit the deck rolling about in the mud, the cops were soon separating us and we were both handcuffed and thrown into some cells near their end, we were shoved together and he was being okay with me chatting away about the game etc, a few more lads were thrown in, a few from Hull and Oldham who had been fighting outside the ground, I only knew one Big Neil Donaldson, a lad I had known most of my life whose family lived near us in Westwood, Neil was a couple of years older than me a tall gangly lad with a very deep voice, his dad was a very hard powerful man originally from Belfast, Big George, very much respected and feared in the area were we lived, he was a good pal of my dad, both being Ulster Protestants, both drank in the Irish Catholic pubs in Oldham, dad often told me no-one ever give Big George any lip.

All the lads who got arrested were bailed by 8.30pm, they contacted my mother who told the cops to keep me there as she didn't want anything to do with me... no surprise there... Neil to be fair told the cops he would leave when they let me go, his loyalty didn't wash with the cops who released us on bail into the freezing winters night at midnight... we asked which way was Oldham, they laughed and pointed up towards the motorway..90 miles...we didnt have any money, the cops just said 'tough'!

It was one of the coldest nights I have ever known Neil just had cap sleeved tee shirt on flared jeans and trainers, I had Harrington levis and slip on loafers, hardly the togs for such harsh conditions, we walked for miles, before eventually noticing a lady putting milk bottles out on her doorstep, we asked her for any old clothes as we had to walk home to Oldham, this lovely lady made us a brew gave us some biscuits and me and big wooly jumper and for some reason Neil a ladies negligee ha ha. I was pissing meself It was so flimsy, we had struggled hitch-hiking but now it would be impossible with Neil looking like a Tranny...

We ended up in a town called Goole in the early hours and found the train station and got our heads don in the waiting room awaiting the first Hull–Manchester train, which arrived at 6-30am, we got on and crashed out, a hour later we were awoken rudely by the guard, we explained we had no money and he told us a transport copper would meet us at Piccadilly Station, which one did, he gave us the option to get someone to pay our fare, which Neil's pal Gnasher did and picked us up and drove us home, top man Gnash!

I was shattered but only had a kip for two hours, cos Latics were playing Blackpool at home, it was a big crowd, 13,000 and Blackpool brought a few thousand fans but there was no trouble and tell you the truth I was glad because I was fucked!

In the spring of 1978 we found ourselves in the latter stages of the Anglo-Scottish cup, in the quarter finals we had a two legged match with St Mirren of Scotland, they brought quite a lot of fans down to Boundary Park but not as many as Hearts 4 year previously which was a disappointment but the away leg up in Paisley on the outskirts of Glasgow was a bit more lively, we only took one coach but most of us who went up were up for a battle with our Scottish rivals, we were very wary as this was near Glasgow which itself had a fearful reputation, our coach arrived at 5pm and we went straight into a pub near the ground, it was full of Jocks, gobby Jocks trying to intimidate us, but we stood firm and the only move they made was as we were leaving for the game one of them threw and ashtray which smashed above our heads, but their normal fans remonstrated with them.

During the match half a dozen of them came amongst us trying to bully us, I nutted their main lad who went down and crawled away Eddy B dropped a couple with them heavy haymakers he cold throw, and that was the sum total of their "we'll kill thae English bas tarts!" in fact after the match which we won on penalties we went back into their supporters club with our players til midnight singing and cheering away.

The semi finals saw us pitched against our Lancashire rivals Burnley, whom we had turned the tide around fully and went up to Turf Moor with confidence but they still came to Boundary Park with as much confidence, Burnley were a tough mob no doubts but we certainly did not fear them anymore, the first leg was at Boundary Park on a Tuesday night and true to form Burnley brought a few thousand fans but sadly none in the Chaddy End, we searched frantically amongst this packed crowd to find them but we could not, apart from one big hard looking lad with a boxers face who no - one could recognise, I tapped him on the shoulder and asked him where he came from ? he said Burnley and I stuck the nut on him and he dropped but as he was dropping he pointed right and finished his sentence and said lane ! Burnley lane was only 200 yards from Boundary Park, he was a local lad and I felt a right cunt, and helped him up and apologised, my pals were in hysterics, the lad was okay about it and just dusted himself down, the match went Burnley's way and they beat us 4-1 and their fans in the away end were celebrating and taking the piss, just before the end of the game about 100 of us went to the back of the away end hiding in bushes in the valley behind that terrace, we sent Yogi and a few young un's to tempt them towards us so we could ambush them, it worked perfectly as Burnley came out Yogi and his pals did reel them in and they set chase and as they approached this boggy bit of grassy verge were we were we ambushed them and dived right into them, it was a great brawl Burnley were game as fuck as usual and we rolled about with them fighting many falling down the slippy hill into the stream the coppers had no idea and we were free to have a right good scrap which we did, no serious damage just a few bloody noses etc, the cops eventually coming with their dogs but by them we had more or less finished and were dusting ourselves down promising each other to finish the job off at turf Lane the week after at the second leg.

Even though we lost the first leg of the Anglo Scottish cup 4-1 we still took a great following to Burnley the week after for the second leg, the town of Burnley was still rocking from the visit of Glasgow Celtic who had not only smashed half the town up but also wrecked Turf Moor, breaking down the fences and using them as spears to throw at the police and fleeing Burnley fans, they caused up to that date the most damage everinflicted by away fan on an English ground and it was in every newspaper and news programmes, the level of violence that night shocked even the most ardent of football fans, there were over 100 arrested and many more ejected, Burnley did not roll over but were overwhelmed by the Scottish thugs aided by many English hooligans who jumped on the Celtic bandwagon Burnley had no chance. So it would be fair to say Burnley's mob would not be too pleased with taunting English fans chanting "Celtic, Celtic" at them.

For this away game at Burnley King Kenny Jones of Failsworth was running a "Invited Thugs" only coach 52 invited tried and tested hooligans, it was testimony to how far me Paul and a few others my age had come to be invited on this "elite thugs" coach for on it was Oldham's finest and many older veterans, me, Paul, Dennis, Loyd and Eddie B were all on board Kenny's coach which picked up at C & A's superstore in Oldham town centre on a wet and windy Tuesday evening at 5pm. Once I saw who was on board I felt confident, there were some very tough lads on, many whom I had looked up to as I grew up on the terraces, lads like Herby and his brother Ray, Kenny Jones and his faithful Failsworth crew. Failsworth was a big Mancunian overspill area on the border with Oldham and all the Failsworth lads spoke in Manc accents which was a world from our broad Lancashire accents, other lads were Spazmo the Chaddy giant a man at 13 with a full beard a big hard bastard, Terry Horton, Shaun Bowskill, Tommy Nolan, Johnny Cleworth, Paddy Costello, Tony Kirton, all game as fuck Chaddy lads ( Chaddy is name for Chadderton a large district of Oldham ) Barry the barrister was on board, Barry's real name was Bartholomew a Cheetham Hill Jew boy who was a barrister but also a football hooligan and he got stuck in wading in with his brolly or cane, he always wore an ankle length Crombie overcoat shirt and tie and highly polished brogues, he never ever got arrested but got lobbed out a few times, he had the patter you see..and no doubt the right contacts, he must have been late twenties in 1978 maybe early thirties, there were a good few Fitton Hill lads on the coach including Big Alan Bambrough.. known as Bambrough the Square because of his old fashioned dress sense, wearing old hobnail boots cheap flared trousers – the rest of country were in straight legs by now and wide lapelled jackets, he was a very heavily built stocky man, with fists like shovels and he was very violent, he once punched a police horse on Sheepfoot Lane that got in his way of smacking some Forest fans. His hand got smashed to bits on the very hard head of the huge horse, but this did not deter Bambrough from wading into his foes that how he fought wading in throwing heavy haymakers left and right, skittling foes, we younger ones used to take the piss out of him for his dress sense and he used to threaten to knock our blocks off, on this particular night on the way he grabbed me around the throat with his big strong hands, he was strangling me and took the breath out of me, thankfully Paul and Eddy managed to drag him off me and his Fitton Hill buddies calmed him down and told him to save for the Burnley bastards we were bound to face....two other lads on bard were big Stu Boardman and a lad called Geordie, now Big Stu was justified as he was one of the toughest lads at Oldham, he was a powerfully built youth 3 years older than me with a powerful build and a knockout punch who dropped loads of away fans in the 70's/early 80's.

He was also the very last Boot Boy at Oldham who still wore his skinners docs and wrangler jacket and his blue and white scarf tied around his neck, he was a throwback to the early 1970's when we all dressed that way, no one took the piss because he was such a pleasant lad, always smiling even when knocking fuck out of away fans, his partner in crime who should not have been on the coach was Geordie, who was a right strange lad, he came from Shrewsbury originally, supported West Ham but followed Oldham, spoke in a ridiculous fake cockney accent and called himself Geordie, he was very lucky that Big Stu was his best mate, and Big Stu looked after him and to be fair they were inseparable, so I suppose when Big Stu got the invite he demanded his right hand man Geordie came along, and Geordie was a laugh we could all see through him and I am sure Big Stu could also.

We arrived in Burnley at 6pm and our coach dropped us off in the town centre and we piled right into the first pub we came across which had twenty or so Burnley lads in who we fucked off right away, most of them clambering over the bar to get away, we knew word would soon get round that we had arrived and we awaited our old foes, the drinks flowed well for everyone apart from me Paul and Eddy B, who drank coke, and by 6.30pm we were bored waiting for Burnley so we went in search of them ourselves, just the three of us, we didn't have to wait long as we headed towards the ground, three big Burnley thugs were walking towards us fists clenched, they were a bit older than us but that didn't bother us, we agreed we were gonna steam into these, the tension was really building, they were gobbing off psyching themselves up calling us Oldham cunts etc, we were relaxed, I was good with my head, Eddy was bound to knock one out and Paul would have no problems getting stuck in, it was perfect timing, they were actually grinning as they raised their fists, I butted the lad in the middle who went arse over tit, Eddy knocked out the one on the left hand side, bang, right hook into side of jaw, lad hit deck and didn't get up, mine was crawling about, moaning, and Paul set about his target, having to hit him a few times about the head and body but he also went down and stayed down, it was perfect timing and we all high fived each other as we strode away victoriously towards Turf Moor.

As we approached Turf Moor we noticed loads of running battles as coach loads of Oldham fans began emptying and Burnley fans were lying in wait, it was "even stevens" with lots of missiles being lobbed at each other and the cops struggled, we piled right into the brawling it was brilliant, over 200 youths and young men fighting each other in the middle of the road, there were quite a few injured and ambulance sirens were filling the cold night air, and the cops were arresting dozens, eventually peace was restored and a stand off occurred and the cops forced us into our part of the Longside, loads more Oldham were turning up in vans, mini coaches and cars plus pouring down from the town centre it was a tremendous turn out for a game we had already lost but terrace pride was the order of the day/night. Inside the ground the atmosphere was electric, it was a great Kop so loud and there was a couple of mini pitch invasions, Oldham were taunting Burnley with Celtic chants which I did not join in with my dad being an Ulster

Loyalist, but it wound the Burnley fans up no end with lots trying to climb over the dividing fence and get into us, it kicked off at half time behind the stand were both sets of fans were clambering over the fence into their foes..

With twenty minutes to go most of our elite thug coach load left the ground early to attack Burnley's side of the Longside, it was very dark and foggy outside and we somehow escaped the cops and climbed over a wall at the back of the Longside like Marines, and we then headed up the steep concrete steps at the back of their end, we got to the top without anyone noticing us then we charged in their mob, who scattered, thinking there were a lot more of us a huge gap appeared and the mass of Oldham fans across the fence were cheering us on like heroes, our bit of fame only lasted about 30 seconds until Burnley realised that there was only 30-40 of us and they all came piling into us, we had a go but got pushed down the steps at the back, the cops set their dogs on us and we had to clamber back over the wall, but by now hundreds more Oldham fans had come to join us, and we rampaged through a council estate smashing windows and cars, etc, the cops were going mad and the alsations were biting loads, we got onto the main road in a 300 strong mob and attempted to go the long way around the ground but the cops held us back but a few brave Burnley fans broke through and had a go but got twatted, the cops eventually forcing us all onto our coaches many of them got their windows put through as we snaked through hundreds of very angry Burnley fans., our coach of "invited hooligans " was a third empty on the way back, ten arrested and half a dozen in hospital and those of us who survived were sporting cut's and bruises..what a night. Big respects to Burnley a town the third the size of Oldham but who not only got bigger gates than us but had as many lads.

Personally in 1978/79 I had completely lost the plot several appearances in court for assaults, criminal damage and affray, I was getting fined and even a 6 month suspended sentence on Friday Feb 2nd 1979, my 18th birthday I got £300 fine and 6 months suspended for two years at 2 –30pm, at 10-30pm that very same night I was once again arrested and charged with Affray, I lasted 8 fucking hours ! I was to get 6 months later that summer for this.

I was also being targeted by two Oldham coppers in particular, one a ginger haired Oldham lad/copper called Rafferty who was always trying to nick me at home games, I was too sharp for him but he was the copper who arrested me on my 18th birthday, what happened that night was I was out at 7pm with about 15 mates who plied me with doubles and trebles all night, as a non drinker I was soon drunk as a skunk and from 9pm onward I had to be carried about the town centre pubs, at 10 ish we end up in what was then a very new pub the Tommyfield, it was packed out and were joined by another ten more mates, I was making my way tot he toilet when I was surrounded by about fifteen lads, one lad brought a photo out of me and his bird from a photo booth, the pic was a couple of years old and me and the bird Viv never went with each other just had this pic, this lad butted me and down I went, I was an easy target I could hardly stand up, while I am down another lad glasses me behind my ear, and blood is spurting out, all of a sudden my twenty odd pals come flying over and a wild west brawl breaks out, I was out of the equasion on the deck with blood pissing out of me, two barmaids somehow got me into the lads bogs to wash me down, as the rest battled, bottles tables chairs etc the new pub was wrecked, the lads we were fighting with were from an ear of Oldham called Lees and as the cops arrived they fucked off to a nearby pub called the Centurion Inn, the cops arrested a couple of our lads, and when the PC Rafferty came into the bogs and saw me on the deck full of blood well he could not believe his luck, I couldn't even speak I was that drunk and as much as the barmaids kept telling him I was assaulted he couldn't stop smirking he kept saying "I've gotcha now ha " and in the back of the cop van I was thrown to join 3 of my pals and one of the Lees lads, we were thrown into the cells, within half a hour we were joined by ten more of my pals and ten more lads from Lees as they carried on fighting in the Centurion, our lads heard they had gone in there and sent Yogi the lookout to have a look, well he did and come out with his nose broke, so the lads piled in and got stuck into the Lees lads, but the cops were soon there and loads got lifted, it even kicked off in the cells until the cops separated us Westwood lads from the Lees lads, over the next few months 22 lads were dealt with in court, all got fined £100 all pleaded guilty, I pleaded not guilty because I was not guilty, so my case kept getting adjourned, the evidence against me was weak, my Solicitor told me the only evidence they have is a lad with short hair and a black Harrington jackets, well in February 1979 most of my mates were Mods/Skins and most wore black Harringtons, I was confident of a walk out.

I tried to keep a low profile for the rest of the 78/79 season I was on bail and a few coppers were on my case, but Bolton away I was it, a van laod of us got there about 1pm and we parked up in the won centre, there was about 15 of us and right away we were spotted by some Bolton fans who didnt fancy their chances but were back withing ten minutes mob handed, we armed ourselves with b ricks n bottles and charged intot he bigger mob of 30 or so who had a go but fled once they knew we were nt backing down and had weapons and were using them, we marched down to Burnden [ark but got attacked several time off big mobs of Bolton, every pub seed to have at least fifty lads, it was very dodgy as ever and a few of us got mashed up, but we ended up at the ground were more and more Oldham lads joined us, we went into the Warbys end but got overwhelmed as per usual, after the match the long walk back into town was madness, and we got it under the big railway bridge and afew more times before we eventually got a police escort to the van which surprise surprise had been smashed up! Fortunately Oldham is only half a hour away, we stopped halfway home in Birch Services for a brew and butty etc..all free of course, as we are heading back to our van one of the lads noticed Len Fairclough off Coronation Street who hd just been involved in a big case for tampering with kids at Bury Baths, we shouted "oi yer dirty pervert" and set off after him, he ran off over some fields we fell about laughing at this so called tele hard man! We then set off back to Oldham but our van was a hire van and we lost our deposit. We survived another mad day at Bolton though, just, and compared our cuts and bruises.

Our final game of this season took us to Charlton Athletic in South London, a great fixture thatexcited many of us, a day and night out in London, a guarantee of fun and games, 15 of our lads from Westwood had pre booked the 7-30am train leaving Manchester Piccadilly to arrive at London Euston at 10-50am, we hit Manchester at 7am and piled into that greasy Itie cafe next to the station entrance, it was already full of Oldham fans all scoffing the cheap all in full English breakfast, there was about 100 Oldham lads on that train with another 150 coming down on the next train ahour later, there were a few scuffles with a group of United fans who ran off, outnumbered ten to one, they can't keep their gobs shut, shouting 'United aggro'!

On the train the cans of lager were soon being opened and the card games began, I soon get bored so went for a mooch up and down the train, noticed quite a few fans of other teams heading for the Smoke, when we arrive at Euston most of us split up and went our own way, us 15 Westwood lads headed for Soho and it's 50p wank booths, how childish ha ha, we just walked about the West End taking in all the sights, it was a lovely sunny day, spirits were high, a few of our lads dived into a pub, me and Paul went for a walk on our own, we were not bothered about boozing, at 1pm we were on Victoria station awaiting our connection to Charlton when a group of Chelsea fans approached us, they noticed me and Paul wearing Union Jack pin badges on our Harrington jackets. One big fucker said.. "oh NF lads, you're okay off you pop" for some reason which I have never been able to expain I butted this cunt who went flying into a newspaper stand, his half a dozen mates were stunned, and me and Paul fled laughing our heads off.

The Chelsea lads set off in pursuit of us, we spent the next half a hour running up and down escalators in and out of shops and hiding behind bins, they wouldn't relent, eventually we found refuge in a busy pub and kept out heads down for a while before eventually coming out checking everything was ok and then got the train to Charlton's ground. It was now 2.30pm and there were over 300 Oldham lads there, a great turn out...the game was a dull end if season meaningkess 1-1 draw, and after the game our tidy mob made our way t the neaby train station, we didn't think Charlton had a mob, of course they chanted but wasn't aware of any thugs. We soon found out that they certainly did as a big mob of 200 or so came charging towards us.led by the biggest Skinhead I ahve ever seen before or since. I'm good at judging heights and this cunt was 6 ft ten and I'm not exaggerating..he was also very powerfully built..we fought back lobbing bottles and bricks into these Charlton fuchers, one half brick hit the big Skin in his head and blood pissed out. He was very angry, the cops somehow shoved us all onto a two carriage small train, we were squashed in like sardines and it's roasting hot, I shoved my head out of the door window for some fresh air, it was that stifling, I could see that big angry looking Skin heading towards me with his mighty fists clenched, a lad behind me called Dutty asked if he could have a bit of fresh air, I said by all means pal. He stuck his ginger nut and it oon came flying back in as this big Skin smacked him, it knocked Dutty senseless, clean out, I felt awful for a few seconds, we soon brought home round as the train set off back to Victoria.

Arriving at Victoria we bumped into various mobs including Leeds, Arsenal, Millwall, Preston, the cops were all over it though, over half of our mob went back on the 8pm trian from Euston, most of us went into the West End and most of them ended up at a pub called the Lion and Lamb in Kings Cross, near to Euston, our train was the last one out, 11.30pm. This train split in half at Stafford with the back of the train going to Liverpool Lime street, the front half taking us to

Piccadilly Manchester.

The Lion and Lamb was a crackin little back street pub with the old piano banging away and a few cockney locals singing along, we had used this pub a few times on London trips, it was a good one to end the night in and only 5 mins walk from Euston, this particular night there would have been around 80 of us in various pub around Kings Cross and Euston, most of us squeezed into the tiny Lion and Lamb, were Al Jones gave us a rendition of " There's only one Simon Stainrod" as the owd lady banged away on the ivories...all good fun.

At 11pm we set off to Euston for the last train home as our mob of 50 or so entered the station we saw a big mob of maybe 70 Everton lads, they eyed us up but nothing was said. In the newspapers the next day there was an article how this big mob of Everton had ransacked a load of jewellers shops after their game at Spurs. As we were making our way down to platform 12 down the big ramp, one of our lads Paul Heap threw a bottle into the Everton mob, who then came flying into us and large scale brawl broke out, it was a great scrap, with loads of one to ones and lads rolling about scrapping. On Platform 11 was a massive train full of Widnes Rugby fans who had been to Wembley that day and they were all cheering us on to do the Scouse bastards!

There was a lull and the Scosuers headed back up the ramp away ffrom us they were met head on by the remaining 30 Oldham lads, the Scousers fled back down the Ramp and right into us, another huge brawl ensued, withthe Widness Rugby fans loving it, a few of our lads got cut up, Dozy Dunc got hit with an iron bar and his face was pissing blood, Geoff Noble was hid under a bench his head pissing blood, a few of us had bloody noses but plenty of Scosuers also got hurt, big Al Cambell got one of those large trollies full of mail bags and went hurtling into a mob of Scousers who went flying, eventually the cops came and broke us up. They lifted Paul Sykes and Dutty who were led off, the cops then put us on the front of the train and the Scosuers at the back, the Widnes fans gave us a round of applause. Paul and Dutty were not charged but were held back until our train had set off, they got on the Widness train and were treated like kings with cans of lager and butties. When they got to Widnes Paul nicked a car and drove over to Manchester Piccadilly, they met us there, they got there half a hour before we did, we couldn't believe seeing them as we disembarked. Meanwhile on the train the inquest went on about our mass brawl with the Scousers, we reckoned we did them, we had a few cut up but so did they but they kept running off before coming back at us. Game fuckers though, after half a hour of the train setting off a group of about ten of us went in search of the Scousers, down the train, they didn't want to know,most of them hid inbetween normal people, but we came across a mob of ten in this carriage, who were giving it all the vee's and wankers sign to us, but they would'nt come out and put their weight against the glass doors, Dennis was seething and smashed his hand through the thick glass windown shattering it and his hand was pissing blood, the Scousers all curled up as we set about them, beating them up. We eventually gave up and went back to our compartments.

Most of us were fast asleep as the train puled into Stafford station at about 3am, the train was due to split in half, when all of a sudden, iron buckets and other implements came smashing through our windows shattering us with broken glass loads got cut up, a few of us got off the train and onto the platform only to see the back end of the train pulling away and these Scousers laughing at us calling us Manc Nobheads and Woolyback Wankers! I don't know what hurt more, being called Mancs or being outwitted and done by the Scouse bastards! You had to admire their cunning though – we may have won the battles but they had the last laugh..

# CLACTON BUTLINS

IN MAY 1979 FIVE OF US decided we were going to work away that summer in the holiday camps, we all went to the job centre together and all hope to be sent to the same Butlins holiday camp, we all chose Pwhelli North Wales as outfits choice of three, only Paul Sykes got Pwhelli, I got Clacton in Essex and Clarky got Skegness, Lincolnshire. Hoof ended up in Great Yarmouth where members of his family had worked for years and Cockney Tim went back to Brighton were he was brought up, we all met up for one last night in Oldham town centre then we all went our own ways and promised to keep in touch, I never saw Cockney Tim nor Hoof again, Clarky did a couple of seasons at Skeggy, Paul did the one season at Pwhelli and I did half the season at Clacton cos I ended up getting 6 months!

I got the train down to London first thing Monday morning but when I was in London I decided to go and visit my dad who I'd not seen for a few months. Dad was working and living at the Isle of Grain in Kent, he was not expecting me, and it took ages to find this huge building site which was 5 miles long, it was a huge power station job, I asked loads if they knew my dad but it was the twentieth person I asked who informed me my dad was in charge of the stores which was about 2 miles walk away across all these muddy fields. Eventually I found him feet up in the cabin having a brew and a butty, we hugged, it was very emotional we were so close but had lsot touch a bit. He was well chuffed to see me, I had a good hour with him before we bid farwell, he gave me £50, which was a big bonus for me, and I promosed to write to him once a week which I did.

I now had to get back to London and then onto Clacton, still a lot of travelling and it was 9pm when I finally walked through the gates of Clacton, Butlins, I handed my sheet in and I was shown my chalet, I was knackered, and it was pitch black in there, I slung my Army bag onto the couch and flopped down, I then heard a murmur coming from the bedroom, "who the fuck is that?" I enquired...it was then I met Miles, a bearded beatnik kind of bloke, "Hi I'm Miles" he said as he offers me his hand, we shook and he informed me we were sharing this tiny chalet, he had claimed the single bed and I had the bed settee, I wasn't bothered and told him I want to get me head down as Im shattered, so was he, we both soon crashed out.

Next morning when I awoke Miles had made me a brecky and a brew - top lad and we got to know each other a bit better, we got on well, he was a middle class young man aged 22 who was taking a year out of university, he came from a village in Oxford and thought he was a Rocker, I soon told him I was a Mod but he had never heard of a Mod ha ha. We had that day to sort out or jobs at Butlins, he was to work in a photo booth all day, what a boring job, all he did was sit in the booth all day were peole picked up photos that had been taken the day before, but he was happy enough and read books all day..

The staff meeting was really busy hundreds of applicants there for the summer season jobs, like thousands before who had gone down this route at various Butlins camps throughout Great Britain, it was/is a true British tradition, I was on my own, as was Miles but many of these people were amongst friends, you could see them huddled and grouped together, laughing and joking with each other, there did seem a lot of idiots there, people who did not look like they were really up for the disciplines of working in teams, just my opinion, I was down as a kitchen porter but as the jobs were being allocated the lady giving the posts out asked if there was anyone with bar/pub experience as a post had come up in the staff bar, it was a higher rate of pay with better hours and perks, I put my hand up and I joined the staff bar team, I had blagged it, I got talking to this Scouse kid called Maccy, I told him I had blagged it and could he help me, he said "no prob lah, it's a piece of piss" and that morning he showed me the ropes, pulling pints changing barrels and all the other things required to be a barman, within a couple of hours I had it sussed and was a fully fledged barman.

There were not many of us Northern lads/girls at Clacton, most were Cockneys, or from the Midlands, most of the lads were footy fans and always asking who I supported, I had no problem in telling them proudly Oldham, they took the piss with us being a small town club, but it didn't bother me, we had the banter, surprisingly I was the only Mod on the staff, given that the Mod revival was already in full flow in London, it grew though as the summer progressed and the Mod holiday makers influenced so many of the staff with their Mod clobber etc. Their were 8 of us on the staff bar team, our leader was called Sophie, a university educated lady who was taking a two year gap, she spoke well and was on the ball, very efficient and good to work for, strong but fair, but she did not mix with us out of work hours, there was five of us manning the bars, me, Maccy the Scouser, Walter from Coventry who was 40 odd recently divorced and a moody man, very sulky, just got on with his job, he always wore his Coventry shirt, Bryn, a Rockabilly lad from Reading, with his big quiff and big turn ups on his jeans, Lucy a bubbly giggly little buxom blonde from Basildon, Essex, she was good fun, Theresa an Irish lady about 25, another quiet lady but very pleasant and finally Dougie an ex army lad now 30 odd and forever going on about his army days whom he had killed and the many campaigns he had fought. His stories did not add up, he claimed to be in wars he was nowhere near old enough to be in, but we humoured him and he was a laugh, whenever he came into work we would shout "left, right, left right", and he'd stiffen up and start marching, we would be in fits, it was a good team.

The first week in the staff bar as the camp itself was mayhem, there were many brawls as many of the new workers just went on the piss and began fighting each other, by the end of the first week over a third of the original workers from the whole camp had been shipped out, expelled for drunkenness, assaults, theft and many other petty crimes, Butlin's was very strict and did not put up with any shit, the week after the next lot to arrive were much more disciplined and things settled down, however I saw an horrific assault in the staff bar when a big black girl glassed a lovely trendy looking lady over a feller she was dancing with. The black girl broke a beer bottle and ripped it up and down this ladys face, blood spurted everywhere, we had to pull down the shutters and close the bar while security sorted it out, half a hour later things were back to normal but this incident sickened me, I was used to violence but never seen a girl being glassed, it haunted me, I never saw either girl again.

Once the knobs had been fucked off Butlin's settled down and was a great camp, my wage was £28 but that was with free digs as much food as could eat, free drinks, (I didn't drink alcohol but could have as much as I required) but the bar staff could also get tips but this was not much as there was not much money amongst the staff workers, the bar staff on the big bars got good tips from the holidaymakers and it was our fellow bar staff from the big bars who would tip us with their tips ha. Our wages would reach £40 most weeks after tips. which was all spends – mine went on clothes, my day off was Tuesday and every Tuesday morning I would get the early train 7am into London and spend the day around Carnaby Street and the West End, I loved my days mooching around London, and it would be a joke on camp at what 60's clobber I would come back in, ha, I soon got he nickname of Carl the Mad Mod, I didn't mind.

I remember the top of the charts the first few weeks I was at Clacton was Bryan Ferry's Dance Away, a great song and we 'd all sing along along to it, another tune from then was the crazy Pop Music by M "Pop Music" ha ha we 'd all sing this also... Butlins was brill, when me and Miles were walking through camp together the lads would shout out, "watch out everybody it's the Mods n Rockers, there's gonna be a riot!" I'd laugh but Miles called them imbeciles in his posh accent. There was loads of parties and even the odd excursion out into Clacton town for a night out, that year Terry Griffths won the Embassy World Snooker Championship, the winner of this was contracted to visit every Butlins camp to do exhibition shows for the punters and staff, there was a draw amongst staff to have the chance to play the World Champion, and I was the winner!

I loved snooker even though I was no good but I was a dirty bastard always snookering opponents and very defensive, very frustrating to play against. Well on the night the snooker room was packed with most of the staff present to see the great Welshman take the piss out of me with his fancy exhibition shots, ha well that didn't happen cos I snookered Griffiths every opportunity and I was booed for my negativity and it took him ages to get into his stride, but soon as I made a loose shot the Welsh bastard destroyed me, I had my pic taken with him and I reckon I played a part in his downfall for he never won the World title again, I had broken his spirit!

June 8th/9th/10th 1979 I blagged 3 days off to come back to Oldham for the weekend, I told my bosses my mother was ill and needed me, the truth was that the Jam were playing in my home town and being a Mod I just had to be there to see this brilliant band, I set off from Clacton Friday morning National Express and was back home by 6pm, at 7pm I was out with my pals regaling in my great life at Butlins, it was good to be back if only for the weekend, I'd been away 2 months, most of my pals were going up to Saddleworth to see the Jam on the Saturday night, I was so excited, Saddleworth was a very nice country group of picturesque villages just outside Oldham were the posh people lived, this concert was being held in a huge Marquee to celebrate the annual Saddleworth summer festival. Normally they would have Brass bands or Morris dancers but someone had the brainwave to book one of the countries most exciting and up and coming bands The Jam.

I was that excited I could hardly sleep that Friday night and I was up bright and early that sunny Saturday morning and put on my US Army Parka and got the bus up to Saddleworth to have a mooch, I was there within a hour and made my way to the site of the concert, I seen the big Marquee in the middle of this big field, I could hear live music and a band was tuning up etc, I went for a peep and was delighted to see the Jam practising, I strode over to the the stage and they took a few moments break, I shouted out hello lads, Ive come up all the way from Clacton to see you in my home town, Bruce Foxton and Rick Butler both said "oh thanks mate that's great and hope you have a good night". Paul Weller said very sarcastically "Oh no not another Muppet!" I was gutted. Butler and Foxton were embarrassed and I just turned away and said "see you tonight" (I still don't know whether the arrogant Weller called me a Muppet meaning a fool or the fact I and most Mods back then wore Army Green Parkas, the colour of a Muppet) however it was uncalled for, rude and ignorant a trait Paul Weller was renowned for. I actually met Bruce Foxton in Newquay in 1983 and reminded him of this incident, he could not recall it but said it was typical of Paul Weller.

It was not going to stop me having a great night though and I went back home to meet my pals to come back later in the afternoon, at 4pm around twenty of us set off from Oldham town centre in our US or German Army parkas, fred perry polos shirts, levis or cords, desert boots, brogues, loafers or boating shoes, we all had neat short styled hair many with crisp side partings, we looked cool we felt cool we were cool we were the Mod's. Arriving in Saddleworth we hit the local pubs which were full of Mods who had arrived all day from all over the North, many coming on Lambrettas and Vespas which looked resplendent all parked alongside each other their mirrors and spot lights glistening in the bright sunlight, at 6pm we had made our way over to the playing fields were the concert was being held, the atmosphere was brilliant and there were hundreds of Mods and Moddettes, there was also quite a few Rockers, Saddleworth was a big Rocker area and many of these got filled in 12 months earlier at an Elvis Costello concert in Oldham town centre at the Queen Elizabeth Hall, scuffles were already breaking out, we of course dived in and attacked any long haired leather/denim wearing Greebos.

The support band that night was Dr.Feelgood and they were fantastic and the packed marquee rocked, when the Jam finally came on the place went wild, every single one of us seemed to know every single word, Weller for all his arrogance was The man, a great song writer who knew how to whip up the crowd, it was one of the very best concerts I have been to, I was so proud it was in my home town, it was roasting and we were all sweating as we jumped and danced about like loonies, the heavy US parkas did not help, more scuffles broke out but that was the norm at most concerts back then, and when the concert finished at 10.30pm the real fighting began, the Rockers had kicked over a load of scooters bang out of order and many paid the price as the Mods went on the rampage. We missed the last buses back to Oldham which was 5 miles away and had to walk back home but there were hundreds walking back and it was great as we all sang Jam songs and others like Clash, Elvis Costello, Pistols and many other popular tunes of the day, it was an incredible day/night.

After such a wonderful couple of days it was a long haul back down to Clacton on the National Express and I arrived back at Butlins at 6pm, shattered but had to do the 7pm—11pm shift, I slept well that night and for the next month carried on having a great time at Butlins, making so many friends and still going up to London every Tuesday. However I got a letter telling me I was due in court on Friday July 9th back at Oldham Magistrates to face the Affray charge after being arrested on my 18th birthday. I seriously considered not going and taking a chance at staying at Butlins and facing the music at the end of the season but the fact my solicitor kept convincing me I would walk and there was very little chance of me even being found guilty persuaded me to make the long trip back home, I somehow blagged another 3 days off but was fast running out of chances, and on the Thursday July 8th I got the National Coach back home again.

Next day I was in court, my mam asked if she should come along to support me, I told her it would be thrown out and I will be home in no time - I got six months! Six fucking months detention centre. My solicitor could not even look at me as the magistrate gave me the third degree of what a menace I was to society, which was true but not on this night I wasn't, I had been assaulted and then glassed and did nothing to justify even being arrested, the sight of the ginger haired copper PC Rafferty smirking as I was taken down really pissed me off, he kept telling me I was getting 6 months, how did he know? Is this system that bent they know what is going to happen before you've even got to court? I was gutted ! they somehow produced six witnesses stating that I had caused all the trouble that night, 2 of those witnessing against me were the two barmaids who had tendered to my injuries as my head was pissing blood, the same two ladies that told the cops it was not me and that I had been attacked! Why did they change their minds? Why did they lie? Other witnesses included the landlord and bar manager, I have subsequently found out that landlord was not even there that night but at a function in Manchester, he didn't last much longer at the Tommyfield or even in Oldham come to that, my mates disgusted at his lies made life very uncomfortable for him and rightly so.

I knew sooner or later I would get sent down, I had so many chances and perhaps needed to be off the streets, but to have all those lying bastards stood up under oath condemning me to six months away from my family, my friends and my great job at Butlins really hurt me.

I never got the chance to go back to Clacton, and I lost all my clothes, I did write to them asking what could be done about getting my clothes back once my time inside was up but they said after a week the clothes were given to Oxfam, fucking Oxfam! I had a belting wardrobe of high quality classic clothes, including half a dozen fred perry polo shirts, 3 Fred Perry jumpers, a few Ben Sherman shirts, a Tonik suit, Italian knit wear tops, 3 pairs of levis, a pair of desert boots and Italian leather shoes which cost me £70 and my beloved US Army parka! Plus loads of personal photos and letters. I was so fucking angry, after a couple of hours in the holding cells I was informed that the van was here to take me to Rochdale's Buckley Hall detention centre, the only good thing about this horrific day for me was the fact I would only be 6 miles from home and would get plenty of visits....the big police van dropped of half a dozen thieves, conmen and drug dealers off at Strangeways before taking me to Buckley Hall Rochdale, it was now 5pm....

☆ ☆ ☆

I HAD NO IDEA WHAT TO expect at Buckley Hall DC, I wasn't expecting anything like this so did not even consider this scenario, I had heard how Detention centres were a short sharp shock environment, a harsher more disciplined version of the Borstal, it was for youths aged between 16-21, the first rung to prison life for those who did not learn the error of their ways, as the van parked up inside the grounds of this big old country hall, I told myself to get a grip, stop feeling sorry for myself and just get on with things, one of the prison guards escorting me tried winding me up saying that the lads in here would eat me alive, they were Scousers and Mancs blah blah blah, I told him I was not one bit concerned about Scousers or Mancs, (I 'd been an active football hooligan for five years I could handle myself and wasn't going to roll over for any cunt.)

Once inside I was ordered to strip and then given my uniform of blue and white striped shirt ill fitting denims and plastic slip on loafers, I was given a bed pack and shoved into a tiny one man cell, an overnight incomers cell, the door was slammed shut, I felt very lonely, very angry and gutted when it all began to dawn at me, six fucking months! 6 weeks to be deducted for good behaviour - I could be out for early November if I could keep my behaviour in check, which was going to be hard given the amount of wankers and pricks in here... within 20 minutes I heard a horrendous noise as hundreds of youths came charging down the corridor on their way to the main hall for their tea/evening meal, most of them forcing their ugly mushes at the little window on cell door to see the latest recruit, most of them threatening me, telling me I was gonna die and they would cut me up etc. I should have known the score but I reacted screaming back at them and trying desperately to remember as many faces as possible, it all became a blur and eventually I just lay on my bed and blanked them out!

I didn't sleep well that night and was glad to hear my cell door be open but shocked to hear the screw screaming at me to get out of my fucking pit, tidy my bed and make a bed pack then get my arse down to the Governor's office, it was 6 am! I did my best with the bed pack - blankets, pillows and sheets all folded perfectly and put together in a perfect pile - the screw threw it on the floor and booted it and told me to do it again! I bit my lip and did so, I really wanted to stick the nut on him. The governor read the riot act to me and told me I was going in Dorm 4 which slept 24 inmates, my job for the foreseeable future was scrubbing floors, polishing the long wooden corridors, at 7am I went to the main hall for breakfast with the other 300 inmates, I got my dried toast, hard fried egg and tiny piece of bacon and a plastic cup of piss weak tea and sat down. No one would talk to me, I looked around to see if I could recognise any of the cunts who threatened me through my cell door window last night. I couldn't so I set about eating the worst brecky I had ever seen in my life.

I soon sussed out who was who, the Mancs who were the biggest group were all sat near each other, as were the Scousers, the rest were the "woolybacks" those who did not come from Manchester or Liverpool, I was a woolyback and fucking proud to be so! The Mancs were gobby cocky fuckers, most looked liked rats, the Scousers were a bit more cooler, better dressed more stylish - even though we all had the same clobber, the Scousers ironed theirs and added buttons on the collars etc, they had a swagger about them, but fly bastards and very sarcastic and spoke in back slang, and were very cliquey, very few Scousers would mix with any Mancs or Woolybacks, they looked down on the rest of society..

I was shown to my dorm and given my bed with a tiny little cupboard for personal stuff and then allocated a mop a bucket and a tin of polish and a heavy duty cloth and ordered to spruce up the long wooden corridors, cons and screws were walking past every couple of minutes and messing up my work, dropping stuff and being cunts, I was pissing against the wind and getting wound up, one big fat lad from Stockport began on me for no reason, he was just leant against the wall asking me questions and after question, where you from shag what you in for shag who do you know shag.. I hated being called shag and asked him to please not call me that, my name is Carl, he said listen shag you don't have names in here, most people will call you the town you come from but I'm gonna call you shag! I was seething and determined to do this fat fucker, I stood up and walked towards him and held my hand out and said sorry pal I'm a bit nervous first day, he brushed my hand away and said stop fucking creeping shag! I ran at him and butted him, his nose bust and he slid down the wall, I wanted to kick fuck out of him but a screw turned up and told me to get on with scrubbing and told fatty to fuck off back to the nob head shop - which was a factory on site were the lower intelligent cons worked making cleaning cloths.

At lunch in the main hall I saw fatty sat with his mates and pointing over, with him were two twins tiny, lads about 4 ft ten and they were giving me the wankers sign, I tried to ignore them, later that afternoon I was on my hands and knees scrubbing the floor when these little cunts set about me, one kicked me the face the other jumping up and down on my back, it didn't hurt these were light and weak as a feather, I threw them off and got up and another screw came and gestured to me to sort them out and he walked away. So I grabbed these two little cuts and smashed their heads together both squealing like the rats they were and scuttling off, fuck me I've got 6 months of this I thought...

I had still not made any pals but at supper 7pm a big lad came and sat by me and asked where I came from, he was called Brendan Kelly and came from Wolverhampton and like me was a football hooligan, he had a nice soft Midlands accent and I made him laugh with my accent and 100 mph talking, he was doing 6 months also and had already done a month, he kept himself to himself and said because of his size no one bothered him, he told me the score, who was the daddy. He pointed a huge lad out with long greasy hair centre parting with crude tattoos up and down his arms and hands, that's Turner he says, a Manc from Gorton he's supposed to be the daddy, he bullies a lot of kids and always has a crew of ten other Mancs with him all rats, always nicking stuff and robbing lads tuck (sweets), Turner had a terrible scar across his cheek which made him look evil, he was always snarling and intimidating lads and even a few screws seemed scared of him, he must have been 6 ft 4, however Brendan said the real daddy and one who Turner would never challenge was Noone whom he pointed out. Noone was a Scouser but a decent Scouser, a big good looking lad, with perfect hair and teeth and had a footballer's build and it was rumoured he played for Liverpool reserves before getting sent down for breaking someone's jaw. He was quiet but controlled the fags and money rackets, Turner didn't have a say on that he just went around bullying, I shook hands with Brendan and felt a lot better for meeting him, a decent lad and I headed to dorm 4 for my first proper night in Buckley Hall, as I approached my bed I noticed a crew of about ten lads together, it was fucking Turner and his Manc rats, fuck me I thought "here we go".

I got the third degree "where you from what you in for" etc etc, the fact I was in for affray gave me a tiny bit of credit I was not a nonce but most of these cunts were thieves, drug dealers and general low lives, as I am being interviewed in walks fatty the twat from Stockport I had butted earlier on, oh fuck me I thought, he began whingeing to Turner how I butted him but Turner and his crew just laughed, but then informed me I had to go through the first night initiation, which was running round the dorm vaulting every bed but I was to be punched and kicked by every lad in there all 23 of them ! I didn't mind this I had been used to it the last 6 years on the terraces and up and down the country by rival football fans, so it was lights out and off I set, I took some serious smacks about the head and went down a couple of times but got round with a bloody nose and a few bruises, Fatty caught me a belter to the back of my head which I am sure he must have enjoyed and Turner the daddy caught me flush on my nose and was the one who bust it, but that was it, I had survived and got myself to sleep which was hard given these cunts giggling all night and telling tales of what they had done and who they know - pricks.

The alarm went at 6 am the next morning and we are all in the yard in line and answering our names, it was very military the screw shouting our names out had his peak cap right above his nose, he looked a tough bastard and I found it this was Sgt Lamb ex-SAS, who no one took liberties with, he was hard as iron and put the fear of god into most people he came across. Once the drill was over we were in the main hall for another shit brecky, I found Brendan and he asked about the bruises, I said I did the fist night initiation, he laughed and said "oops I forgot to warn you about that." "It was fuck all", I said, "I've survived Molneux 1976", he laughed out loud at that. I was fed up being in there amongst this horrible lot but Brendan palling up with me made things easier, that day I had two strokes of luck whilst scrubbing the floors, one was when big Nooney the Scouse daddy came talking to me, talking to me in a nice manner, he told me he had heard I butted the fatty from Stockport and that I had done initiation run with no complaints. I had gained respect already, he said don't trust Turner he s a fucking Manc rat and If I get any shit off anyone come and see him, which was nice but never going to happen, I looked after myself and took what I had to but a lovely gesture none the less and I trusted him which was rare with him being a Scouser but he was genuine.

Later that day one of the senior screws approached me and began talking to me about Oldham he was also from Oldham and we both knew many of the same people, he knew my mam who was a famous pub entertainer and he seemed a good feller, he said I will sort you a top job out soon enough just bear with me, I felt better already, that night in the dorm no one said anything to me just left me alone reading a book, next day after brecky in the main hall my name was called out to visit the governors office, in I went to this grand room and I was asked if I would like to be the tea boy - which was one of the very best jobs in Buckley Hall, basically I had to brew up for the screws in their staff room and also provide brew and snacks for visitors, I could have as many brews biscuits and sandwiches as I wanted, I had an extra 2 hours a week visiting as a perk you only had 2 hours a week normally, and I was to be reallocated to the Stock dorm, the smallest dorm but most prestigious this is were the farm lads slept, who had the best job best hours and best perks. There were 7 farm lads and the tea boy in here, only the most trusted lads got on the farm, one of the perks we all had our breckys a hour later than everyone, and as much as we wanted only lads on their last six weeks and 6 monthers not 3 monthers could get on the farm, and they were all good lads.

I accepted the job and was well chuffed, the current tea boy showed me the ropes he was due out that week, he was telling me the score but warned me that I would have to smuggle out cigs, biscuits sugar and any loose change to give to the daddy Turner, all tea boys had to keep the daddy sweet, I thought this fucking tea boy ain't keeping any fucker sweet! Ok, I said to this lemon, just show me how it all works and I told him not to tell anyone Im taking over his job I didn't want anyone knowing til I was out of 4 dorm.

I did tell Brendan that evening though and I told him Turner's getting fuck all off me, I'm not a thief I am a fighter and I'm not risking such a good job for a rat like that, he warned me he wouldn't be very happy, I said fuck him, he laughed, and said you ve got some bottle.

Three days later I swapped dorms and moved into the Stock dorm, the beds were bigger the blankets and sheets a lot better the pillows more fluffier we had much more room for our personal stuff and we could have posters and photos on our walls, it was like Butlins only bigger and better sleeping conditions. I met the lads and they were all sound as a pound, all just looking forward to going home and over the next few months experienced some very emotional scenes as lads had completed their time inside.

The tea boy job was a doddle and I got on with most screws whom I had laughing with my quick fire humour it was great reading all the newspapers they had and supping all them brews and scoffing them biccies all day, I enjoyed supplying the visitors visiting their sons, some very tearful scenes, I also clocked the odd passing off contraband between visitors and cons but that was nowt to do with me, it was well known that I was now the new tea boy and a few rumours flew about that I must be a grass/informer for getting such a top job so soon. This is the mentality of these low life rats, I didn't give a fuck what they thought I knew I was never gonna be a grass for anyone, I was all about looking after myself the best way I can but even though I was not a criminal would never grass anyone up.

That Sunday afternoon we are all in association which is when you get a few hours off and just doss about the main hall watching tele or playing cards etc, relaxation time, I was sat with Brendan, we both noticed Turner and his Manc rats looking over whispering to each other, Brendan said be careful Carl I can sense something naughty here, 2 minutes later over comes Turner with his crew and they surround me, Turner said "tea-boy I want some fags and sugar from the staff room go and toddle along and get them". "Sorry pal," I replied, "I'm not nicking nay stuff for anyone". He then began calling me a grassing cunt etc and then nutted me in the side of my face, I grabbed his long greasy hair swung him round and smashed my plastic mug in his face several times, we rolled about fighting, tables and chairs went flying but I had the better of him until the screws broke us up, they took me through one door and Turner the other way, I was chuffed though to feel so many lads patting me on the back saying well done and a few cheering me, even a few screws said well done as I passed them, I was taken to the staff room cleaned up and I feared the worst but was told my job was safe they knew I had knocked Turner's thieving request back and they admired me for that, but warned me he would avenge this.

For the rest of the day the inmates looked at me many putting their thumbs up, others warning me to be careful Turner was a snidy bastard and had lost face and would not let it go. Big Nooney asked if I would be okay, I told him thanks for the concern but I will be okay, that evening I was tucked in my bed at about 9.30pm under my blankets, the lads in the dorm were all chuffed I had stood up to the big bully, I felt relieved when the doors to our dorm was locked by the screws at 9pm, but all of a sudden the door flew open and in bursts Turner with 2 of his pals and as I tried to get from my bed I got wrapped up in my blankets and Turner pummelled me, relentlessly punching me hard very hard, to the verge of unconsciousness. I then heard a voice, "okay Turner that's enough back to your own dorm". A fucking screw had allowed him in after lock up, bang out of order, my face was a mess and I was aching for days, but I refused to name him to the governor, I took my punishment however out of order. I had to take 3 days off tea boy duty they did not want visitors seeing my face mashed in, but I was back 3 days later.

In the main hall people were speaking in hushed tones, Turner and his cronies were sniggering, I just grinned and bared it, a few weeks later Turner was due for release on the Wednesday morning, the night before was football night in the gym, seven a side, I asked the gym teacher Mr Walsh a very tough looking strong man if I could be in the opposite team to Turner, he laughed and said "yeah course you can lad", he knew the score, it was the first time I had been to the football night you had to go on a waiting list, captain of my team that night the Blues we wore blue bibs was none other than the shamed Liverpool reserve Nooney. I told Nooney I was gonna crunch Turner, he laughed and said "good on yer lah" It didn't take long for my opportunity to arise, as soon as Turner got the ball I was into him I went right through him lifting him off the floor, he crumpled to the floor, whingeing at Mr. Walsh, "foul sir foul boss". "Get up yer big soft bastard," Walshy said. Everyone laughed including members of his own team, he got up and gave out the big threats. "I'm gonna do yoh Oldham yer sheep shagging bastard!" I laughed at him and said bring it on, I relished a good hard game of football, I was a very tough tackling player and feared no one on the pitch, for the rest of the night I got stuck into him and hurt him and he lashed out a few times but missed each time, he knew it was his last night and didn't want to get in trouble and lose days so he had to take some ferocious tackles, I was loving it and teasing him, "Hows that Manc?" I would taunt him.

Next day he was gone and good riddance, Nooney was now the official Daddy and loved me and made sure I got into the Wednesday afternoon football team, Buckley Hall were in a midweek industrial league were we played police teams firemen teams and ambulance teams plus a team from Hindley Borstal and Strangeways Young prisoners, it was a good hard league and we were top four team Nooney was a class act our midfield general, I was the ball winner, won it and gave it to Nooney to spray about like Glenn Hoddle. Two screws also played for us, Mr Walsh and Mr Hutchinson both gym screws both big hard bastards, they nicknamed me "animal" because of my hard tackling, at our home games we would have a good crowd and they would chant "animal animal " whenever I crunched an opponent, I was now accepted as one of the top lads in Buckley hall although I had a few more scraps during my time there.

My time in Buckley Hall flew, I had it easy to be honest, I ate well, had a top job, good lads in the Stock dorm every 6 weeks it changed but whoever came in were behaving and on their last few weeks, I organised talent competitions to allay the boredom, singing, telling jokes, magic tricks etc, we had a right laugh and when my last six weeks arrived I was on the farm gang and glad of it. I loved the outdoors the weathers and smells, our farmer screw was called Tasker and he came from Oldham and he was sound with me, but a bit of a cunt with the others, during my final weeks a blonde haired punk from Burnley calling himself Sputnik came into our Dorm, he would not join in any of the fun and as just being a dick all the time, always robbing stuff, nipping over to the shop facing the farm for fags which was out of bounds and could have had us all done. I told him to get a grip and he told me to fuck off , I wanted to batter him but I was so close to getting home I had to take his gobbyness, one day I caught him grobbing in my cup of tea as we were milking the cows, Tasker the screw also saw him and told me I've got five minutes to sort him then he was coming back, Tasker walked away and I ran and butted Sputnik, we both fell in amongst the cows and dung as we rolled about, he tried biting me but I nutted fuck out of him, the cows were thrashing about kicking out with their hooves connecting with both of us, Tasker eventually comes back and boots us both in our stomachs winding both of us, really took the wind out of me and this Burnley cunt. Tasker then sent Spuntnik to the Governor's office and he got taken off the farm crew, when I got back to my dorm he had ripped all of my letters and photos of family etc, what a twat! I was gutted.

He used to smirk as he walked by me or saw me in the hall, I wanted so much to do him in, again, on my very last night I could not sleep, next morning Friday November 7th 1979 I was having my final brecky only this time in the main hall with the other 300 or so inmates, I was due to be released at 9.30pm, I finished my brecky and returned my dirty plate to the servery and guess who is in there washing pots. Sputnik the Burnley Punk. I butted him smashing his nose, he went down screaming but I was gone, collected my personal belongings and marching down Buckley Lane to freedom to catch the bus to Rochdale centre and the number 9 bus back home to Oldham. I was back home for 11am fit strong and carrying a giro for £24!!!!

Paul my pal was waiting for me at home and it was great to see him and we went for a mooch up the town centre, but then I went down Manchester to watch Quadrophenia at the cinema for it had come out in the summer and everyone was on about what a top film it was and given I had brought the Mod revival back to Oldham in 1978 and by now half the town was Mods I just had to see it, in fact I loved it that much I watched it twice over that afternoon. I also bought a blue beat hat for £12 and wore it that night as I went out with loads of my mates, we were all Mods, suited and booted looking like extras from Quadrophenia, apart from Jimmy the Punk, that night was brilliant we saw three Mod bands in three pubs and ended up at an all night Mod party, was packed out with great 60's tunes and Mod revival tunes, was just like being in Quadrophenia I thought I was in heaven.

THE VERY NEXT DAY Saturday November 8th 1979 Oldham were playing Chelsea at Boundary Park, there was bound to be trouble. Chelsea still attempted to take every end and they would be in the Chaddy, I was determined to keep out of trouble at the footy especially I was targeted now by Oldham cops so had to keep a low profile, and this day I went into the main stand paddock and watch things unfold, it seemed watching from afar I could see exactly what was happening, it was exciting like watching a film, Chelsea only had a couple of hundred in but I could spot them as they mingled and knew within seconds the roar would go up and it did, but Oldham's much bigger numbers swamped Chelsea and forced them down the terracing towards the pitch, they fought valiantly and it was so hard not to climb into the Chaddy and get involved, very hard, but I stood firm, and was proud of Oldham in effect doing Chelsea, the cops eventually restoring order making a few arrests and ejecting the Chelsea mob taking them around the pitch to the away end.

As the cops were escorting them past the paddocks I noticed one big plain clothes officer dragging this Chelsea lad up the pitch but really punching and kicking him, this copper wore black trousers, light blue shirt with dark blue tie and black car jacket, looking every inch the plain clothes copper we were all used to only it was my pal Brandon! I couldn't believe my eyes. Brandon latched onto our Westwood mob about 12 months ago, he was a bit older than us and middle class, his parents owned a sprawling farm on the moors above Oldham, but he loved the football violence and the Mod scene so he started knocking about with us, he was always wedged up, buying us drinks and meals etc and buying top Lambrettas, none of us knew what he did for a living nor ever asked just accepted his many favours. Five minutes later he's walking back down the pitch and into the Chaddy End, I couldn't wait to meet him and asked what was going on? Was he really a copper? Fuck me I hope not, otherwise a lot of us were fucked, we got up to all sorts of naughty stuff in his company, as it turns out, he was a fraudster and a few months later got ten years for a massive fraud he was involved in, this day he had the mad idea to dress up as a plain clothes copper, he even had a fake ID card, he just wanted to arrest a Chelsea fan, he said he booted fuck out of the Chelsea fan then just threw him outside after taking him through the players tunnel, no one questioned him.

From getting released from detention centre for a couple of months I was determined to keep out of trouble, which was so hard, because football violence was still rife and being a Mod attracted many enemies along the way, apart from our natural enemies the bikers/rockers, skins were turning against us, now the original skinheads were just a harder younger version of the 60's Mods and dressed very similarly and were into the same soul/reggae tunes, these were the ideals I based myself on from 1976 but by '78 most skins were now punk orientated, into punk music, glue sniffing and dressing terribly, with no emphasis on style, they wore their docs up to their knees and their jeans not much lower, they all wore those green flying jackets and they were miles away from what I thought a skinhead should look or behave like, Mod was my life, I realised this is what I wanted, smart clothes, great music, scooter rallies, live bands and many parties, it was between 1978—84 a fantastic scene and one that I totally immersed, I was the perfect age 17—23.

As desperate as I was to keep out of trouble, inevitably I crumbled and was soon back scrapping, but it wasn't with rockers, rival hooligans or the piss pot mid twenty bully boys from the town centre pubs it was the Perry Boy's, who were a modern day version of the Mod's, where as we Mod revivalists based our clothes ideal and music tastes on the 1960's the Perry Boys, so called for most of them began wearing Fred Perry polo shirts in the late 70's, but we Mods were also wearing perry's as did the original Mods in the early 60's then the skinheads of 69—71, so they were hardly fashion innovators, but by 1980 they began wearing their own brand of clothing mainly sportswear and labels like fila tacchinni Adidas, kagoules they had awful hair, mainly over one eye, they were forever flicking their hair out of their one eye, we called them flickers or Johnny one eyes, another hairstyle popular with them was the pudding basin cut, awful ! they looked very effeminate and most of them were very skinny, handy for the amount of running they did ! the vast majority of these whom we called " Boys " came from Manchester, they copied Scousers who were two years ahead of them, they seem to come from the border areas and outskirts of inner city Manchester, the border towns of Failsworth Moston and Middleton which bordered Oldham were full of these "boys " and between 79-82 clashed many times with the

Oldham Mods, mainly at Oldham Civic hall when bands like Madness, Secret Affair, Salford Jets, Dexy's Midnight runners etc were performing, another trait of the "boys" was they greatly exaggerated the Mancunian accent, it was very embarassing and cringey and older genuine Mancs also would cringe, there were a few "Boys " in Oldham who followed Man City and most Manchester "Boys" seemed to follow City whereas their Scouse counterparts followed both Liverpool and Everton, United despite their much bigger numbers were very unfashionable lot, many still wearing flares, centre partings and tank tops !

The "boys" hunted in packs and were like rats, after several beatings they asked us for a truce and we agreed and for a couple of weeks it was quiet, but one bank holiday Sunday there was an all day Mod event at Romeo and Juliets night club in Oldham there were hundreds there and about 40 scooters parked up outside, it looked wonderful, well these rats came while we were all inside dancing and kicked over and smashed up all these lovely scooters, bang out of order, as soon as we are outside they fled on foot all the way down to Manchester, we gave them a torrid time over the next couple of years, Oldham became a no go are for any of the twats, they gave Oldham a very wide berth!

1980 arrives, and it was great to be 19. The charts were full of great tunes Specials, Madness, Secret Affair the Beat Selector, Dexy's, Lambrettas all recreating the great ska blue beat sound and beat sounds of the 1960's, life was sweet, I managed to keep out of trouble apart from clipping the odd Manc "Boy", I actually did not go to many Oldham matches for the rest of the 79/80 season in a vain attempt to avoid the violence I craved for, one match I went however was Wrexham away in the spring of 1980, the night before Friday me Paul and an older lad called Tuts decided we were gonna hitch hike through the night, it was only 70 miles away but we fancied a laugh, at last orders 11pm on the Friday we called into the Lancashire Vaults, a notorious Rockers pub on the edge of Oldham town centre, they always had Rock bands on in here and it was full of smelly greebos, we were wearing donkey jackets and flat caps ha for the long night ahead of us, and we fitted in amongst the non stylists, we had a couple of pints and the last thing we saw as we were leaving was Alan Jones who had waist length hair and was more of a hippy but a violent hippy who loved a fight, he was our mate but we lost touch after school we became Mods he became a hippy, Al as we knew him was also a football hooligan and a real loyal fan who travelled all over the country, he was forever chanting "there's only one Simon Stainrod!" Oldham's best player back then, he was getting ejected by the landlord chanting this as we were leaving, it made us chuckle.

We got to the motorway junction for midnight and soon got a lift to the nearby Birch Services, 5 miles away, we settled down for a brew plus any grub we could swipe, after half a hour we saw a coach load of Northern Soulies unload and come on for a brew etc, they looked ridiculous in them vests and very baggy trousers that no one else in the country had worn since the mid 1970's or at least shouldn't have been doing, they were loyal to their music and clubs it was a whole different scene to what we were into although the Mod scene soon encompassed this wonderful sound which actually originated back in the 60's via the Mods back then - at 2 am we went to try and get a lift, and nothing came for a hour and it was getting cold, eventually this Capri screeched to a halt, we ran down to it, and this billy big time bloke with crisp white shirt open exposing his hairy chest and solid gold chain beckoned us in saying I can take you as far as Chester. We had a home made sign saying North Wales, he was clearly pissed and I was not very happy but Tuts and Paul convinced me to get in, this fucking idiot drove at 110 miles a hour with the music blaring out Meat Loaf, Rolling Stones and Queen!

I closed my eyes and prayed we arrive in one piece which somehow we did, we thanked him then sighed a hug sigh of relief, it was now just before 4am and still freezing. We dossed about Chester this wonderful historic city til 6am when we found a cafe and had some brecky, then had a mooch about before getting a bus the short distance over the border into Wales and we arrived in Wrexham at mid day, we decided to go to the train station because we knew loads were coming in on the "service trains " from Piccadilly and at 1pm we could hear the muffled chats from this distance and as this train approached we could see all the arms and scarves and heads hanging put of the window but the first one we saw was Al Jones his long hair blowing in the wind and he had a can of lager in his hand was shouting "there's only one Simon Stainrod " it made us chuckle, there was over 200 lads on that train and we were told another 200 on the next one coming in, but the cops were soon on our case and horded us all into the ground by 1.30am, a long wait til kick off, there were no Wrexham fans to have a go at.

The game passed without much incident but was a good following from Oldham and after the match we went in search of Wreham fans to no avail, they were not coming out to play I didn't really want to get involved but did not want to let my mates down, the cops shoved all 400 of us on the train back to Manc and it was standing room only and few carriages got smashed up by the usual vandals, as soon as the train pulls into Victoria station, me Dennis, Paul, Eddy, Loyd and Mark Kelly broke away from the mob cos the cops were being heavy handed, as we are walking down these stairs we bumped into half a dozen " boys" with their silly flicker haircuts and cagoules etc, Kelly said " come on yer Manc bastards let's be having it " one of them a big heavy built lad in a pink polo neck shirt said " don't insult us we are Bolton not fucking Mancs". We couldn't believe our luck and said, even better yer

Bolton bastards and we flew into them but these were game as fuck. We thought we were good and always backed each other and had been in so many situations over the years but these lads were mates and really fought back.

It was such a long brawl that brought a huge crowd of onlookers, everyone of us including all of them was cut and bleeding, it was a very hard fight and eventually we called it a draw, and even shook hands, even laughing as we limped away, fuck me they breed them tough in Bolton!

That was my first football related fight since I came out and the buzz and adrenalin was still there although I did mange to steer clear until one of the last away games of the 79/80 season when in April we went to our old Lancashire rivals Burnley, we began arriving as early as 10-30 am and found a pub near the market which opened early, by mid day there was over 200 of us in here, we were ballooning singing and chanting and getting all giddy when the landlady eventually snapped and threatened to bring Julian down to sort us out, we all rolled about at the thought of some wimp called Julian taking on 200 hooligans, Robbo the mad Werneth nutter said " go and fetch Julian love " she did, 2 minutes later she came down with the biggest most ferocious snarling dog you could imagine, Robbo crumbled, we all did and made our way out, it looked like he could eat us all and wanted to but we cracked up laughing at the normally fearless Robbo turning white and apologising like fuck!

A couple of our younger lads told us a pub not far away was full of Burnley fans and not only that it was a big bikers pub with over 30 bikes outside, well happy days most of us were Mods and thought we were in Quadrophenia and set off for this pub, there was about 50 of em outside this pub and we ran towards them many launching bottles, they ran inside the pub and sadly a few Oldham lads then kicked their bikes over which I was not happy with and ironically the main instigator was a lad called Fudge who was a biker himself! The greasers boarded up the front door of the pub but we broke it down and pursued them through the pub, they fled out the back and down a canal but only the odd one got caught for the kicking, we then marched triumphantly towards Turf Moor our mob growing as we got nearer, as usual Burnley had a big mob waiting and some serious running battles occurred, the cops were out in force with their alsations and a few on horse back, Robbo was telling everyone he was gonna knock a horse out ha ha, and he threw a wild hay-maker at this police horse flush on the jaw, the horse did not budge a inch, just neighed, Robbo was screaming in agony as his hand was smashed to bits, and he had to go to hospital and have a plaster on it, it was hilarious, Robbo should stay clear of big animals.

# THE OLDHAM JACK RUSSELLS

FOR SOME REASON OR OTHER Oldham has consistently produced very tough aggressive short men, our Rugby teams are renowned for producing so many little tough as teak scrum halves for years, nasty aggressive snarling little buggers, also many small boxers have done our town proud over the years - this trend continued at Oldham Athletic during the 70's & 80's. From the very first hooligan I ever saw in action Slouk, the little hard as fuck Ukrain lad from Glodwick Mob, never saw him take a backward step. Others include Ian McGrat, a year younger than me only small bit stocky and toothless well no front teeth, game as they come, you just knew when it kicked off he'd be flying in with no worries about size and numbers, Rorcoe the ex Man United hooligan who changed to Oldham late 70's cos he knew there was far more action here, this gobby slighkty built small Manc was the most cocky confident bastard ever, he soon made his mark and was a great little character. Joe Ashowrth from Royton a professional hooligan who followed City, United and Oldham in his quest for violence, about 5ft 4 inches and frightened of nothing, he'd go right into battle no questions asked. Dally had the same stamp as Joe, same age a couple years younger than me, from the rough Limeside estate had a boxers face well a losing boxers face ha but brave as fuck. One of the Oldham nine sent down in the famous Oldham Race Riots of 2001 - the charismatic Mouse of Glodwick only five foot tall a natural leader, in first led by example but also well switched on, very much respected. Johnny Murphy, The Mighty Atom of Werneth, game as fuck totally fearless and a voice like a fog horn, when he went charging in chanting Oldham Aggro you'd have thought there were fifty coming at you! Egghead of Holts, a real rough tough battler, you'd never think he was a hooligan to look at but he loved a scrap and could do some damage...Robbo Watson was only about 5ft 6 at tops but one of the gamest and most respected lads at Oldham in the 1970's, another one with the broken nose face of a boxer...so many more great little battlers who never let us down.

I worked away that summer in Newquay, a wonderful resort in Cornwall, I had the best time of my life down there between April and August 1980. I got their by train, Oldham were playing at QPR this particular Saturday and were taking a "Special Train" down, I assumed that Newquay wasn't too far from London and I jumped the train to London and was gonna make my way to Newquay from there. Fuck me it was another 300 miles away, I knew I should have concentrated more in geography, I arrived in Newquay at 8.30pm on this warm night, Adidas sports bag slung over my shoulder I walked the short distance tot he promenade on the lovely night, a slight sea breeze cooled me, as I got to the edge of this cliff and looked over the wondrous harbour festooned by the most gorgeous sunset I had ever seen tears filled my eyes at such beauty, I really was in paradise, it was so clean.

I found the flat were a couple of my pals were staying Tony Howe and Tuts and within a few days had secured a job, Tony and Tuts were homesick and went back home but there were quite a few from Oldham down here, in fact most of the holiday workers came from up North, Bolton, Manchester Scousers Sheffield Barnsley and Nottingham providing so many seasonal workers, we soon all became mates and any football rivalries were rightly put to one side, one Oldham lad who was in his second season let us down, Big Neil Donaldson, the lad who got arrested with me at Hull, well he didn't want to know any of us Oldham lads and girls, he knocked about with a lad from Nottingham called Spanner who was a great lad and mixed with us all but Neil didn't and not only that kept telling everyone he was from Manchester and was even claiming to be a fucking United fan by now, he had the strongest Oldham accent ever and the Mancs used to take the piss asking him were he came from in Manchester, it was pitiful, for Neil was a good lad and we went all over the country following Oldham since kids.

All the seasonal workers would meet up and drink in pubs like Newquay Arms, Sailors bars, Red Lion, Berties and Atlantic bars, and on Sundays we would have a mass game off football usually north v south, great games and laughs, I ended up seeing a great girl called Debbie, we were a couple and got on great and when a few of my mates came down for a week in June they were shocked to hear that Deb was from Bolton!

I got heavily involved with the local Mods and most Saturdays we would travel to Plymouth for the All Nighters in a Mod club called the Metro off Union street, which was very famous what a place that was, so vibrant, one of the busiest places I have ever seen, every pub was packed out with sailors, prosses, good time girls, stag and hen nights, it was kicking off all night but I wasn't interested, I was well into the music by now dancing all night or as long as I could do, given that I never took any stimulants, I often fell asleep but could still hear the music pounding away, and one time about 5 am I was half asleep and the tune Police and thieves by Junior Murvin came on, it was an incredible few moments, it was so surreal, I was floating to this great Reggae classic that was lifting me in body and spirits, I felt such a wonderful feeling of well being, it was one of many fantastic memories form the best time of my life.

I made the heart breaking and very regrettable decision to leave Newquay in August to come home for my younger sister Karen's 18th birthday, I wished I had have stayed down there for I was in paradise and never experienced a better place or time in my life, it left me though with some fantastic memories.

We played Burnley in a pre season friendly and took loads up, I was part of a three van convoy that lft Oldham at 11-30 am, two transist and a big box van, msut have been at least 70 of us, as we are dring hrough Rochdale we stopped at a garage and all of a sudden 5 lads came flying out of a pub launching bottles and ash trays at us! Cheeky fuckers, they ran back in and bolted the door, but that soon got broke down and they were beaten to fuck by about ten of our lads, we had to chuckle though at their "bottle".

The game itself was a typical Lancashire derby on and off the pitch the players got stuck in to each other as much as the fans, and the flying tackles just wound up the fans as much as ever, missiles were thrown to and fro as per usual, lots of ejections and a few arrests, at the end of the game it really kicked off in and around Turf Moor, Burnley as ever game as fuck but so were Oldham and many brawls broke out with many injured on both sides, we had the upper hand for a while charging through the town centre but they came back at us and eventually had us backed into the bus station, were our vans were parked, the cops eventually getting us back out of town, we unloaded in Rochdale and went for a mooch and Moggy and his Rochdale pikeys were waiting for us as usual until getting overwhelmed again! But they would have been happy to pick a few off, this evening we bumped into a 40 strong stag party from Leeds who actually attacked our much bigger mob lobbing pint pots and ashtrays - we ran them back into the Flying Horse and got in there and smashed em to bits, all their fancy shirts suits and ties shredded and blood stained.

Blackburn was once a very rough ground to go to no matter who you followed, in the early 70's they sorted out teams such as Millwall, Man City, Bolton, Sheffield United and many more, however by the end of the decade they were somewhat of a joke, we certainly had no respect nor fear of them and hadn't for a long time, so much so that this game early on in the 1980/81 season we decided to make an assault on their end the Blackburn end, three van loads of us, around forty paid into their end just after kick off on the late summer night, we knew we didn't have the numbers to stay in, most of our fans were already massed up in the away end the Darwen end, but by going in there and getting in amongst them we were laying down the challenge, so in we go and not one lad said anything as we made our way to the top of their end where their mob was, in fact Blackburn fans began melting away as they knew we were Oldham despite not having any colours, as we got to the top up went the roar, 'OLDHAM OLDHAM!' and we charged into them, they scattered and there must have 3-400, all falling over each other, they did not know how many there was of us but we all went wading into them.

The big gap appeared and we just stood in there laughing at them, only when they saw there was only 40 of us they came back but even then we held em off for a bit, but in they came, one of our top lads Pete Hilty got a crash helmet smashed into his face busting his nose then he and big Bruno got arrested by the cops and dragged around the pitch, and got heavy fines, that ended Hilty's hooligan career, the rest of us got escort back to the Darwen end were we got a standing ovation from the 2000 Oldham fans massed in the Darwen end, it was pitiful and not one of us got hurt despite being outnumbered ten to one... I just wished a couple of hundred of us would have got in we would have taken it over and stayed the whole match, as it was it was a gesture and Blackburn had to come to Oldham and do the same..would they ? at three quarter time hundreds of us left early to try and take that end again but the cops held us off but Blackburn were not interested and would not come out to play, we marched back into the centre 2 miles away triumphant.

The tide had turned full circle..

ONE OF THE FIRST GAMES of the 1980/81 season was Cardiff

City at home, Cardiff had a very tough reputation and we had not played them for years but the last time they came there was trouble in our end and after the game, we did not know if they were gonna bring a lot up for this game, but we were suorised to see that there was about 60 of them in the Spinners Arms, our pre match local back then, it was only mid day and Harry the landlord had let them all in at 10.30am, and they were all pissed up and singing their tits off. To be fair to Harry he had them all in the games room leaving the main room to us Oldham fans, by 1pm our room was also full as word got round about these mad Taffies in the Spinners, for the next hour or so it was just rival chanting, but their constant "we fucking hate England" was winding us up - we had to use the same bogs at the back of the pub and there was the odd scuffle in here but nothing serious.

At about 2.15pm a you Cardiff fan walked into our room and smacked Yogi of all people, Yogi wasn't the brightest and jsut stood there with blood trickling down his nose. Another young Oldham lad cracks this cheeky Welsh lad then in came the rest of the Taffies from both sides, armed with pots, pool cues, ash trays etc, there was nowhere to run it was just a mad free for all, we picked up stools and waded in, the figh lasted a full ten minutes with all the windows going through and the bar was was ransacked. During the fight a Taffy stuck a broken coke bottle into my chest, it was one of those old heavy glass coke bottles, it was stuck in a couple of inches or so, I was in shock, when the fight fnally spilt outside, Graham, Harry the landlords son came over to me and told me to lie down as he pulled the bottle out of my chest, well the torrent of blood flew up and hit the ceiling, I then lost conscienous and the next thing I recall was being in the back of the ambulance with nurses pressing nto this wound, also in the ambulance were Jimmy Ragg and Dave Green both who had been potted and needed stitches in their heads and a Cardif fan who had ben hit with an iron bar and had a deep wound in his face.

I was operated on that evening, I was panicking and asked the nurse how bad it was, she said I was very lucky as the deep hole was right on the joint of my chest and shoulder, a inch or so inside it cold have been fatal. I had dozens of micro stitches inserted inside the wound and was kept in over the weekend, rumours were flying around town I was dead, ha...but it was close I suppose. You would think that would put me off football violence for life but there was still fire in my belly.

# ENTER MAD MICK...

IN SEPTEMBER 1980 the word around Oldham was of this big lad my aged 19 who was knocking out everyone who had a name/reputation, that summer this lad had knocked out dozens of so called hard lads or lads who got in his way, especially the wannabe Mancs of Failsworth, and a few twenty odd year old bouncers from the towns clubs. This lad was called Mick Carolan, known as Mad Mick, he loved this name and that's how he introduced himself, Mick's story is the old classic of a lad bullied at school but growing up bigger and stronger than all his tormentors, Mad Mick avenged every single lad or man who bullied him, from the age of 18 he shot up to over six feet two and filled out like a prop forward, he had hands the size of shovels and a knock out punch, he was angry very angry and many paid the price for crossing him.

Well I had never met him but was aware of his fast growing reputation and the fact I was one of the lads about town was aware that he would come in search of me sooner or later and this is what he did, it was a Thursday night and it was Mod night at the Harlequin pub in Chadderton, packed out in the upstairs function room, we were dancing and posing to the sounds like Green Onions, Booker T & the MG's, Down in the Tube station, the Jam, Too much too young, Specials and On my Radio by Selector, when all of a sudden the whispers began, "Mad Mick's here!" His reputation had preceded him, he was like some kind of bogie man, we all rush down the fire escape to the back garden of this pub and there he was large as life, this big imposing figure complete in oversized crombie overcoat, the boxers face and the toothless grin.

Ooops.. I got pushed to the front of him and I said to him, Hi Pal who are you? he said "I'm Mad Mick". "Oh hiya Mick, how mad are you?" the chuckles began. He said "I'm this mad" and I expected him to attack me, but he turned around and ran arms outstretched into a waney lap fencing panel and brought it down with him on top of it, he got up and dusted himself down and everyone fell about laughing, I put my hand out and said, "nice to meet you mick, I'm Carl" and with that we shook hands and had a chat. He told me he wanted to be a hooligan and I was the lad to see, so I invited him to meet us that Saturday lunch time in Oldham town centre as we had a very big game and guaranteed trouble as we were playing Sheffield Wednesday and with that he was gone, grinning like a Cheshire cat... phew!

At Saturday midday me and about ten pals met up town and along came Mad Mick with his pal Punk Tommy, I explained at 1pm we will walk to the ground and maybe bump into a few Wednesday fans en route but I also expected them to come into the Chaddy End. The last time we played them they took the Chaddy End..at 1pm we set off marching the mile or so to Boundary Park, halfway down we bumped int half a dozen Weds fans, they didn't look keen so i said leave these lads, but Mick knocked two clean out! I told Mick there'll be loads in the Chaddy End and he didn't have to smack everyone he saw, he said "I've come to knock out Yorkshire bastards and that's what I'm gonna do" and he knocked a few more out on Sheepfoot Lane, all you could hear was this big clumping sund and then see a Weds fans twitching on the deck. As we gets near the ground we could hear the rival fans in the Chaddy End and we ran the last 100 yards or so to join in the fray, soon as we are hit we are battling, charging into each others mobs across the top of the Chaddy End, it was great, during a lull I saw Mad Mick with his back to a wall breathing heavily, he couldn't get his head around the fact no one gave a fuck for his size and strength, this was a different game, all about bottle and cunning.

It always amuses me when critics of football hooligans say things like oh they are all shithouses, cowards, can only hunt in packs blah blah blah. Funnily enough many of these critics are your hard men about town, doormen, bodybuilders, rugby players etc lads with no interest in football and no idea about football hooliganism, I accept there are a lot of wankers at the game, lads who preen about stay in the back ground once it kicks off and good at pushing and shoving but for all those of us who fought on the front line we had courage and fighting skills which had to be admired under extreme situations.

These so called hard men would not have the bottle on the terraces where no respect for size and reputation was shown, I've seen these so called hard lads venture down to Boundary Park and when it's kicked off they have crumbled, got out of the road, even left the ground, such was the level of violence, they are okay on the doors dealing with drunks and with back up from other doormen. They are okay going for a one on one down a back alley knowing full well they have a big advantage being much bigger and stronger than their opponent, Rugby players are fine mauling and brawling on the field of play knowing full well it would be broken up, football violence on the front line was a very dangerous game, knowing you could be stabbed or kicked to death, dozens of punches and boots piling into you often rendering you unconscious, and then those god forsaken trips away from home, being attacked for hours before during and after the games, most of the time Oldham got hammered away from home, we did not have the numbers for many games, I still have nightmares of some of the situations I found myself in.

Your average so called hard man probably has ten fights all his life, ten! His name and reputation can be cemented forever by that if he wins all or most of them, some days I had at least ten fights in that one day, taking many many blows, I'm not alone there were many like me at Oldham and indeed up and down the country, I've worked out I fought fans from over sixty teams (sixty!) from all four divisions, and many of them many times and many of them many times in one day/night! We are talking hundreds of brawls, fights punches and kicks swapped, hit with all kinds of weapons and that was just in a ten year career! Some hooligans have been at it for over forty years!

I have seen some incredible scenes of bravery at the football games, young, small lads taking on giants and often outnumbered, getting kicked to fuck but dusting themselves down and going back into battle. These are the kind of people you want in the trenches during war time, you can't put muscle on a heart, you either have courage or you do not and plenty of football lad's had incredible courage.

Of course the cowardice of ten on to one happened many times, and yes I would be guilty a few times, but this was the law of the jungle and as I got older I tended to search out the main lads of away teams, I am sorry for any innocents who got caught up in the rampages, but this was few and far between, the vast majority of football hooligans only wanted to fight other hooligans, I will say this and I mean it, if Victoria Crosses were only ever dished out for extreme courage in battle then quite a lot would have been dished out on the terraces in the 70's/80's.

As kick off approached in the Weds game they began taking over, they outnumbered us three to one and were coning in from both sides and up the middle to take the Chaddy End, but this day Oldham stuck together and fought gallantly, in fact it was the bravest and most courageous defending of an end Ive ever seen, the Weds fans all seemed like giants, men in their 30's and 40's, but we reppled them and yes our normal fans got stuck in and our own coppers encouraged us to get stuck in, despite several attempts at taking our end Weds were eventually ran out of our end, and clambered onto the pitch in their hundreds, the away end was almost full with Weds fans aswell and lets not kid ourselves if they had all got intot he Chaddy End they would have taken it, but that day we won the day before the match, "you'll never take the Chaddy!" we roared at them, I was so proud - ironically later on in the game Sheff Weds fans rioted to such a level that the game was held up for 20 minutes, the Yorkies attacked the police and their then manager Big Jack Charlton pleaded with them to stop, he was ignored, he left the pitch in tears, more and more police arrived and it was a full on riot. One cop got rendered unconscious by a big lump of concrete ripped up from the terrace, eventually the game finished, but there was still serious crowd disorder - us Oldham fans wisely chose not to take them on after the match - there was the first ever government enquiry into the events at this match and it was becasue of this game that steel fences were erected around all pitches to stop invasions - nine years later these fences were torn down because of the disaster at Hillsborough when 96 Liverpool fans were crushed to death - how's that for a coincidence?

Despite our recent success on and off the terraces we did come unstuck the odd time, a good example was at Rotherham of all places, we took a big mob and went on a bit of rampage before the game but could not find many Rotherham fans to play, but in the game we noticed how many they had in the adjoining paddock to our allotted end, they seemed very aggressive with a couple of mini pitch invasions. We were looking forward to seeing these outside after the game, fair play to them they came looking for us after the match and we had a big clash with them on the car park, the cops sorted it out and we got into our transit van and went in pursuit of them, there was 15 of us, Eddy was driving and me and Dennis were in the front with 12 very game lads in the back, we did not have to wait long for action, we were stuck in a traffic jam when out of nowhere came all these Yorkies, many of them armed with bats and various other weapons, they wrenched the back doors open and began dragging lads out, we had to get out to help but we were surrounded and we couldn't get out and these fuckers smashed our windows and tried to drag us out beating us about the head with these bats, it was horrendous, only the sound of a police siren stopped this classic ambush, but most of us were done in, we were desperate to avenge it but the cops escorted us out of town over the moors, and these cunts never come to Oldham in the return match and we never got the chance to play them again as they got relegated.

Another time we came unstuck well our little crew did was Leicester City, the season before we played Leicester in the FA Cup on a Monday night and they came in droves smashing several pubs up and rampaging on Sheepfoot Lane after we had defeated them, they had us that night, we wanted revenge the season afterwards, they did not bring the same numbers but about ten of us went to look for them on the coach park after the match, it was very foggy but we spotted a van with a few likely looking lads climbing into the back of it, so we attacked this van but they burst out of the back doors armed with hammers chisels and pick axe handles, and knocked fuck out of us, my hands were smashed to fuck as I protected my head and a few of our lads got cut up badly and we had to bail out, these sorted us out good and proper, they were armed and ready and game as fuck.

Barnsley was always a dodgy place to go to, but always more so on a cold winter's day and on this freezing foggy day we got ambushed as we came out of our end onto that big shale car park, it was so dark you couldn't see who was attacking you but they came from everywhere, men women and children, no weapons just out and out sluggers, the cops did fuck all but watch this planned assault, we fought back but were heavily outnumbered and were we come from it's deemed out of order to hit women but there were loads of Barnsley women attacking us, so a few of them got dug, not by me, but you could hardly blame those that did these women were wild, scratching eyes and biting, it only stopped when they got bored, we could not wait to get them back to Oldham but they never turned up but next time we went there to that god forsaken hole we took loads and hammered loads in the town centre before and after the game, we did avenge that one.

Amongst all this fun and games were moments of classic comedy truly hilarious moments, one of my favourites was whn we played Blackburn Rovers at home on Boxing Day, we decided that seeing as they very rarely came for trouble nowadays we would have a fancy dress party, by now we were going into our supporters club which was directly behind the Chaddy End, the Clayton Arms, loads of us dressed up as the usual suspects, Elvis, Hippies, Julius Caesar, Hitler, and various other celebrities. My pal Paul and Vic Scan, Loyd's brother who was a 6 ft odd half caste lad, a very muscly athletic lad, well they were both dressed as prostitutes, with wigs, stockings, sussies, bras stuffed with socks and ladies clobber and high heels, they looked ridiculous and could hardly stand up, the were also carrying handbags, well twenty minutes before kick off we left the club to go to the match en masse all dressed up, as we are leaving the club doors a mob of about fifty Blackburn thugs came towards us, we couldn't believe our luck, but the way we were dressed made it awkward, but never the less we piled into them and a mass brawl ensued.

God knows that they thought? But the funniest was seeing Paul and Vic wading in swinging their hand bags, knocking loads over, but once they were down the high heels went into them we were cracking up laughing as were the watching cops and even a few Blackburn fans saw the funny side of it, it looked so uncouth as both got their tights laddered, it lightened the mood and Im sure a few Blackburn fans must have had some weird nightmares about this for years after!

Another funny one was when we played Burnley on a night match at home, well this young girl called Debbie latched onto me in the game and after the game we are walking up Sheepfoot Lane, and she's giving it all "Ooh ive heard of you your hard aren't you, you've got a big reputation" Well I was milking it to impress her and not denying this, she was a bonny 'un, so I was saying yeah yeah I like rumble etc and as I'm saying that this massive Burnley fan walked by with a couple of his mates, she said "yeah but I bet you wouldn't have a go at someone that big!" I said size never bothers me and with that I tripped him or tried to, he turned round and lamped me right between my eyes and knocked me clean out! I awoke to her straddled over me asking if I was okay? She couldn't stop laughing and it's fair to say she never bothered with me again, ah bless her.

There were loads of girls in the Chaddy End and all the top lads were popular with them, the girls loved the bravado the fighting and the gamest lads, also a lot of the Oldham girls would mingle with the away fans, many times trapping off with them, but when it came to the fighting the Oldham birds always backed their home town lads, girls I remember from the 1970's include, Shaz, Kathy, Carol, Skip, Nat, Salmon Pam, Dirty Donna, Fat Joy, Pauline, Donna H, Karen, Loz, Elaine, big Deb, Sheila Blige, little Jenny, Jackie Gee, loads more..

IN MARCH 1981 something I had dreamed about but never ever thought could happen was when we made an assault on Bolton's end. Now we had gone into their famous Lever End in '77 but we were kids and knew it was just a gesture and as it was they were all in the away end awaiting us and really gave it to us for having the cheek to dare go into their end, but by 1981 we were all aged around twenty – twenty five, no longer nervous teenagers but experienced veterans of football violence, Bolton no longer held any fears for us and more to the point we relished facing our old foes, this particular match was a Tuesday night game but it was still light at kick off, there were three van loads of us, 2 transit vans, a large box van which held about 30 lads and a few car loads, we had a mob of around 70/80 - all game lads, a few were carrying weapons, home made coshes etc, we arrived late on purpose twenty mins after kick off, Bolton by this time assembled in the Burnden Paddock alongside the Railway Embankment open end terrace were away fans went.

Now if I'm being honest Bolton were not the force of yesteryear they had recently been relegated from Divison One and were on a downward slide which would see them tumble through the leagues, but they had as many as we did if not more, they got bigger crowds it was a much bigger town and most lads in Bolton were Bolton fans unlike a lot in Oldham who followed United, City and Leeds, everything went to plan, there were no coppers about and we walked down the back of the Burnden paddock, amazingly we all got in through the late turn style with out being noticed.

A couple of Bolton who were at a cafe bar got smacked, and then we made our way into their end, our intention was to get in behind, them then attack them and hold our place for as long as possible, it was going great as we mingled amongst them, they'd never expect us to be so bold, all of a sudden there was great excitement as Oldham fans in the away clocked what was going on and Bolton began looking around to see what was going on so we had to start scrapping, the chant went up 'OLDHAM - OLDHAM - OLDHAM!' Bolton scattered most of them running not knowing how many there was of us, a few old long haired grizzly Rockers stayed and slugged it out, but most of them ran to the bottom of the terrace until they sussed how many of there really was and then they came back but for a few minutes we held the top of their end, but they overwhelmed us but we went down fighting like fuck cheered on by our supporters over the fence, the cops eventually got us out and into the away end were we were once again treated like heroes, Bolton were livid and will deny this til their last breath but it happened and briefly we took them on and scattered them in their own end.

After the match we were driving around for a hour picking mobs of Bolton off, Meggy ploughed into a mob of them in his car, skittling them, we were jumping out of the vans and cars every few moments attacking Bolton fans, we went into all their rough estates and attacked any lads aged 16 - 25, it was revenge time for all the times they had made our lives hell, we hurt a lot of lads that night - never was revenge so sweet.

Whilst I was still very active in 1981 I began to feel depressed at the end of the Saturday's antics, it was draining me and as I reflected on the pain I inflicted and indeed taken I began to question it, the aches and pains were taking longer to go away, I would have incredible lows but the incredible highs I was still getting at the game and linked to the game were still outweighing the lows, I was reaching an age where most football lads retired, early twenties as many got married and had families or the spells inside slowed them down, but I loved the camaraderie amongst my friends, I loved the adulation and respect I received for my courage, leadership qualities and loyalty to my friends, football team and town, I had all the qualities to be a soldier for Queen and country and did indeed try to join up when we went to war with Argentina in 1982, they knocked me back because I had been inside, so I shrugged my shoulders and went back to war on the terraces as much as I was doubting it.

# 1981-82

**B**Y 1981/82 NEW LADS were coming through as many of the older lads faded away, lads like the West Street boys, CBC (Chaddy Boozing Crew), Middleton led by the loud n'brash Colin Moore, what a mob they had game as fuck with their strong Manc accents but they loved Oldham, more young uns came from Failsworth more Mancs but loved Oldham, Royton Wanderers, a young up and coming firm from Royton who followed Oldham, City and United in pursuit of excitement, lads like big Pete Buckley, and his pals from Waterhead, Hollins with good lads like Hammy Si Boss, Dave Bourne, Ronnie Davies, Jarvis all been about a bit but young lads were latching onto them and following Oldham, there were many more and it was great see and it swelled our numbers both home and away.

1981/82 season was lively, we took a massive mob up to Huddersfield on the train one lovely Saturday afternoon, and rampaged from mid day til kick off, loads got arrested, the cells were full of Oldham fans who had smashed up pubs and robbed tills in shops and attacked Huddersfield lads, from that day on Oldham and Huddersfield became big rivals and both teams brought big mobs to their rival towns with both firms gaining results.

We also took a big mob to Bradford and took on their famous Ointment Squad, they held no fear for our young ones and those of us who recalled how rough it was back in '76 and come a long way since then and toughened up, and we went to Bradford with confidence and was in and out of their town centre pubs all day with very little opposition, they got stuck in at Valley Parade but after the game we fought them and gave as good as we got, once more the heavy handed West Yorkshire police arresting loads of Oldham fans, there was a young Jewish solicitor in Oldham called Joe Newman who loved representing the Oldham hooligans and was kept very busy during the 1980's, he was corrupt and eventually got sent down in the early 1990's for bending the system, via legal aid and got 9 months and was in Kirkham open prison same time as me, I was only in for a month for non payment, it was good to see Joe who was very popular giving out legal advice to the cons for treats like sweets, pop, stamps and other bits n bobs, Joe was also a very useful footballer and represented the Prison football team.

# Y VIVA ESPANA

IN JUNE 1982 I made the decision to go an watch England during their World Cup campaign in Spain, I had booked a one way boat ticket a couple of months prior Plymouth—Santander, a big port in the Basque region of Northern Spain; me, Tony Greaves and Shane Clegg, my relationship with Caron had broken down and I just wanted some adventure, we were due to sail on the Monday morning, the day before I was running about trying to raise some funds for the trip to Spain, all to no avail, on the Saturday night I told myself I was not going, but when I woke up very early Sunday morning I wanted to go, I asked my then girlfriend Linda if she had any money whatsoever, all she had was her bus fare back to Manchester, £1-50 in 15 ten pence pieces, I convinced her to walk the 7 miles home and lend me that - £1 fucking fifty! That's all I had when I met Tony and Shane, and an old adidas bag with a few bits of clobber toothpaste and a couple of books, I never saw the lovely Linda again.

I met up with Tony and Shane and we decided to hitch-hike to Plymouth as the boat wasn't sailing til Monday morning so we had a full day/night to get to down there, I told them I only had £1-50 and that I would get by off my wits and wasn't after any money off them I knew they had scrimped and saved, we got a lift off Tony's dad to Birch services Sunday morning, then we soon got another lift off a school teacher down to Hilton Park services, where I ragged the food on sale, that was a free lunch, already I was living off my wits, I robbed bags of sweets and chocolate bars also, I was stocking up, Hilton Park services just north of Birmingham are the biggest services in the UK, when we went to hitch hike further there were dozens of others hitch hikers all with their placards to their destination. It seemed hopeless, we decided to split up and meet in Plymouth, after a hour the queue was going down a bit, it was a nice day so  wasn't bothered, all of a sudden this big box van came swerving towards me, this lad leaned out of the window and shouted, "hey Oldham get in the back with yer mates!" as I did Tony and Shane had sorted this lift out to Plymouth these lads who were from Bury were also booked on the "Pride of Bilbao" the boat taking us to Spain. There were about ten Bury lads in the back and three in the front, result!

We arrived in Plymouth at around 5pm and ended up on Union Street the famous vibrant street full of pubs and sailors and good time girls, there were hundreds of England fans already here, from various football teams, we met up with six Bolton lads I recognised a couple of them, Dave a short stocky lad with a big tache was always at the front when we were fighting each other and my old enemy the feather cutted ginger kid from the 70's who by now had a flicker hair style, he was called Donny. We laughed at the amount of times we clashed with each other, we found a pub playing Northern Soul and settled there for the night, these Bolton kids bought me a few cokes and Donny slipped me a fiver after I explained my situation to him, at the end of the night hundreds of England fans headed towards the docks for the 8am sail the next morning, me, Tony and Shane dossed down in these decrepit old bogs, there were loads of England fans just sleeping anywhere they could.

It was a restless night and I was awake at 5 am and went for a wash and just mooched about watching all the England fans arriving, all the different football teams from all over the country, many of whom I had clashed with over the years but now we were one as we headed to Spain, the mother country of Argentina who we were still at war with! The sight of so many Union Jacks filled my heart with joy, I found a greasy Joe's cafe and had myself a full breakfast, and read the morning papers, at 7am me Tony and Shane boarded the "Pride of Bilbao" I was so excited and proud, I felt like we were going to war, all the press were there clicking away with their camera and film crews, there were 2000 of us on that boat and pictures the next day adorned the front pages with images of us, calling us "Maggie's Boot Boys" set sail for Spain ha ha I loved that headline... Once on board I went off on my own, Tony and Shane wanted to be together I sussed that much out and I was fine with that, I didn't want them carrying me I would sort myself out.

I went on the top deck as we sailed out, heart was beating with pride, never mind "Pride of Bilbao" I was pride of Oldham and felt as though I was representing my town abroad! I set about finding some food and robbed the kitchens, of bread, ham, cheese and biscuits and just found my own little space on the top deck and scoffed away as the sea mist blew about me, it was a fucking choppy sail, through the bay of Biscay, notorious seas at the best of time, this huge boat was being tossed about and loads were spewing up including me, it was a 24 hour crossing and now it was late afternoon and I went to the main bar were most England fans were on the piss, all singing and chanting their teams songs, most big teams were represented and plenty off smaller teams, Chelsea and West Ham had the most maybe 100 each, but Bolton, Forest, Newcastle and Leeds also had large numbers of lads, sadly there were only three from Oldham, me, Tony and Shane and them two were trying to keep a low profile. Not me though I told everyone who I was and where I came from, at about 7pm a big Cockney got up on the stage grabbed a mic and announced that he wanted a member from each team to get up and sing one of his clubs songs, well I was soon up volunteering, I could see Tony and Shane cringeing but I was so proud of my hometown team, I was about fifth up and the lad asked me where I was from and what as I gonna sing. I told him Oldham and the Bolton fans booed and hissed me so I decided to sing "Latics from Lancashire " now Tony and Shane sunk behind their seats, ha ha.

" We are the Latics from Lancashire, we are the team Man United fear, altogether we will make it clear, oh so clear, we ran Bolton in to the ground, their own supporters wouldn't make a sound cos some fucker told em that this team from Oldham are theLatics from Lancashire!"

I got a standing ovation even the Bolton fans cheered me and a few lads threw coins onto the stage which I gladly scooped up, about a tenner's worth, it was a great craic but it eventually kicked off with Chelsea and Bolton before the rest broke it up, Tony and Shane went to the Casino for the night and around mid night Tony found me and gave me a tenner as he had won a good amount on the roulette. What a day that was, I was on passenger only Tony and Shane had a cabin but no room for me, I was okay and found myself a nice little room full of warm fluffy towels, the room was heated and I had a great kip despite the boat bobbin up and down.

Breakfast was served from 6am and was part of the ticket price and self service yes! I was a big eater and demolished it, me and Shane sat down at this table, there was another bloke sat the with a trilby on, reading his newspaper, after a minute I nudged Shane and whispered, "that's Bobby Moore " and lo and behold it was our greatest ever footballer and World Cup winning captain chatted away to us no airs and graces sound as a pound and signed loads of autographs for fans, what a lovely man. After breakfast I got chatting to some West Ham fans who promised me a lift into Bilbao were the first three World cup games were being held, Bilbao was about 50 miles away from Santander, Tony and Shane had sorted themselves a lift out (a bit of a theme here eh) the West Ham lads were great and loved the fact I had come with just £1-50 in my pocket and when they dropped me off gave me twenty pounds between them, a lovely gesture.

When I arrived in Bilbao this wonderful vibrant city I went for a long walk taking in all this architecture, eventually made my way to the main railway station were I had told Tony and Shane I would catch up with them, when I found the station bar it was full of England fans hundreds all singing away, I found Tony and Shane who informed me they had sorted themselves some digs out, no offer of me on the floor but there you go, I got chatting to 2 Pompey lads, Mark and Aidey lads my age, we went for a mooch about and began ripping bars and cafes off, over there it was all on tab and trust, you had a chalk board next to were you ate and drank, they trusted you that much you wrote your own order down and what you had. Fuck me we couldn't believe our luck, we ate like kings and just disappeared into the night, we kipped in bank door holes for the first few days, the first game was not while Sunday we had a few days to go, each day I would meet up with Tony, Shane and more Oldham lads who had come by train or car to Spain. On the Friday Tony and Shane announced they were going to a resort about 20 miles away called Laredo, I went with them but they informed me they had a hotel booked and were sorted out, I said I will sort something out, as soon as we got there to this lovely resort which was full of England fans I bumped into my cousin Gary Walker, a great lad a few years older than me and a fanatical Man United fan home and away, he was with about twenty Burnley Reds and Burnley fans, he had no hesitation on letting me doss down with him and gave me some money, top lad.

Laredo was great and more and more Oldham fans came here, including big Colin Shaw one of Oldham's most respected fans, he had a massive Union Jack with OAFC emblazoned across it and that flew from the highest mast in the town centre square, looked brilliant – there was also loads of Northern Ireland fans based there who we all got along great with. I loved it here and all the rival fans got along, on the Sunday the day of our first match v France in Bilbao we all left this resort on buses early in the morning, of course I did not have a ticket but as determined to get in the game by hook or crook, Bilbao was teeming with both England and French fans the mood was upbeat, it was a scorching day, I met up with the Pompey lads and we did our usual trick of gaining free food and free drinks from these trusting Basques, who to be fair actually supported Britain in our war with Argentina and many flew Union jacks in support, the Basques hated the Spanish!

We made our way to the ground a couple of hours before kick off none of us with tickets, the crowds outside the stadium were huge with a big police presence gun toting cops, a big mob of West Ham fans were going about asking who everyone supported, and if any said Man United they got attacked, fucking bang out of order, saw quite a few United getting beaten up, it sickened me, I don't like United but we were all here to support England. We saw Ken Bailey the England supporters mascot dressed up in his union jack top n tails etc, he was creating a big stir with the French and locals, all wanting pictures taken with him, I then noticed a swarthy looking Basque man selling tickets, a tout, I told the Pompey lads im gonna snatch some off him and run away through the crowds, I approached him and said "how much tickets " with one hand in pocket as if I was getting money out, he was grinning with very bad teeth, he looked a handy fucker with scars all over his mush and a thick bandit tache, he said in broken English,,," teekets five mill!  (£25 ) I said I want four please, he warily pulled four out I pretended I had a bundle to hand over and then I snatched the four tickets, and away I went running like fuck through the crowds, I heard him briefly shouting "bastardo bastardo!" After a few minutes I took a breather on this hill, I was knackered and spewing up, then my Pompey mates turned up crying with laugher telling me they saw it all unfold, and that the Spick gave chase but fell over and loads of tickets fell on the floor and England fans were scooping them up!

I felt bad for about ten seconds then handed the Pompey lads 2 tickets then gave the other one away to a Sunderland fan asking for any spares, these tickets were for the end behind the goals which was half French and half English, no segregation but everyone got along there was no trouble and I have to say when they sang their anthem it was hairs on back of neck job, really stirring stuff, it was roasting though over 120 degrees that day and I was so thirsty, there were signs in the bogs saying under no circumstances drink the tap water, I thought fuck that I'm drinking s much as I can and I did, and it didn't do me any harm, just before kick off I had another stroke of luck when a bloke in the seats above me asked if I would put his banner on the fence behind the nets, just to the side,  which I did no problems, it had his company name on and he and his mates were from Sheffield. I tied it up and it looked great and would get the TV exposure he craved, when I got back he handed me an envelope and it was two tickets for the next two games, Kuwait and Czechoslavakia, what a result.

This game against France was fantastic, Bryan Robson scoring in the first 30 seconds and we went on to win 3-1 brilliant! What an atmosphere and thankfully no trouble with the French, I really did not want to fight them, after the match thousands of jubilant England fans poured into the city centre to celebrate, jumping in and out of the fountains, great scenes and many Basques joining in with us including many Basque ladies, many of them blondes, we got the last bus back to Laredo and continued our celebrations in this quaint little resort, what a day.

Our next game was the oil rich Kuwaitis, and on that Wednesday morning in Bilbao centre I had another stroke of luck when I bumped into some pals of mine from back home, lads from Werneth the next district to Northmoor where I came from, I had hung about with these lads many times in particular Willis a bespectacled lad a year older than me and even though he looked a nerd he was very game a good lad with great personality - the birds loved him and he owed me a big favour. For a few months earlier he was looking at getting sent down for GBH, but I stood for him in Crown court and lied through my back teeth and gave such an outstanding performance in his defence that after he got an absolute discharge, his barrister told us both that I had won him that case, not the barrister, me...the barrister said you were looking at three years there. Willis could not thank me enough and his eyes lit up when he saw me come into the bar he was in with his mates, I told him my story how I came with £1.50 and got by on my wits and generosity of friends and my cousin etc, he said well from now on you will want for nothing, he was wedged up and he lashed me with drinks as much food as I wanted even bought me some clobber and best of all said you are now staying with us in our apartment in Bilbao and we will drive you home when it's all over.

We beat Kuwait and loved seeing all those big fat billionaire Sheiks supporting Kuwait, after the match I went back to Laredo for the last night there and collect my belongings, we had a great night and it was very emotional because there were lads there who had become friends and I would never see them again, we were all in good spirits as were the Northern Irish who had also won, I got on great with them and told them my dad was from Northern Ireland which impressed them.

Next morning I went to Bilbao for the next part of this wonderful adventure, met the lads in this city centre bar which we made our base, it was a great bar the staff loved us and the local birds came in and mingled with us, it had an English juke box and loads of England fans came in and out all day and night, it was facing a beautiful fountain which lit up in various colours at night time.

Bilbao was such a vibrant and lovely city with lots of nice bars and restaurants, they seemed such nice people lot nicer than the Spanish and a lot better looking it seemed, our apartment was on the edge of the city a taxi ride away but we stayed in this bar til midnight every night, eating full chickens and drinking plenty of wine and lager. Most of the England lads were coming in telling us tales of this wonderful red light district only a short distance away from our bar, how beautiful the ladies were and offered their services for only one mill (a fiver) so one night I went for a mooch, this street was a long snaking steep hill and every five yards there were these dolly birds in their mini skirts and tight tops and they were beautiful well most were there was the odd exception.

I walked up and down for half a hour before one gorgeous lady convinced me to choose her, she was only short maybe five four, she had tight satin shorts on and a crop top, exposing her toned belly, she had sporty legs and a lovely smile, jet black hair and ruby red lips, she as a stunner. "Englaise fucky fucky?" I gulped, "how mucho?" I asked heart beating like a drum, "for you handsome, only one mill", I soon produced the one mill note and she grabbed my hand and we walked a short distance down this backalleyway, there was a taxi rank here and loads of taxi drivers smoking yapping and laughing, the laughs got even louder as we walked by hand in hand, I wondered what was so funny? We entered this big old scruffy house which had no lights on and this pross handed over the one mill to a fat owd lady sat on a chair in the hallway, we then climbed up these stone stairs and down another hallway I could hear the grunts and moans of us sad bastards like me, we entered this large room with a double mattress son the floor, it was pitch black apart from a shaft of moonlight pouring in through the window.

She began kissing my neck and chest getting me all aroused, she ripped off my shirt and rubbed my now hard cock, we fell onto the mattress and I took off her top and began to kiss her small but firm breasts, I then started kissing her lovely sporty legs form the knees upwards, across her thighs, she was moaning and groaning eyes closed, I parted her thighs then pulled her tight satin shorts to one side, and the sight of two small but defiant testicles popping out filled me with absolute horror and shock, I froze briefly, I then began apologising? This tranny was trying to pull me back towards it! I felt sick, I grabbed my shirt and ran out of the room spitting out and shouting argh argh ! as I fled the building all these taxi drivers were rolling about laughing at my predicament.

I returned back to our cafe—bar all flustered but I wasn't about to confess and I just sat in a corner mulling over what had just happened, eventually I felt the urge to come clean get it off my chest and I confessed to the fifteen or so England lads in there including my 3 Oldham pals, they burst out laughing then most of them admitted they had been there every night and most of them were trannies! I went home early had a shower disgusted with myself...and them.

A few days later the centre of Bilbao exploded in a carnival atmosphere as thousands of England fans poured into the centre and fountains - we had won the war. Argentina had surrendered in the Falklands, TV Images of Maggie Thatcher flashed form all the bars and cafes, many Basques joined in the celebrations hugging and kissing us and dancing in the streets with their green union jack flags, it was fantastic, many of the cafe owners were handing out cakes and sandwiches, we partied late that night into the early hours.

However the next night me and Willis name came unstuck, we went for a walk in the old town, which was a maze of old steep narrow streets, we got lost, all of a sudden we spotted half a dozen lads one had a Union Jack draped over his shoulders, with Halifax Town FC emblazoned across it, we went to talk to our fellow countrymen but they were locals, and Willis asked the lad with the flag were he had got it from, he brushed Willis aside who then smacked him cos he knew he had nicked it, two of them closed in on us with flick knives, lashing out at us, we had to bolt, but these Spick bastards would not let up screaming obscenities at us, we were running round in circles and dead ends, we had to launch bins at them to get away, I shit myself, I did not want stabbing to death in a foreign country or any fucking country come to that, eventually we found our way back to our bar were we got a mob of England lads together and went searching for these greasy cunts, but after half a hour gave up and went back to the safety of our base camp, we never ventured out alone again.

I went to one more match v Czechoslovakia, the final one in group stages, enjoyed the game and the craic afterwards but only stayed a few more days as the lads gave me the option of getting a lift home with them in the car or heading down to Madrid for the next stages, I decided to go home in the vain hope I could raise enough funds to fly to Madrid the week after, it never happened, our last night in Bilbao was emotional as the local girls we befriended came and cried their eyes out, the bar owner laid a load of butties and free drinks on for us and we had a bit of a party and bid farewell to these lovely wonderful Basque people. The trip home took best part of two days and was hard, I loved my time in Bilbao and Laredo, it was a fantastic time and the people were great, to say I set off with £1.50 I didn't do bad – I saw all three games put a stone on with eating all them full chickens etc, trapped off with three gorgeous Basque girls, met loads of England fans from other clubs, got a great tan and had the time of my life, I landed back in Oldham with £22 on me!

During the rest of the summer of 1982 I reflected on my football hooliganism, I had met so many rival football fans and got along great with them, had no inclination to fight them, not even the French our natural enemies going back centuries, I began to question the futility of wanton football violence..

# BOLTON AGAIN

IN SEPTEMBER 1982 WE PLAYED Bolton Wanderers in the League cup at home, they did not bring many and certainly none ventured into the Chaddy End but we were reliabl informed a couple of vans and cars were parked facing the Spotted Cow pub on Middleton Road, so we made our way after the match to confront our old enemies, when we got there we charged into them, and they fled, I felt a bit bad because Dave and Ginger were amongst them , the Bolton lads on the boat to Bilbao and lads who we had a good drink with on the Sunday night in Plymouth, we did not catch any which was a blessing there was over 100 Oldham and only about 30 odd of them, when we got back near the pub I saw a white Capri overturned and smashed up, really trashed, it belonged to a tall half caste Bolton fan who was seen parking it up, I felt even worse now, why smash his car up? It was brand new aswell, once more my conscience was questioning this nonsense.

A couple of weeks later we played Chelsea at home and the Clayton Arms was full of them and loads of us but we all got along, singing England songs and swapping tales of the World Cup. Greenaway, their cheerleader, was in there with his zigga zagga chant and the banter was brilliant, I much preferred this kind of craic to fighting nowadays although a few Oldham still wanted to attack them in the club or as they left, but we talked them down, outside pre kick off we all walked up as one mob they carried on to the away end with a few going into the paddock next to the Chaddy End, we mobbed up as usual at the floodlights and watched the game, at 3.30pm a load of lads and men began coming through the turn styles, they were not smart enough dressed to be Cockneys and we thought "who the fuck are these" about fifty got in and we asked them who they were, they said "calm it down yonnohs (Manc name for Oldhamers) we are here to sort Chelsea out for yoh!" Ha ha ha... yeah right. With that we set about them bouncing them back down the concrete terracing, they were climbing out of the ground to get away, loads got dragged back in and filled in, it was a combined mob of Manchester United and City fans, amongst them was was a well known lad called Bull-Dog a fat City fan who got his fat nose splattered, he was staggering about in a daze with his nose pissing blood, and other one who got sparked out was Eddy Beef an infamous United hooligan known for jibbing trains, quite a lot got twatted as we engulfed them, we couldn't believe our luck, and their fucking Manc arrogance, as the last few were clambering out of the ground a well know City thug called George Lyons from Failsworth who was about 30 then told us that if City ever get relegated we will turn this shithole over!

We were well pleased with ourselves with fucking the Mancs off, but two of our top lads were falling out with each other, ha both arguing like fuck who broke Bulldogs nose, Eddy "one punch " Benedek claimed it was his punch that splattered his nose but little Johnny Murph claimed he broke Bulldog's nose, it was hilarious. If I was a betting man I'd have to say Eddy delivered the devastating blow but maybe Murph also punched him aswell,  never the less the gobby Mancs came unstuck and the Chelsea fans in the paddock saw it all and loved it, and praised us, the Mancs hung about outside til the end of the game and tried to take on Chelsea who true to form also knocked fuck out of them, it was not a great day for the Mancs and one of the very few times they have combined together.

We played Preston next home game and fair play to them they made an attempt to take the Chaddy End led by Eccles Jerome their big half caste top boy, there were loads of half castes amongst them and they were game but we had too many and we fucked off onto the pitch, a few weeks later we went up to theirs on a Tuesday night match, we had a few hundred and there were a few scuffles in that park next to the ground before the game, we all piled into our end the away end and were delighted that it was half full of Preston and series of running battles broke out, during a lull a big gangly blonde lad stepped forward arms outstretched and I ran in and nutted him, down he went and Oldham ran Preston across the terraces, we took this end with Preston down at the bottom of far side of this end, at half time this blonde lad I had nutted was with tow coppers looking for the lad who nutted him, what a wanker, he wanted to scrap, amazingly he picked out Kenny Jones, who is 6 ft tall heavily built with long black hair, I was slightly built back then curly fair hair 5 ft 9 fuck all like Kenny. As the cops were dragging Kenny away I tod the cops it was me but they wouldn't listen, Kenny told me to leave it he'd get away with it in court which fortunately he did do, after the game Preston got their act together and got the better of us on that park, they had it sussed and knew all the angles, plus there were that many darkies it was hard to see them until they were on top of us. Quite a few Oldham got arrested aswell....

My involvement with the footy aggro was becoming less and less from 1982, I was still on the scene and I was still ploughing in when the need arose but I had stop searching for the enemy, the depression after a long day's fighting running about chanting etc was taking it's toll on me, I felt burn out, I did not have the desire nor energy of my youth, I had seen so many men broken by years of football violence, many turning to alcoholics, druggies, mental health issues, divorces and dropping out of society, I was getting wiser and seeing all this destruction around me and it played on my mind, my natural instincts were to always defend myself and attack if I thought I was about to be attacked I would never ever lie down for any man but it all came to a head when we played Leeds United in January 1983 at home, now for some reason we had never had any large scale disorder with Leeds, I don't know why because they were rampaging up and down the country in the 1980's and they would be in anybody's top five mobs in the country, nobody took liberties at Leeds.

This game was a non-event on and off the pitch they had brought loads but made not attempt on our end and I did not hear of any trouble before the game, after the match we were walking up Sheepfoot Lane when we noticed about ten of them all dressed up in latest football fashions and looked lively lads, we crossed over to mingle in with them and then I struck one wearing a light green Pringle golf jumpers and a deerstalker hat, he hit the deck and gap opened he then got himself up and asked why I did that and I didn't have the answer, I felt so embarrassed, I apologised and walked away disgusted in myself.

My pals Dennis, Eddy, Loyd etc set about them and shouted me back to get stuck in but I walked head bowed and feeling sick, they did not question me when they saw me later and I did not explain myself, it may have been a shock for them and they all carried on for years later although Eddy slowed down, I had reached the end of what was an incredible journey as a football hooligan, from a nine year old gobsmacked onlooker with my childhood friend Paul to by the time I was 13 chucking bricks and getting closer and closer tot he front line, I had been stabbed just a week before my 13th birthday by a Burnley fan and stabbed in the chest in 1980 by a Cardiff fan, I had been hit with bricks, iron bars, bottles chairs, tables and various other implements, I had my nose broke several times cheekbones smashed fractured skull broken both my hands my wrist, ribs, been rendered unconscious a few times I had been kicked to fuck stamped by large numbers and

I had somehow survived as did many others, it was a hard game back then, it gave me the ultimate thrill for so many years but eventually the lows came and it all came crashing down that cold winters day. I had made the name I craved for a kid, I was respected on the terraces and was game and loyal, but now it was all over – or was it? Because two more situations were to occur and even though I had no intention of fighting or taking a beating I was powerless to stop. It was a blip but a very painful blip.

In Easter 1984, the Thursday before Good Friday, we went on a stag do at Bernard Manning's club in Harpurhey Manchester, my life long pal Ste Ragg was to be married, we got a double decker bus to take us there, 40 odd of us mostly football fans, it was as ever a great night with Britain's funniest comedian and the club was packed out, afterwards we were all outside awaiting our bus when a mob of about twenty Burnley fans began chanting, our lot began chanting Oldham and it was just a bit of old fashioned banter, but then the Burnley lads came charging into us and attacking us, so then a mass brawl breaks out, I got stuck in as I wasn't seeing my mates being hammered, so we rolled about as you do, I got up when I saw one big bald headed Burnley fan sat on top of Terry Forsyth and was pummelling Terry, I ran over and threw a right hand haymaker at this feller and it smashed right into his head knocking him over, Terry then set about him and hammered him, but I was in agony my right hand was smashed to bits, the pain was excruciating, a horrible dull but very painful feeling I just knew I had broken it, the cops soon arrived and broke the fighting up and packed us on to our buses.

When we got back to Oldham I went to the Infirmary with my hand and my fears were proved correct it was broken and they put a plaster on it, I got out of their at 7-30am, shattered, they gave me some strong pain killers, supposed to take two three times a day I gobbled about 8 down – not a wise move! I went to bed for a few hours then woke up at midday groggy as fuck. I felt really ill but Latics were playing Manchester City in what was one of the our biggest ever games, City had been relegated and I chuckled at what George Lyons had threatened us with "if City get relegated we will smash your town and ground up".

In Oldham town centre there were loads of Oldham hooligans

milling about awaiting their Manc enemies, here is Dicky's story, Dicky was a Young Guvnor from Chadderton who went everywhere with City and was a member of their notorious hooligan mob the Young Guvnors.

*"About fifteen of us City fans from Chaddy went into town (Manchester) early that Good Friday to meet up with the Young Guvnors, we had it in mind to go to Oldham on the train wreck the town and take the Chaddy End. It was awkward for us from Oldham as we knew so many of the Oldham lads and knew they would avenge us personally but I could not turn my back on the Guvnors I had been with them through thick and thing for two seasons now and they were my family my pals, my brothers. We had a huge crew in Manchester that morning at least 200 and we go the train up to Oldham Mumps their main station, on the way up the lads were joking about Oldham and how easy it would be taking the piss out of the yonner. I tried to tell them Oldham is a rough town and it won't be easy and they had a big mob at Boundary Park, I was laughed at, dismissed... but we Chadderton lads knew we were in for a rough time..."*

*"As we departed the station just south of Oldham town centre we were met with a hail of bricks by a load of scruffy kids from a high bridge, they had a few hits but ran off, a few City were laughing saying is that Oldham's mob.... I cringed at such ignorance... we then marched up Yorkshire Street through Oldham town centre, cocky as fuck, but when we came to the Artisans, Grapes and Mess House pubs loads of Oldham came out throwing bottles chairs and ashtrays at us, it split our mob in two, loads got cut up, these were not just hooligans with Oldham but Teddy Boys in their 40's Punk Rockers, Builders, Bouncers, and even women, attacking us, it was mayhem they caught us unaware and we got twatted, the other half didn't do much better as they ran into Oldham's mob, a strange mixture of rockers, skinheads, punks, mods, beer monsters, rough birds and lunatics. They were lobbing bottles and jumping on our backs and the cops were nowhere, what we thought would be an easy stroll was turning into a nightmare, loads got hammered some ending up in hospital we knew there would be thousands more City pouring into Oldham but in the town centre we came unstuck big time. We had to make our way to the ground in little mobs but even that was dodgy as we had to negotiate our way through two rough council estates and past a few Oldham pubs, we finally arrived a the ground totally knackered after all the chasing and attacks en route."*

As for me I knew there would be loads of trouble in the town and en route to the ground aswell as in the ground, but I was determined not to get involved, for one my hand was in plaster and my arm in a sling, I was in agony and so groggy, and really didn't fancy the game, but I went and was in the ground early before 2pm, a good hour plus before kick off, outside the ground there were thousands of City fans milling about but only the odd scuffles, a lot of verbals but nothing too heavy.

In the Chaddy End there were maybe a couple of hundred young Oldham lads at the top of the Chaddy, lads aged 14-18, the away end was filling up quickly with thousands of City fans, it looked very impressive, I found myself a quiet spot, and was now looking forward to the game but all of a sudden hundreds of City appeared in the Chaddy End, most of them Casuals/Boys, with their flickers, mushroom haircuts, cagoules and adidas sportswear, they stood out like sore thumbs. They moved towards the top to take the Chaddy End but Oldham's young guns held them off, they would not budge, the City fans then began attacking normal fans older blokes and the kids who were not hooligans, ths disgusted me, and when I saw ten of them attacking Mad Frank Ashton a man then in his thirties, I went wading in, Mad Frank was a legend in Oldham a proper hard nut, heavily tattooed and one of the original Glodwick mob from the late 1960's, typically Frank went down fighting but was kicked to fuck and Im sure he was slashed, his face was pissing blood as he was stretchered out of the ground, the image of him on the stretcher appeared in many of the next mornings daily newspapers, the *Daily Mail* showed Frank and the headline made many of laugh out loud. "Innocent victim of football violence" Ha ha Frank had given plenty of stick out over the last twenty years or so and went down fighting until overwhelmed.

My plaster cast on my hand came in handy it was like having a brick attached to my hand and I knocked loads of Mancs out in the next hour as I got stuck in the mass brawls, running battles and hand to hand combats, fights were breaking out ever minute or so, and to tell you the truth I was loving it, the adrenaline was flowing I felt ten feet tall and I witnessed some incredible scenes of bravery from my fellow Oldham fans who were heavily outnumbered, maybe 3-1 and we had a massive mob in by kick off, City were like rats appearing from every angle, most of them with one hand in their back pocket to convince us they were carrying blades, well one of our top lads was carrying a blade and cut three City fans up, he got away with it, there was plenty of blood shed, the St John's ambulances were as busy as they had ever been, there were loads of arrests from both sides and even as rival fans were being ejected up the side of the pitch, they were still fighting each other, it was mayhem, the cops could not control the rival fans, and City remained in the Chaddy End throughout the whole match in various mobs, snipin Oldham fans who passed them to go to the bogs or for a brew, City had more than enough to take the Chaddy End that day in the Chaddy but Oldham's pride and sheer courage held firm despite being outnumbered, but if all the City fans in the away end had come across the pitch they would have taken us no danger, but what a lot of them did was to attack innocent fans in the Ford stand, climbing up a ladder and chasing these innocent family people out of their seats, a despicable act that may have given them the big headlines but in reality they were shithouses coward attacking easy targets, they should have been in the Chaddy End fighting with the rest of their mob, a lot of those innocent family fans walked out of the ground that day and many never came back.

Meanwhile fights were breaking out throughout the match in the Chaddy End, but towards the end many Oldham fans melted away as more and more City came into the Chaddy End to bolster their already huge advantage, near the end of the match twenty of what I consider Oldham's finest grouped up and left the ground to pick off City thugs, we ploughed into a mob outside the ticket office and they crumbled, but then a mob of around thirty young black lads came at us, a few brandishing blades and we got on our toes, I told the lads to run through the nearby estate of bungalows entice this mob to chase us and when we find something we could hit them back with we'l get into them, well lucky enough we saw a garage door open it was full of garden tools, pick axe handles staves, brushes, shovels, rakes etc, we grabbed them then ran at the City lads who backed off for a while but then came back with their blades, once again we were on our toes, they chased us for over a mile over moorland, and as much as I begged these top twenty Oldham lads they did not want to take these black lads on,

I was gutted, embarassed and near exhaustion as the medication I had taken earlier began to wear off, we lost the black lads and made our way to the town centre heads bowed like beaten troops, we made our way to our town centre base the Hare and Hounds, but as we get there it's full of gloating City fans many of them outside goading us to try and take it back, we had no chance, if we approached it they would have showered us with bottles and ash trays, there was a ramp into the pub so it was nigh on impossible to get past them, we tried to entice them to come to us but they were not daft, they had our pub and it was up to us to try and get it back, a few bottles were lobbed at them but they laughed at us, it looked and was pitiful, we decided to call it a day, and melted away to the comforts of our homes, I was absolutely shattered physically and mentally, I felt weak emotional and depressed, I hated the fact I had got back involved I hated the fact that City took the piss after the match and hated the fact twenty of Oldham's best lads allowed a much weaker and less experienced mob run us, maybe it was time for all of us to retire?

That was my last time involved in football violence well the last time I made the choice to fight, of course there was the odd blip over the years but that was just me looking after myself or a friend (s), it had all become too much for me, it had beaten me, the buzz no longer there, the thrill diminished, the camaraderie gone, there were a lot of good young guns coming through who very impressively fought off City and fought City many times home and away for the next twenty years, but it was over for me.

I had managed to avoid trouble for two years even though I still went to many games and still loved the craic at away games but kept out of the violence, but in November 1986 I came unstuck at our home game v Middlesborough. At 2.30pm that day a mob of a hundred or so of them came charging through the Chaddy End, I wanted to get away from this very violent rampaging mob who were lashing out at anybody in there way, I tried to make my way under a crash barrier but got trapped by fleeing Oldham fans, my head and body was stuck out, well it seemed that every single one of the hundred Middlesborough fans booted me about my head and body, I was in and out of consciousness the dull thuds of the boots and some punches raining down on my, many it seemed in slow motion, I could taste the polish mixed in with the blood, I could feel my skin being ripped as wounds opened, I thought I was gong to die, it seemed to go on forever, I vaguely remember the Jam classic A Town called Malice being played over the tannoy, which must have geed the Boro thugs even more, I came round as Im being stretchered around the pitch as I heard the concerned voices of the police saying "this one's straight to hospital he's taken some serious damage!"

My god how bad was I? I felt terrible but no more so than the many other serious kickings I had taken over the years, I was put straight into a waiting ambulance outside and whisked to hospital, the sirens blaring didn't do me any favours, the next couple of hours is a blur, and the first clear memory I have is being cleaned up then stitched around my eyes and a couple of head wounds. I ached terribly and the nurse ran through my wounds, I had cuts around my eyes two deep head wounds, broken cheekbone, broken nose (again) broken teeth, broken ribs, broken fingers, broken wrist, both my eyes were black and blue I had boot imprints all over my upper body and head, one of my ears was three times it's normal size, I was in hospital for 4 days but off work for three weeks, it was the very worst kicking I had ever taken and I had taken a lot, it scared me, I was close to being kicked to death.

I don't hold a single grudge to Middlesborough fans, it was not personal and I had lost my football hooligan instincts that had been good for me so long, yeah I had taken beatings and many blows but the amount of fights brawls I had been involved with over the years I had been very lucky but my luck ran out that day. I stopped going for a while just picking games out, I certainly avoided the potential bloodbaths but by the late 80's these were few and far between, the tragedies of Hillsborough, Heysel and the fire at Bradford shocked the whole football world, people should not be dying at football games, I watched the Heysel tragedy unfold on the tele, it was horrific, I don't blame the Liverpool fans, like so many do, it was hooliganism, and there but for the grace of god go I. How many times has there been large scale mass brawls across terraces, but the Ities fled, the coppers fled, and the decrepit terracing crumbled, this is why people died, no Liverpool fan went to that game to kill anybody, it was sickening and awful god bless the Juventus fans - RIP.

I also saw the Bradford fire disaster unfold on tele, it scared me, so many innocent people dying in that fire, for some reason this horrific day in football does not get the publicity as other tragedies, which in itself is very sad - RIP.

# WHERE ARE THEY NOW?

Slowk, now aged 60, has lived in Benalmadena, Spain for past ten years. He ran a bar called Churchills for a while with fellow Glodwick Mob lads and Oldham fans Keith Partridge and Steve Ramsden.

Meat Pie Fred aka Roland Shaw: Passed away in 1994 aged 48, good turn out for his funeral, as the mourners were throwing lumps of sand into his grave someone tossed a meat pie into the grave, which we all cracked up laughing at, he would have loved it - RIP.

Jimmy Kirt: Passed away in 2002 aged 54, arguably Oldham's most influential fan, a great character his funeral was huge and the cortege even circled Boundary Park were players and staff stood outside and clapped as it passed by, a wonderful gesture, at the crematorium there were fans from many other teams in attendance in the packed out crowd, Jimmy's humour shone through even in death as the coffin was sliding through to the furness, the classic 60's tune Fire, by the Doors played, everyone burst out laughing and applauded this wonderful man.

Kenny Jones now aged 58 still going to the games looks well, cut the fighting and boozing out now, not been arrested for a few seasons, he is now a diabetic and looks after himself a lot better, still very chirpy and wise cracking.

Herby now aged 57, had a bad accident at work about 2004 and has to walk with a stick now, he is partially sighted and does not get to the game anymore, we held a benefit concert for him raising a couple of grand, despite his condition he burst into the pub did a roll splits and a backward flip as the DJ played a Northern Soul tune, legend!

Happy Harry now aged 56, last seen in 1980 on his hands and knees beckoning hundreds of West Ham fans to take him on, they did, rendered him unconscious, he has not been seen since, apparently he fled to Ireland and lives in a Monastery,

Gill Dock now aged 65, I never got to meet the King of the Chaddy End 1964-1970, but I drink with his son, another giant but a gentle one, Gill is still grafting as a builder and is still one of the most respected men of his generation.

Paul Sykes now aged 52, my best childhood friend and right hand man through my teenage years, he got out of the footy violence early and was a very good amateur footballer, he settled down and married with two kids, we phone each other every now and then but have lost touch as friends.

Danny Standring now aged 56, does not go to the game anymore unless he can blag a free ticket. Danny DJ'd for years around Oldham but last few years has been involved with the Army veterans, despite his little bald rotund figure he has always been popular with the ladies, his claim to fame though was when Oldham played Ipswich and he walked on the pitch and sat down in the centre circle during a protest against our then chairman. It was on all the Sports channels and most newspapers... he has fed off that since and still get drinks bought him some 15 years on!

Robbo Watson now aged 53 a shadow of the man he was. Painfully thin his body ravaged from years of hard drug abuse, it is amazing he is still alive, most of his co druggies have passed away, but he was so tough and maybe he has the same inner strength as outer strength he once had, not been game for twenty odd years apart from very rare appearance, it's always good to see him but also sad.

Johnny Murph now aged 53, still goes to the game, a great little character who works hard and plays hard, out every weekend with his lovely wife Bernie on the pop, soul events, concerts, any event where the drink flows and the craic is fierce.

Mouse aka John Kennedy. now aged 55, the little man with the big heart still a loyal Latics fan, still very much respected town centre character, despite losing some very close friends and his lady still manages to keep his chin up.

Mad Frank Ashton Passed away 2008 aged 60, Frank had been battling alcoholism for a long while and went missing for nine months only for the remains of his body to be found in an old house, his death shocked the town, this tough proud man was no more, he had a great turn out for his funeral and hundreds from all backgrounds turned out to pay respect - RIP.

Big Graham Hall, now aged 54, still a huge man mountain, never really recovered from losing his brother Harry in a car accident in the early 80's, Graham turned to drink but still see him now and then and we have a laugh reminiscing, this gentle giant who was not so gentle with away fans.

Terry Horton now aged 55 terry had a stroke a few years ago and his speech and mannerisms are very slow, it is so hard to see this once super fit strong and tough lad struggling to speak or get by, he goes to the game now and then but need the aid of a carer, very sad.

Spazmo, now aged 55, this giant of a man retired early from the footy and has been a prison officer for many years, no doubting keeping them in check, they would be foolish to take this big strong hard hitting man on. His son is in touch on Facebook and loves hearing tales from the 70's about his dad, there are plenty.

George Kowal now aged 54 - spent a few years in the British Army and his colleagues all agree he was the most inept soldier ever to serve Queen and Country spending most of his times in prison, however since he was dishonourably discharged he has been a security guard for many years, he is a bad gambler but has a beautiful 10 year old daughter and seems very happy.

Eddy B – One Punch now aged 52 this hard hitting one punch phenomenon not only became one of Oldham's most successful builders he actually sponsors the biggest and newest stand at Boundary Park which is named after his company Leesfield Developments, he still goes to most games and is very happy in life - he got away from the footy violence in his early twenties.

Dennis Wright now aged 52, Dennis had links for many years with the FYC. Oldham's late 80's & 1990'S Casual hooligans, he was a doorman for a few years in Oldham town centre, he kept himself fit and looks well, he still goes to the game.

Loyd Scan now aged 51 not in the best of health but another successful businessman who has property both in the UK and New York, this once very fit athletic sportsman has put some weight on but is still sharp as a tack, he makes to odd appearance, he was once barred from ALL Oldham's pub's, he was also a doorman for a few years.

Ian Mcgeary—Max now aged 52 this calm witty heavy punching Roytoner, still goes to the game, he is also heavily involved in cricket, he was always one of those quiet ones not to mess with, a lovely lad, very popular and on the ball.

Jimmy Rafferty now aged 66, Jimmy the original 60's Mod has suffered mental health this past decade or so, in and out of institutions, not been seen for about five years, the last time I saw him was one midweek lunch time shouting and bawling in Weatherspoons, he was ejected. Jimmy remains one of THE funniest and most popular Oldham fans who ever stepped foot in Boundary Park - apparently now living in Rochdale, he refused to watch football when they became all seater stadiums.

Dozy Dunc now aged 53 he retired in 1977 after being arrested three games on the trot and getting 3 months detention centre, that slowed him down apart from the odd appearance, has been a Hippy world traveller for most of his adult life.

Jimmy the Punk now aged 50, still remains a Punk and has lived in Leeds most of his life, got a great job in the theatre creating sets, still goes to every game despite living 30 miles away, top man.

Clunk now aged 47, this former Royton Wanderer has had a fantastic life a professional drummer, playing in bands such as the Glitter Band and backing many other famous musicians, he has played in many bands up and down the country and throughout Europe and is a very much respected musician/drummer, still goes to the odd game.

Mark Kelly now aged 52 this fearless cool as fuck trendy hooligan left the UK for Spain ten years ago and has settled down over the their and loves it in the sun, makes the odd appearance but keeps in touch on facebook.

Gaz Hammy now aged 50, was still active up until recently one of the most respected football lads in town, he s certainly put his shift in, looks good and a proper loyal Oldhamer still gets to a few games.

Si Boss - now aged 48, for the last ten years Simon has been wheelchair bound this big hearted lad has took this on his chin and still remains one of the most popular lads in Oldham, he has many many friends up and down the country and plenty from Hibs, possibly THE most inspirational Oldham fan of all time.

Colin Shaw passed away in 2005 aged 48, this big tough but gentle man's passing shocked the town and especially all Oldham fans, he represented us as the fan on the board, he was a great man so influentially and very much respected, his funeral was huge and very emotional.

Mad Mick now aged 51, stopped going to the football in his mid twenties and played amateur Rugby league well into his forties, always kept himself fit and healthy, see him every now and then and he 's happy in life..

Shane Clegg now aged 56, landlord of the Greyhound Inn close to Boundary Park and a Latics pub on match day, Shane is a big England fan and has been to many games watching them. Does not got to Oldham now but they are still in his heart.

Paul Heap Heapy passed away in 2002 aged 46, in a hostel for alcoholics. A very sad lonely death, he would have had a great turn out for his funeral but it was the same day as Oldham played at QPR in the Division Two Play offs semi final first leg. Once Heapy stopped going to the match he lost the will to live, for he lived for the game and craic

– RIP.

Egghead now aged 51, one of the gamest lads ever at Oldham, he stopped going manyyears ago but his bravery will never be forgotten, bit of a wheeler and dealer nowadays, he is happy..

George Cragg now aged 54 Craggy was one of the main lads from late 70's through most of the 1980's a big heavy lad with a knock out punch, always had a good crew with him, came off the very rough Abbeyhills estate, he has lived in Blackpool for many years now and owns a couple of large hotels, always looks after his fellow Oldhamers.

Ian McGrath now aged 49, works for Oldham Council sorted his teeth out and now has a full grin, lovely feller who retired many moons ago but is still fondly remembered and well respected by many.

Stez, now aged 55, still alive n kicking and still in his home town village of Shaw, although Stez fell out with Oldham and chose Rochdale one can never forget the courage he showed leading his big mob the Shaw Gawbies into battle many time for Oldham and I for one will always respect him.

Big Stu, now aged 54, has lived in Stockport for many years and sadly victim of MS and apparently is housebound, his name always crops up when we reminisce about the good old days, the last of the Boot Boy's certainly made his mark.

Al Campbell, now aged 57 now retired and living in Morecambe due to ill heath, still comes to the odd game and always great to see such a top man and Chaddy End legend, still wearing Doc Martens and still highly polished, big Al never stopped being a skin.

Rem now aged 48, the fighting Punk, he was a huge lad made his name in the early 1980's running about with Mad Mick's rough arsed bunch of council house tearwaways. Rem was a New Age traveller for many yars and still dresses like one, he is a waste removal man and van and was once in a Punk band called Motown Vampires, he has recently released a book of poems, Obnoxious Rhymes in Obnoxious times.

Ste Badby, passed away in 1983 would now be 53,

Me now aged 51, I have led a very colourful life; I am a father, grandfather, divorcee, promoter, DJ, author of seven books to date, lost my curly locks aged 30, in love with a beautiful lady and very happy,. I don't go to the game now apart from very rare appearances, I've fallen out with the game, it does not excite me anymore but have so many wonderful memories, met so many great people.

COLIN BLANEY
"Iconic scally book" - Salford Star

# GRAFTERS

## THE INSIDE STORY OF EUROPE'S MOST PROLIFIC SNEAK THIEVES

### COLIN BLANEY

ISBN: 1901746 925 - 9781901746921
£9.95 - PAPERBACK - 352 PP - 16 PP PHOTOGRAPHS
PUBLISHED: 1ST JUNE 2012

Colin Blaney's 'Grafters', originally published in 2004, was a ground breaking exposè of the links between criminal gangs and footba: hooliganism. In the intervening period the book and the phrase hav become part of the lexicon, defining a generation of professional thieves wh used the cover of their fellow football fans to earn a fortune.

Eight years on author Colin Blaney returns with an updated version of h: criminal memoirs and recounts his experiences as a personality in the murk media world that accompanies public relations - principally his shady dealing with tabloid journalists, TV producers and researchers. In Colin's words he wa thrown in at the deep end to "Swim with the sharks".

It's all a far cry from Colin's adolescence in the council flats of Nort Manchester. As a child he burgled warehouses and factories. As a youth he joine the bootboys of Manchester United's Red Army, rampaging across the countr As an adult he learned to dip with the Scouse pickpocket gangs, sell dope t Rastas in the Moss Side shebeens and sneak-thieve from shop tills with his ma Collyhurst crew.

But Continental Europe offered the greatest lure. The gang moved t Amsterdam which became their HQ for the next twenty years. They stole Role watches in Switzerland, peddled Ecstasy in Spain, kited credit cards in Belgiur flogged bootleg tee-shirts in France and snatched designer clothes in Hollan Blaney and his Wide Awake Frim served time in half the jails in Europe and the went back for more. They were on a riotous, non stop rollercoaster ride - unt they finally hit the buffers.

ORDER FROM WWW.EMPIRE-UK.COM FOR JUST £8 INC P&P